The Development of Capitalism in Russia

This book provides a broad survey of the development of capitalism in Russia from the collapse of the soviet economic system to the present, and includes the results of substantial new research on the working practices of a wide range of Russian enterprises. It surveys, briefly, the old soviet system, and goes on to chart progress through the early post-soviet period, when neo-liberal theorists' 'shock therapy' did not lead to the immediate development of a capitalist market economy. It demonstrates that, far from promoting a transition to capitalism, the economic crisis of the 1990s reinforced the typical characteristics of soviet management. It identifies vertical and horizontal lines of division and conflict within the Russian enterprise and concludes that, while the practices of senior management have been radically transformed, changes in personnel and production management have been much more limited. The book concludes with a discussion of the wider implications of the Russian experience, addressing the question of whether or not a specifically Russian 'variety of capitalism' is emerging.

Simon Clarke is Professor of Sociology at the University of Warwick. He has been co-ordinating research projects in the field of labour and employment with colleagues in the former Soviet Union since 1991 and has published extensively with his colleagues in English and Russian. His current research focuses on trade unions in the Former Soviet Union, China and Vietnam.

Routledge Contemporary Russia and Eastern Europe Series

The Development of Capitalism in Russia

Simon Clarke

Routledge
Taylor & Francis Group

LONDON AND NEW YORK

First published 2007
by Routledge
2 Park Square, Milton Park, Abingdon, Oxon OX14 4RN

Simultaneously published in the USA and Canada
by Routledge
270 Madison Ave, New York, NY 10016

Routledge is an imprint of the Taylor & Francis Group, an informa business

Printed and bound in Great Britain
By Biddles Ltd, King's Lynn

British Library Cataloguing in Publication Data
A catalogue record for this book is available from the British Library

Library of Congress Cataloging in Publication Data
A calalog record for this book has been requested

ISBN 978-0-415-36825-4 (hbk)
ISBN 978-0-203-02806-3 (ebk)

Contents

1 Introduction

This book is based on the findings of a research programme carried out in collaboration with local research teams affiliated with the Institute for Comparative Labour Relations Research (ISITO) in Russia since the early 1990s, funded primarily by the British Economic and Social Research Council (ESRC) and INTAS. The research on which this book is based was carried out in two phases. The first phase, in 1991–5 in collaboration with Peter Fairbrother, involved intensive longitudinal case studies of the restructuring of management and labour relations in traditional enterprises in four Russian regions.[1] This research identified the continuity of traditional soviet management practices and the constraints on change imposed by the struggle to survive in a collapsing economy. This research was reported in a large number of publications in English and in Russian and forms the basis of the three introductory chapters of this book, which cover the central issues in theorising the transition, the characteristics of the soviet industrial enterprise and the key features of the survival strategies of traditional enterprises in the 1990s.

The first three chapters provide the context for the analysis presented in the rest of the book, which is based on the findings of a more recent research project, again funded by the ESRC, from 2002 to 2006 in collaboration with Tony Elger and Veronika Kabalina and our colleagues in ISITO.[2] This project has been based on intensive case studies of fifty-two successful enterprises of all property forms in a range of branches of the economy in seven regions of Russia in order to identify the characteristics and limits of management restructuring in the new conditions of economic recovery since the default of 1998 and has identified both persisting soviet legacies and radical innovation in management practices. A team of researchers worked intensively in each enterprise over an extended period of time, interviewing senior managers, line managers and workers, observing the work of the shops and conducting documentary and

[1] 'The restructuring of management and industrial relations in the Soviet Union' ESRC award L309253049 and 'The restructuring of management, labour relations and labour organisation in the FSU' INTAS-93-1227.

[2] 'Management structures, employment relations and class formation in Russia' ESRC award R000239631. I am very grateful to Tony Elger for his helpful suggestions and careful comments on the manuscript of this book.

archival research. The project has generated a wealth of data and a wide variety of analytical papers prepared by our Russian colleagues, which provide the basis for this book.[1]

The discussion of our research findings begins with an account of the changes that have taken place in the corporate management of our case-study enterprises. The research has concluded that the principal pressure for change in management practices and employment relations comes from the external environment, so the greatest changes have come in, and been driven by, those parts of enterprise management dealing with that environment, particularly sales and marketing. Similarly, change is more radical in enterprises which are owned by outsiders, and particularly those owned by Russian or foreign corporations, and tends to proceed from the top down. This is not so much because the managers of corporations are more competent than the managers of insider-owned companies, as because the owners are more unequivocally oriented to maximising the profits that they derive from their assets.

While there have been substantial changes in the practices of corporate management, it is very rare for the reform of management and labour relations in Russian enterprises to have penetrated the sphere of production and personnel management, even in foreign-owned enterprises. For this reason, the rest of the book concentrates on the examination of the barriers to change found in these spheres by exploring the characteristics of personnel management and the reform of payment systems, before looking in more detail at the contradictory pressures imposed on line management.

The adaptation of Russian management and employment relations is by no means a process free of conflict. However, conflict is not dramatic and does not appear primarily between employer and employees. The lines of conflict tend to coincide with the extent to which the traditional technologistic orientation to production of soviet management has been confronted with an economic orientation to profitability. This appears horizontally in the relations between marketing and production management, and vertically along a line which moves down the enterprise as reform proceeds, initially between senior management and outside owners and subsequently between senior management and middle and line management. In many of the most advanced enterprises line managers find themselves torn between conflicting pressures from senior management and from the labour force they are required to manage, variously coming down on one side or the other. The integration of line managers into the management

[1] Research methodology, interview data, case-study reports and analytical papers can be accessed at go.warwick.ac.uk/Russia/manstruct/management_structures.htm. A set of papers has been published as Кабалина В. И. (ред.) *Практики управления персоналом на современных российских предприятиях*, Москва: ИСИТО, 2005. I draw heavily on these project materials in several parts of this book. I have checked back with the original data, so any errors that may remain are undoubtedly entirely my responsibility. I am also grateful to Guy Standing and Tatyana Chetvernina for giving me access to the data of the Russian Labour Flexibility Survey (RLFS). All other statistical data are those issued by the State Statistical Service, Rosstat, formerly Goskomstat, unless otherwise stated.

hierarchy is a major problem facing the senior management of Russian enterprises.

This ambiguous position of line management is one reason why there is not yet a coherent managerial middle class and no clear lines of class division have yet emerged in Russia. Potential conflicts between labour and capital are dissipated within the management structure. Workers continue to appeal to their line managers, rather than the trade union, when they experience problems, and their line managers usually represent the grievances of their subordinates within the management hierarchy. In rare cases in which line managers have been more thoroughly assimilated into the management hierarchy, industrial relations tend to become more conflictual.

One aim of the project was to address the question of whether a specifically 'Russian' variant of capitalism is developing, which integrates features of company management borrowed from the leading capitalist countries with features of the organisational culture and employment and personnel practices inherited from the soviet past. Although current management structures and practices are strongly marked by the coexistence of the old and the new, we are sceptical that this marks a specifically Russian model of capitalism, in the sense of a distinctive set of institutional arrangements which provide a stable basis for the sustained accumulation of capital, rather than a transitional stage in the adaptation of Russian values, institutions and practices to the imperatives imposed by global capitalism. Of course, the legacy of Russia's past will never be extinguished, but it is premature to assess which features of that past are consistent with the sustained accumulation of capital, which features might constitute barriers to such accumulation and which features might provide the basis of effective resistance to the rule of capital. As Marx noted in *The Communist Manifesto*, 'the history of all hitherto existing societies is the history of class struggle', and the struggle continues to shape history into the future.

The reason for our scepticism about the emergence of a stable Russian model of capitalism is the conflict outlined above, in which there is a clear tendency for capitalist management values and practices to penetrate ever deeper into the Russian enterprise, with the most radical change being in foreign-owned companies and the least change being observed in insider-controlled traditional enterprises. There is certainly some tendency to preserve traditional features of personnel management in response to the expectations of workers, particularly in the paternalistic provision of social and welfare benefits, but these expectations are largely confined to older workers, young workers being preoccupied with the size of the wage and having little interest in funeral benefits or access to sanatoria. This underlines the significance not only of change within particular enterprises, but of the fall and rise of enterprises and the way in which this intersects with generational changes in by-passing old expectations and institutional practices.

Changing management structures and practices is much easier in enterprises which are undertaking substantial investment programmes, which both require the introduction of new working practices and facilitate their acceptance by being associated with improved wages and working conditions and better prospects. This is the principal reason why management change has proceeded further and more smoothly in foreign-owned enterprises and in the oil and gas, electricity generation, and metallurgical sectors than in those branches of the Russian economy supplying the domestic market.

Our case studies suggest that the Russian economy is acquiring a dualistic structure, with modern management practices and technology employed in the export-related sectors, while producers for the domestic market rely for their survival on the skill and experience of an ageing labour force to operate worn-out plant and equipment. Both sectors face an increasingly acute problem of a shortage of skilled workers as traditional industrial training systems have collapsed and younger people have no interest in making a career in industry. This links to the more fundamental question facing Russia, of what future the country has in the global capitalist economy, other than as a supplier of fuels and raw materials.

Finally, the project studied a number of dynamic new private enterprises and found that these shared many features familiar from SMEs in the capitalist countries, of being under-capitalised, operating on the margins of legality, having highly concentrated managerial decision-making, with insufficiently formalised management practices and an excessive reliance on the owner-director and being highly prone to fragmentation in the event of intra-managerial conflict. While the new private sector fills an important niche, it is not in a position to fulfil the task assigned to it by some commentators of regenerating the Russian economy.

The book by no means covers all aspects of the research, but rather focuses on a number of central issues in the areas of corporate management, personnel management and production management. Our findings are consistent with a substantial body of research on the development of Russian enterprise management structures and practices over the past fifteen years, mostly carried out by Russian researchers on the basis of official statistical data and enterprise surveys, but add the depth that can only be provided by detailed case-study research.

2 Theorising the transition

There has been a great deal of largely inconclusive discussion over the past twenty years around the appropriate theoretical framework within which to conceptualise the transformation of the former state socialist economies. The commonly used notion of 'transition' has often been questioned as doubly problematic. On the one hand, it is a teleological notion in implying that the process is determined by its end point, whereas critics have emphasised the dependence of the process on the initial conditions, summed up in the notion of 'path dependence'.[1] For this reason some commentators prefer to use the term 'transformation' rather than 'transition'.[2] On other hand, it begs the question of the characterisation of the end point of transition. The transition is most commonly characterised as the 'transition to a market economy', which is usually a euphemism for the transition to capitalism, but this leaves open the question of what kind of capitalism is developing in Russia. Is the capitalism that is emerging in Russia modelled on one of the existing 'varieties of capitalism'?[3] Or does Russian capitalism have its own original character, based on the incorporation of capitalist practices into soviet/Russian traditions, values and institutions? If this is the case, how does Russian capitalism measure up to its competitor varieties of capitalism when it confronts them on the world market?

Michael Burawoy rightly pointed to the dominance of a 'politicised' view of the transition from socialism to capitalism, which focuses on political programmes while neglecting their real consequences.[4] Most commentary on the transition in Russia has been based on a dualistic interpretation of the transition in terms of the interaction of liberalising reforms and state socialist legacies, the latter being seen as barriers to and distortions of the former. Recognition that the

[1] David Stark, 'Path dependence and privatization strategies in East Central Europe', *East European Politics and Societies* 6(1), 1992: 17–54.
[2] Michael Burawoy, 'Transition without transformation: Russia's involutionary road to capitalism', *East European Politics and Societies* 15(2), 1999: 269–90.
[3] Peter A. Hall and David Soskice (eds), *Varieties of Capitalism: The Institutional Foundations of Comparative Advantage*, Oxford: Oxford University Press, 2001.
[4] Michael Burawoy and Pavel Krotov, 'The soviet transition from socialism to capitalism: worker control and economic bargaining in the wood industry', *American Sociological Review* 57, February 1992: 17.

path of liberal reform is not necessarily strewn with roses has been accommodated within a vulgarised notion of 'path dependence', according to which the path is littered with obstacles inherited from the past which have to be assimilated or removed, but the past plays a purely negative role in such an analysis. This analysis underpins a voluntaristic interpretation of transition as the outcome of political conflicts between reformers and conservatives. In the first half of the 1990s discussion focused on the role of the 'young reformers', who assumed a pivotal position in successive Moscow governments under Yeltsin, and their western allies, who set the agenda for the involvement of the international financial institutions which provided and financed the blueprint for reform. Assessments of the Putin regime have been much more ambivalent, ranging from those who give Putin credit for institutionalising the achievements of liberal reform in a law-governed state, to those who see him as embedding the corruption of the Yeltsin years in the authoritarian apparatuses of a kleptocratic state. However, a voluntaristic and dualistic approach, which analyses the emerging forms of capitalism as a synthesis of an ideal model and an alien legacy, fails to identify the indigenous roots and real foundation of the dynamic of the transition from a state socialist to a capitalist economy and so fails to grasp the process of transformation as a historically developing social reality.

The theoretical basis of this kind of dualistic analysis has been provided by the classical liberal analysis of the development of capitalism out of feudalism provided by Adam Smith. Many commentators have compared the soviet system to that of feudalism in being based on the appropriation of a surplus by the exercise of political power. For Adam Smith and Friedrich Hayek the central feature of feudalism was the distortion of the natural order of the market economy by the superimposition of political rule, and the transition from feudalism to capitalism depended on sweeping away the political institutions of the old regime in order to establish the freedom and security of property – what Smith referred to as 'order and good government' – which would allow the market economy to flourish as the expression of unfettered individual reason. This was the ideology that informed the neo-liberal project of the transition to a capitalist market economy in the former state socialist economies.

Smith, in *The Wealth of Nations*, had provided a blueprint for a liberal reform programme, but had been very pessimistic about the possibility of such a programme ever being adopted against the resistance of popular prejudice and vested interest:

> To expect, indeed, that the freedom of trade should ever be entirely restored in Great Britain is as absurd as to expect that an Oceania or Utopia should ever be established in it. Not only the prejudices of the public, but what is much more unconquerable, the private interests of many individuals, irresistibly oppose it. . . . master manufacturers set themselves against any law that is likely to increase the number of their rivals in the home market . . . [and] enflame their workmen to attack with violence and outrage the

proposers of any such regulation . . . they have become formidable to the government, and upon many occasions intimidate the legislature.[1]

Despite Smith's pessimism, within a generation of the publication of *The Wealth of Nations* the mercantile system had collapsed and the system of regulation had been dismantled by the state itself, not on the basis of the triumph of an enlightened individualism but on the basis of a social transformation which had radically altered the balance of class forces and undermined the old regime.[2] In the same way, the liberal theorists of totalitarianism were taken completely by surprise when the apparently all-powerful soviet state disintegrated, not as a result of any liberal critique but under the weight of its own contradictions.[3]

The promotion of 'shock therapy' by the young reformers was motivated by a similar fear to that of Adam Smith of the power of the old regime to block reform, the idea being that a radical programme of liberalisation and privatisation would completely destroy the old system and all possibilities of resistance, in the expectation that a new system would arise, phoenix-like, from its ashes. In reality the battle promoted by the young reformers between the 'new Russians' and the 'red directors' turned out not to be a battle between the new and the old orders, but a struggle over the appropriation of public assets in the disorder of transition. The old system was certainly destroyed but it was replaced not by 'freedom of trade' and 'order and good government' but by a corrupt kleptocracy in which great fortunes were made by the theft of public property and the diversion of public revenues.

In retrospect even the most ardent liberal reformers in the Former Soviet Union came to recognise that they had put too much emphasis on destroying the old regime and too little on establishing 'order and good government'. However, the failure of the liberal reformers does not lie merely in their political misjudgement, but is rooted in the dualistic model of the transition derived from Adam Smith's ideal liberal model of a capitalist economy. According to this model, the freedom of the market and the security of private property and the person are sufficient conditions for a dynamic capitalism to develop on the basis of the universal pursuit of individual self-interest. For this model the previous system had no dynamic of its own. It is defined purely negatively as a barrier to change which must be destroyed, so that a new system can be created out of the fragments set free by its destruction. This model does not recognise that the individuals who are creating the new system are characterised by values, motivations and perceptions that are marked by their own past and that they act within the framework of institutions and on the basis of a disposition of resources inherited from the past. The past is not merely a barrier to the achievement of the glorious future (a depiction shared by the Communist Party

---

[1] Adam Smith, *The Wealth of Nations*, vol. I, London: Dent, 1910, pp. 414–15.
[2] Simon Clarke, *Keynesianism, Monetarism and the Crisis of the State*, London and Brookfield: Edward Elgar, 1988.
[3] Simon Clarke, 'Crisis of socialism or crisis of the state', *Capital and Class* 42, Winter 1990: 19–29.

of the Soviet Union and the 'market bolshevik'[1] neo-liberal reformers), the future is simply another stage in the development of the past. What is at issue is not the transition or transformation of one system into another, but the historical development of the existing system. The driving force of this development is not the spontaneous expression of individual self-interest, but the incorporation of the Former Soviet Union into the global capitalist system through the progressive integration of the soviet system into the structures of the world market. It is not to Adam Smith or Friedrich Hayek that we should look to understand the development of capitalism, but to Smith's most cogent critic, Karl Marx.

Contrary to the expectations of the neo-liberal theorists of 'shock therapy', the collapse of the soviet system did not lead to the rapid and spontaneous development of the institutions and practices typical of a capitalist market economy. This has led some critics to doubt whether Russia was in transition to industrial capitalism at all. Michael Burawoy, for example, argued that the collapse of the soviet system had led to the transformation of the 'relations of production through which goods and services are appropriated and distributed', but had reinforced the traditional soviet 'relations in production that describe the production of those goods and services'.[2] What was emerging was 'merchant capitalism' which, far from being a stage in the development of bourgeois industrial capitalism, tends, quoting Marx, 'to preserve and retain [the old mode of production] as its precondition'.[3] This led Burawoy to characterise the developmental trajectory of the Russian economy as one of 'involution', akin to Weber's 'booty capitalism', in which profits are extracted by banks and trading monopolies while nothing is reinvested in production, which continues to be conducted in traditional soviet ways.[4] Richard Ericson has similarly characterised the emerging system as an 'industrial feudalism'.[5] Clifford Gaddy and Barry Ickes argued in an influential, if overblown, article that 'Most of the Russian economy has not been making progress toward the market. . . . It is actively moving in the other direction'. Industrial enterprises have adapted 'to protect themselves against the market rather than join it', characterising demonetisation as a way of sustaining the derelict soviet economy although, as David Woodruff has argued, this was a perfectly rational response to neo-liberal policies.[6]

---

[1] Peter Reddaway and Dmitri Glinsky, *Tragedy of Russia's Reforms: Market Bolshevism Against Democracy*, Washington, DC: U.S. Institute of Peace Press, 2001.

[2] Burawoy and Krotov, 'The soviet transition from socialism to capitalism', p. 18.

[3] Ibid., p. 35.

[4] Michael Burawoy, 'The state and economic involution: Russia through a Chinese lens', *World Development* 24, 1996: 1105–17.

[5] Richard Ericson, *The Post-Soviet Russian Economic System: An Industrial Feudalism?*, Helsinki: Bank of Finland, BOFIT Online 8/2000.

[6] Clifford C. Gaddy and Barry W. Ickes, 'Russia's virtual economy', *Foreign Affairs* 77(5), September–October 1998: 53–67; David M. Woodruff 'It's value that's virtual: bartles, rubles, and the place of Gazprom in the Russian economy', *Post-Soviet Affairs* 15(2), April–June 1999: 130–48.

These arguments are reminiscent of those invoked in the debate among Marxist historians around 'the transition from feudalism to capitalism', where the point at issue was whether or not the development of a market economy necessarily precipitated the collapse of feudalism and the transition to capitalism in early modern Western Europe. The debate was first engaged between Maurice Dobb and Paul Sweezy,[1] and was then resumed by Bob Brenner, with Dobb and Brenner arguing, against Sweezy's 'neo-Smithian' approach, that merchant capital made its profits by buying cheap and selling dear, and was not interested in how its commodities were produced.[2] While merchant capital eventually penetrated into production in Western Europe, increasing world trade led to the reinforcement of pre-capitalist modes of production in the rest of the world: slavery in the Americas; feudalism, with the 'second serfdom' in Eastern Europe and debt peonage in Latin America; and household peasant agriculture and landlordism in the 'underdeveloped' world. According to Burawoy, in a repetition of the 'second serfdom', the incorporation of the soviet system of production into the world capitalist market led not to the dissolution but to the reinforcement of soviet relations in production.

While Burawoy's analysis is certainly supported by the experience of the 1990s, it is doubtful that the analysis can be applied to the former state socialist industrial countries over an extended period of time. The fundamental difference is that the slave plantation, feudal estate and peasant household were largely self-sufficient and so were able, within limits, to secure their continued reproduction and to continue to produce a surplus, to be appropriated in the form of commodities for sale by merchant capitalists. State socialist industrial enterprises, on the other hand, depended on the state socialist system of distribution for their inputs of parts and raw materials, for the payment of wages and provision of means of subsistence for their workers and, most importantly in the longer term, for investment to sustain or expand their productive capacity. The collapse of the state socialist system, therefore, implied the collapse of the conditions for the reproduction of the industrial enterprise and so for the reproduction of Burawoy's system of merchant capitalism or Ericson's industrial feudalism.

Burawoy is quite right to insist that the collapse of the soviet system led to a transformation of what he calls the 'relations of production', without leading to any fundamental change of the 'relations in production'. He is quite right to argue that the rise of capitalist intermediaries initially reproduced and even reinforced the 'soviet' character of the 'relations in production', and he is largely right that institutions and households resorted to 'involution' and increasing self-sufficiency in their struggles to survive,[3] although they survived

[1] Rodney Hilton (ed.), *The Transition from Feudalism to Capitalism,* London: NLB, 1976; Maurice Dobb, *Studies in the Development of Capitalism,* London: Routledge & Kegan Paul, 1946.

[2] Trevor H. Aston and Charles H. E. Philpin (eds), *The Brenner Debate: Agrarian Class Structure and Economic Development in Pre-Industrial Europe,* Cambridge: CUP, 1985.

[3] Michael Burawoy, Pavel Krotov and Tatyana Lytkina, 'Involution and destitution in capitalist Russia', *Ethnography* 1(1), 2000: 43–65.

primarily by cutting consumption and expenditure, rather than by finding new productive resources.[1] However, the system of merchant capitalism that he describes is not sustainable. If profits are extracted by banks and trading monopolies and are not reinvested in production, the production process will gradually grind to a halt as plant and equipment wear out and are not replaced. This was indeed, as we shall see, the tendency in Russian industry through the 1990s, and the prospect was one of continuous economic decline, potentially reducing the Russian population to a nation of 'urban peasants', with low or no wages, at best surviving on the produce of their vegetable plots, reducing Russia to an 'Upper Volta with missiles'. The only alternatives were the transition to an industrial capitalist system through the penetration of capital into production or the reconstitution of a centrally planned economy. Until 1998 these alternatives were no more than programmatic dreams of the political extremes. However, since the 1998 financial crisis, there has been a marked penetration of capital into Russian industry and an upturn of industrial investment, as an increasing number of industrial enterprises have been taken over by Russian holding companies, which purport to be the standard-bearers of capitalist management structures and practices in Russia, and even by foreign investors.

The appropriate model for the theorisation of the transformation of state socialism is not merchant capitalism or industrial feudalism, but Marx's account of the development of capitalism in Western Europe. The development of capitalism, for Marx, was not Smith's realisation of individual reason but an expression of the development of commodity production within the feudal order, which was hugely accelerated by the dispossession of the mass of the rural population, who became the wage labourers for capital and the consumers of the products of capitalist industry and agriculture.[2] The dispossession of the rural population by force and by the commercialisation of agriculture provided an ample reserve of cheap wage labour which could be profitably employed by the capitals accumulated at the expense of the landed class through trade and plunder. At this first stage of capitalist development, however, capitalists did not change the handicraft methods of production which they had inherited, so the subsumption of labour under capital was purely formal. Competition between capitalist producers forced them to cut their costs, but they did so not by transforming methods of production but by forcing down wages and extending the working day. Capital only penetrated the sphere of production when competition between producers induced and compelled them to revolutionise the methods of production in order to earn an additional profit, or resist the competition of those who had already done so. It was only with the 'real subsumption' of labour under capital that the characteristic dynamic of the capitalist mode of production got under way. Nevertheless, in the peripheral regions of the emerging global capitalist economy, alongside the destruction of much traditional handicraft and subsistence agriculture, the subsumption of

---

[1] Simon Clarke, *Making Ends Meet in Contemporary Russia: Secondary Employment, Subsidiary Agriculture and Social Networks*, Cheltenham: Edward Elgar, 2002.

[2] Karl Marx, *Capital*, vol. I, part VIII.

production under capital remained purely formal, based on the intensified exploitation of pre-capitalist modes of production.

The process described by Marx as that of 'primitive accumulation' was interrupted in Russia by the October Revolution, but it was completed in the soviet period when the peasants were dispossessed and transformed into wage labourers, not for capital but for the state, which launched a programme of industrialisation based on the introduction of the most advanced capitalist technology. This has led some to characterise the soviet system as 'state capitalist',[1] which leads to a view of the transition as involving merely a transition from state to private monopoly capitalism through the transfer of juridical ownership of property in the privatisation programme. However, the social form of the production and appropriation of a surplus in the soviet system was quite different from that characteristic of the capitalist mode of production, and the dynamics of the system were correspondingly different.

The contradictions of the soviet system

The soviet system had many features in common with the capitalist system of production. It was based on advanced technology and a high degree of socialisation of production, which was the social and material basis of the separation of the direct producers from the ownership and control of the means of production. As in the capitalist system, labour was employed by enterprises and organisations in the form of wage labour and the production of goods and services for individual and social need was subordinated to the production and appropriation of a surplus. However, the two systems differed fundamentally in the form of the surplus and correspondingly in the social organisation of the production and appropriation of that surplus.[2]

The soviet system was not based on the maximisation of profit, nor was it based on planned provision for social need. It was a system of surplus appropriation and redistribution subordinated to the material needs of the state and, above all in its years of maturity, of its military apparatus. This subordination of the entire socio-economic system to the demands of the military for men, materials and machines dictated that it was essentially a non-monetary system. The development of the system was not subordinated to the expansion of the gross or net product in the abstract, an abstraction which can only be expressed in a monetary form, but to expanding the production of specific materials and equipment – tanks, guns, aircraft, explosives, missiles – and to supporting the huge military machine. The strategic isolation of the Soviet Union meant that no amount of money could buy these military commodities, so the soviet state had to ensure that they were produced in

---

[1] Tony Cliff, *Russia: A Marxist Analysis*, London: Pluto Press, 1970.

[2] This section draws heavily on the analysis I developed in Simon Clarke, Peter Fairbrother, Michael Burawoy and Pavel Krotov, *What about the Workers? Workers and the Transition to Capitalism in Russia*, London: Verso, and Simon Clarke, *The Russian Enterprise in Transition: Case Studies*, Cheltenham: Edward Elgar, 1996.

appropriate numbers and appropriate proportions, and correspondingly that all the means of production required to produce them were available at the right time and in the right place.

The system of 'central planning' was developed in Stalin's industrialisation drive of the 1930s in a framework of generalised shortage, including an acute shortage of experienced (and politically reliable) managers and administrators. The system was driven by the demands of the state for a growing physical surplus with scant regard for the material constraints of skills, resources and capacities on production. The strategic demands of the five-year plan would be determined by the priorities of the regime, initially the demand for the means of industrial investment and ultimately by the demands of the military apparatus, which would then be converted into requirements for all the various branches of production. These requirements came to be determined in a process of negotiation between the central planning authorities, ministries and industrial enterprises.

The bureaucratisation of the planning system from the 1950s represented a significant and progressive shift in the balance of power from the centre to the periphery as the negotiated element in plan determination increased, at the expense of its exhortatory promulgation and repressive reinforcement. Alongside this, the single-minded orientation of production to building industrial capacity and meeting insatiable military needs was tempered by a growing concern for the material needs of the mass of the population: the expansion of housing and social consumption from the 1950s and of individual consumption from the 1960s, which was linked to the increasing role of material incentives in stimulating the energy and initiative of the direct producers and securing the reproduction of the labour force.

Soviet social relations of production were supposed to overcome the contradictions inherent in the capitalist mode of production in being based on the centralised control of the planned distribution and redistribution of productive resources. However, the soviet system was marked by its own system of surplus appropriation and associated contradictions. Enterprises and organisations negotiated the allocation of means of production and subsistence with the centre in exchange for the delivery of defined production targets, the surplus taking the form of the net product appropriated by the military-Party-state to secure its own expanded reproduction.

The fundamental contradiction of the soviet system lay in the separation of production and distribution which led to a contradiction between the production and appropriation of the surplus. The development of the forces of production was constrained by the exploitative social relations of production, and it was this specific contradiction that underpinned the collapse of the 'administrative-command' system. The central planning agencies sought to maximise the surplus in their negotiations with ministries and departments, enterprises and organisations over the allocation of resources and determination of production plans. However, the enterprises and organisations which were the units of production had an interest in minimising the surplus by inflating the resources allocated to them and reducing their planned output targets. The softer the plan that they could negotiate, the easier it was for the enterprise directors and their line managers to induce or compel the labour force to meet the plan targets. Since neither the worker, nor the enterprise, nor even the ministry, had any rights to the surplus produced, they could only reliably expand the resources at their disposal by inflating their demand for productive resources, and could only protect themselves from the exactions of the ruling stratum by concealing their productive potential. Resistance to the demands of the military-Party-state apparatus for an expanding surplus product rested ultimately on the active and passive resistance of workers to their intensified exploitation, but it ran through the system from bottom to top and was impervious to all attempts at bureaucratic reform. The resulting rigidities of the system determined its extensive form of development, the expansion of the surplus depending on the mobilisation of additional resources. When the reserves, particularly of labour, had been exhausted the rate of growth of production and of surplus appropriation slowed down.

The fundamental contradiction of the soviet system was between the system of production and the system of surplus appropriation. The centralised control and allocation of the surplus product in the hands of an unproductive ruling stratum meant that the producers had an interest not in maximising but in minimising the surplus that they produced. The contradiction between the forces and relations of production was also expressed in chronic shortages. Enterprises were oriented purely to meeting their formal plan targets, not to meeting the needs of their customers. Thus, while the centre could allocate rights to supplies, it could not ensure that those supplies were delivered to the place, at the time, in the quantity and of the quality desired. The endemic problems of shortages and of poor quality of supplies were an inherent feature not of a system of economic planning, but of a system based on the centralised allocation of supplies as the means of securing the centralised appropriation of a surplus.

Like capitalism, but in a quite different way, state socialism was a system within which the practice of individual rationality led to socially irrational outcomes. These irrational outcomes were not defects that could be remedied by introducing reforms into the system, for they were inherent in the system itself.

The transition to a market economy

As in the case of feudalism, the contradictions inherent in the soviet system meant that money, the market and quasi-market relations developed spontaneously out of attempts to overcome the contradictions of the system and were tolerated, however reluctantly, by the authorities.

First, even if the supplies allocated to an enterprise by the plan were adequate, securing these supplies was a major problem, for the resolution of which enterprises used informal personal connections with their suppliers, often backed up by local Party *apparatchiki*, and came increasingly to draw on the services of unofficial intermediaries, the so-called *tolkachi* (pushers), who were the pioneers of market relations within the soviet economy. The central directives which nominally regulated inter-enterprise transactions within the soviet system were therefore only realised in practice through exchanges within networks of personal, political and commercial connections.

Second, Trotsky's early attempts at the 'militarisation of labour' were unsuccessful and, although wages were regulated centrally, workers were always in practice free to change jobs in search of higher wages. Labour shortages put increasing pressure on the centralised regulation of wages as employers sought to attract the scarcest categories of labour, so that wage-setting had to take account of labour market conditions, with 'coefficients' providing higher wages in priority branches of production and in the more remote regions.[1]

Third, although social reproduction was as far as possible subordinated to the imperatives of production, with housing, items of collective consumption, a wide range of social and welfare benefits and the right to buy goods and services which were not on free sale being provided through the workplace, labour power was partially commodified and workers were paid a money wage with which they bought their heavily subsidised means of subsistence and which they saved in the hope of acquiring the right to buy consumer durables, to take a holiday or to provide for retirement. Money in the hands of workers lubricated the black market for consumer goods and for the private production of agricultural produce for the market which was tolerated and even encouraged, with rural producers being allowed to sell their own products on the *kolkhoz* markets, which provided a basis for more extensive market transactions.

Fourth, the need to acquire advanced means of production from the west meant that the Soviet Union had to export its natural resources in order to finance its essential imports of machinery. Although the state retained a monopoly of foreign trade, this made the soviet system very vulnerable to fluctuations in world market prices and so to the instability of global capitalism. The 1930s industrialisation drive was made possible by the massive export of grain forcibly expropriated from the peasantry, which led to the devastating famines of the 1930s. By the Brezhnev period the Soviet Union had become dependent on its exports of oil and gas to finance its imports of machinery and even of food. In 1985 fuel accounted for more than half the Soviet Union's exports, with another quarter being accounted for by raw and semi-processed raw materials, while machinery accounted for a third of imports and food for one-fifth. The share of world trade in the net material product of the Soviet Union increased from 3.7 per cent in 1970 to almost 10 per cent in 1980 and a high of 11 per cent in 1985, while oil and gas production doubled between 1970 and 1980. At the same time, the Soviet Union saw a sharp improvement in its terms of trade, the net barter terms of trade improving by an average of 5 per cent per annum over the period 1976–80 and 3 per cent per annum between 1980 and 1985, helping to offset the decline in productivity growth and allowing the Soviet Union to increase its import volume by one-third, while export

---

[1] Simon Clarke, *The Formation of a Labour Market in Russia*, Cheltenham: Edward Elgar, 1999, Chapter One.

volume increased by only 10 per cent.[1] The improved terms of trade also made a substantial contribution to the buoyancy of government revenues through the price equalisation system. This opening of the soviet economy to the world market, and the corresponding political processes of détente, were by no means a sign of fundamental change in the soviet system, but were rather the means by which change was constantly postponed as the soviet system was sustained by the vagaries of world capitalism.[2] However, such favourable circumstances could not last: production of gas and oil peaked in 1980, so that the Soviet Union was increasingly dependent on improvement in the terms of trade to sustain its economy. When the terms of trade turned sharply against the Soviet Union from 1985, the system moved into a deepening crisis.

Proposals for reform of the soviet system were always based on providing direct producers with material incentives to increase production and to make suppliers more responsive to the needs of consumers. Such reforms necessarily implied giving more independence to enterprises and allowing them to retain a portion of the revenue received from the sale of their output, which necessarily implied in turn an increasing role for money and market relations, since producers had to have the freedom to dispose of the incentive funds put at their disposal.

The dilemma that all such reforms soon presented to the centre was that they necessarily eroded centralised control, so even if they were successful at encouraging the development of the forces of production, this was at the expense of the erosion of the system of surplus appropriation. Moreover, once reform was set under way it tended to acquire a dynamic of its own, as enterprises which had received a taste of independence demanded more. For these reasons, every reform initiative prior to Gorbachev had been reversed in order to preserve the system. In the same way, Gorbachev also came under pressure to reverse his reforms, but Gorbachev's reforms soon acquired an unstoppable momentum, particularly as the erosion of the administrative-command system of economic management undermined the authoritarian political system with which it was enmeshed.

The 'transition to a market economy' was not an alien project imposed on the soviet system by liberal economists, but was an expression of the fundamental contradiction of the soviet system. Gorbachev never had a coherent reform programme. Perestroika was reactive, pragmatic and fragmented, each reform responding to pressures created by the previous stage of reform. The first stage of market reforms sought to improve the balance of external trade by ending the state monopoly of foreign trade, licensing enterprises and organisations to engage in export operations and to retain a portion of the hard currency earned. The idea was that this would give industrial enterprises an incentive to compete in world markets and to use the foreign exchange earned to acquire modern equipment. In practice it provided a windfall for exporting enterprises, at the

[1] IMF/World Bank/OECD, *A Study of the Soviet Economy*, three volumes, Washington, DC, Paris: IMF, World Bank, OECD, 1991, volume I, pp. 86, 105.
[2] Marie Lavigne, *The Economics of Transition*, second edition, Houndmills: Macmillan, 1999, p. 55.

expense of the state, and opportunities for those with the right connections to make huge profits by acting as intermediaries.

Once the precedent had been set, other enterprises sought the right to sell above-plan output on export or domestic markets, and to retain a growing proportion of the proceeds. This aspiration was met with the proposed replacement of plan deliveries by state orders at fixed state prices, with the control of prices replacing the control of quantities. But the emergence of new structures of distribution further undermined the centralised control of the system. Allowing enterprises to sell on the market provided an alternative source of supply to the centralised allocations which the state could not guarantee, and if the state could not guarantee supplies, why should enterprises continue to deliver their state orders when they could sell more profitably at market prices? Thus the development of market relations undermined the control of the centre, created a space for the development of capitalist commercial and financial enterprise and precipitated the collapse of the administrative-command system. Rather than resolving the contradictions inherent in the soviet system, the 'transition to a market economy' brought those contradictions to a head. While market reforms might provide an incentive for enterprises to develop the forces of production, the loss of centralised control undermined the system of surplus appropriation by removing the state control of supply which was the basis on which the state extracted the surplus. The surplus which had been appropriated by the state was now retained by enterprises and/or appropriated by the new financial and commercial intermediaries that arose to handle the emerging market relations.

The collapse of the administrative-command system of economic management under the pressure of growing demands for economic independence also undermined the centralised political system of which it was an integral part as national and regional authorities asserted their independence of the centre. Yeltsin ruthlessly exploited these tendencies in his struggle with Gorbachev, but once he had seized power in Russia his priority was to strengthen rather than to undermine a centralised Russian state. If the Russian Federation was to survive, it was essential to detach the state from its responsibility for the economy, which meant that it had to give free rein to the market relations and market actors which had emerged. Yeltsin's decision to free wages and most prices from state control at the end of 1991 was no more than a recognition that the state had already lost control of wages and prices, since by the end of 1991 nothing was available to buy at such prices.

Corporatisation and privatisation of state enterprises were equally inevitable consequences of the disintegration of the administrative-command system, merely a juridical recognition of what had already become a fact: these enterprises had already detached themselves from the administrative-command system of management which no longer had any levers of control over them. Privatisation did not give enterprises any more rights than they had already appropriated for themselves, while it allowed the state to abdicate all the responsibilities to them which it no longer had the means to fulfil. Thus, the ideology of neo-liberalism and radical reform was little more than a rhetoric to cover what was essentially a bowing to the inevitable.

Integration into global capitalism

It is tempting to see the rapid collapse of the soviet system and the equally rapid emergence of market relations as a cataclysmic event marking a radical break between the past and the future. However, although very few people had expected any such dramatic developments, in retrospect we can see that the pattern of collapse and emergence was prefigured in the developmental tendencies of the soviet system which expressed its fundamental contradictions. The Stalinist system had been created on the basis of exhortation and repression, backed up by dramatic political penalties and rewards to encourage workers and managers to superhuman effort, but even under Stalin it had proved necessary to allow a role for material incentives and horizontal quasi-market relations in an attempt to compensate for the deficiencies of a repressive authoritarian system. With the bureaucratisation of the system from the 1950s repression was increasingly tempered by negotiation, through which the Party-state was compelled to accommodate to the material and social barriers to intensified exploitation, while attempts to overcome the deficiencies of the system by providing material incentives to workers and managers necessarily implied the expansion of market relations and the further weakening of centralised control. This was the stumbling block of reform throughout the Brezhnev period, during which the failures of the system to provide the material elements of its own reproduction were compensated by an increasing reliance on the world market for supplies of food and machinery. As export growth slowed and the terms of trade turned against the Soviet Union in the 1980s the new wave of reform was unleashed, the dynamic of which rapidly eroded the entire economic and political system. The course of reform, from ending the state monopoly of foreign trade to abandoning state control of prices and wages, was not simply the transition from an administrative-command system to a market economy in Russia, but was more specifically a process of integration of the soviet economy into the global capitalist economy through its subordination to the world market.

The collapse of the soviet system transformed the environment within which enterprises and organisations had to operate. Enterprises and organisations were now subject to the constraints of the market: in order to reproduce themselves they had to secure sufficient revenues to cover the costs of wages and the purchase of means of production and raw materials and, to the extent that they did not receive subsidies and subventions from government, this could only be achieved by selling their products as commodities on the market at a price sufficient to cover their costs. To this extent, enterprises and organisations were subordinated to capital through their subordination to the rule of money, but this did not have any immediate impact on their internal practices and procedures, which did not immediately adjust to the capitalist demands of profit maximisation. In the first instance, the immediate priority of the workers and managers of enterprises and organisations, who in the majority of cases were soon to be recognised as their owners, was to secure their own reproduction. The watchword of the 1990s was 'survival'.

The integration of the soviet economy into the global capitalist economy provided opportunities for some and presented barriers to others. The opportunities were primarily seized by commercial intermediaries, who were able to make enormous profits through arbitrage as a result of the disparity between domestic and world market prices, reflecting differences between domestic and global production conditions. This was the basis of the 'primitive accumulation of capital' during the late 1980s and early 1990s, which led to the rapid growth of new capitalist companies in trade and finance. The emergence of private commercial and financial capitalist enterprises represented a change in the form of surplus appropriation, or at least a change in the identity of those appropriating the surplus, since the appropriation of the surplus was still based on the exercise of monopoly power and divorced from the production of the surplus. The new capitals were formed by the commercial and financial intermediaries which had their roots in the interstices of the soviet system and had been given free rein by perestroika. They appropriated their profits by establishing the monopoly control of supplies which had formerly been the prerogative of the state. They acquired this control on the basis of rights assigned to them by state bodies and they maintained their control by the corruption of state officials and enterprise directors, backed up by the threat and use of force. This was not a matter of the corruption of an ideal capitalist system, it was a normal adaptation of capitalism to the conditions it confronted. However, the change in the form of surplus appropriation was not matched by any change in the social relations of production.

The surplus was not appropriated on the basis of the transformation of the social organisation of production or the investment of capital in production. It was appropriated on the basis of trading monopolies, above all in the export of fuels and raw and processed raw materials (which by 1998 made up 80 per cent of Russian exports) though also in domestic trade. It was appropriated through the banking system, which made huge profits through commercial intermediation and speculation in currency and government debt. Meanwhile, the bulk of enterprise profits were annihilated by taxation, leaving little or nothing to pay out as dividends to shareholders. The windfall profits which enterprises could make in the late 1980s when they could buy at state prices and sell at market prices were annihilated by the liberalisation of prices at the end of 1991. With the collapse of the soviet system, enterprises inherited the land and premises, their capital stock and their stocks of parts and raw materials, which substantially reduced their costs and enabled many to remain in profit by trading on their inherited assets. But by 1996 the majority of enterprises were loss-making.

This is the phenomenon that Burawoy characterises as 'merchant capitalism', in which capitalists make their profits through intermediation, exploiting the divergence between Russian and world market prices, without making any investment in production. But the merchant capitalists were not the driving force of the development of the Russian economy and society through the 1990s, they were merely the intermediaries with global capital. The experience of the 1990s was the experience of integration into the capitalist world market, into a system dominated by the dynamics of capital accumulation on a world scale. The first stage of Russia's incorporation into global capitalism from the late 1980s was as a source of fuel and raw materials, extracted and processed by traditional soviet enterprises on the basis of existing production facilities, with virtually no productive investment in the expansion or even the renewal of production capacity, but the dynamics of the Russian economy through the 1990s showed that this phase of pure exploitation could not be sustained. Continuing economic and social collapse was quite possible: Russia would not be the first country to suffer from 'the development of underdevelopment'.[1] But the default and devaluation of the 1998 crisis transformed the terms of Russia's integration into the global economy, reduced the opportunities for rentier capitalism, and provided more favourable conditions for economic growth and social stabilisation based on the penetration of capital into production. While the first stage of the incorporation of Russia into global capitalism was associated with the purely formal subsumption of production units under capital, the penetration of capital into production opens up the possibilities of their real subsumption and the systematic subordination of the production process to the logic of capital.

Following the Smithian logic, the neo-liberal literature places most emphasis on 'order and good government', in the form of corporate governance structures, transparency and the rule of law, as the conditions for the renewal of economic growth in Russia, but it is notable that the recovery since 1998 has not been based on or associated with marked improvements in corporate governance, accountancy and legal practices. These institutional arrangements are undoubtedly important for outside investors, who need to be able to evaluate investment opportunities and have some guarantees of being able to exercise ownership rights, and so the large Russian companies which want to get access to international capital markets have, at least formally, adopted international practices. But just as important for the direct investors who play the predominant role in productive investment in Russia is the development of appropriate management structures and practices which permit the subordination of the production of use values to the production and appropriation of surplus value. It is these structures and practices that are the focus of this book.

What management structures and practices are appropriate for Russia? Recent discussion of the 'varieties of capitalism' has shown that capitalism can adapt to a wide range of institutional and cultural contexts. In different countries and at different times, and even within the same country at the same time, capitalism has shown itself to be compatible with different systems of financing (stock markets, retained profits or bank-lending), different forms of regulation of labour relations (individualistic, collectivist), different payment systems

---

[1] André Gunder Frank, *The Development of Underdevelopment*, New York: Monthly Review Press, 1966.

(money, in-kind; individual, collective; piece-rate, time-based), different forms of social and welfare provision (employer-based, state-based, insurance-based). But to compete, capital has to subordinate production to the production of surplus value. This means that it has to install systematic management structures and practices through which it can obtain relevant information and take and implement appropriate decisions. These are not purely formal bureaucratic structures, they are social structures through which the divergent interests of different managers and workers have to be subordinated to the accumulation of capital. The ultimate barrier to the production and appropriation of a surplus is the resistance of the direct producers to their exploitation, but this resistance does not necessarily appear immediately as such, and class antagonism certainly does not necessarily result in class polarisation and class confrontation. To what extent has capital penetrated production in Russia and what are the barriers to this penetration? This is the focus of our research.

In the next two chapters we will first look more closely at the social relations of production as they manifested themselves in the soviet industrial enterprise and then look at the main characteristics of the response of those enterprises to the 'transitional crisis' of the 1990s. We will then examine in some detail the development of systems of corporate management in Russian enterprises since the 1998 default before looking more closely at personnel management, wage systems and the role of line managers. We return to the question of the character of and prospects for Russian capitalism in the concluding chapter.

3 The soviet industrial enterprise

The legacies of the soviet past were deeply embedded in the structures and practices of Russian industrial enterprises and organisations. These structures and practices were adapted to achieving the tasks set for the enterprise within the environment within which it had developed and they had shown a remarkable stability throughout the soviet period.

> *The great strength of the soviet factory, from an organisational point of view, is that it has been the only stable structure in all of soviet industry. Ministries and their subdivisions have been split apart, lumped together in new combinations, and then once more splintered. This process continued steadily over a period of three decades.... In all of this shuffling, only the plant organisation was left alone.*[1]

Just as the industrial enterprise had persisted through the soviet period as an island of stability in a sea of change, so it provided the stable reference point for managers and workers in the face of the collapse of the institutions of state socialism and the incorporation of the Russian economy into the structures of global capitalism. This is not the place to provide a theoretical and/or a historical account of the development of the soviet industrial enterprise. In this chapter I simply want to identify those characteristics of the soviet industrial enterprise which mark it out from comparable capitalist industrial enterprises and which provide a legacy and perhaps a barrier to the development of Russian capitalism.

The external environment

Many of the distinctive social and technological features of soviet enterprises and organisations were determined by characteristics of the external environment within which they had been created and had developed. The collapse of the administrative-command system transformed the external environment, but many of these features were embedded in the enterprise and

---

[1] David Granick, *The Red Executive*, New York: Doubleday, 1960, pp. 161–2.

remained as a legacy of the administrative-command system even after the latter had collapsed.

The central characteristic of the system in which enterprises and organisations were inserted was that it was built around a distinctive but fundamental contradiction. This derived from the fact that it was a centralised system of surplus appropriation in which the central authorities, ultimately directed by the Politburo, sought to maximise the material surplus extracted from enterprises and organisations under its control, while the enterprises and organisations at every level sought to maximise the resources at their disposal in order to secure their own expanded reproduction. This contradiction was expressed in the annual negotiations over the plan, as the central planning authorities sought to maximise plan deliveries and limit the resources allocated to the achievement of the plan to the minimum necessary, while ministries, production associations, enterprises and organisations at all levels sought to minimise their obligations and maximise the resources at their disposal.

From a purely economic point of view, agents throughout the system were seeking to maximise production costs, but from their own point of view they were seeking to maximise the resources at their disposal to secure their own reproduction. The more resources the enterprise can claim, the more it can produce not only for the plan but also for its own needs. It can produce new plant and machinery for its own use, goods for local consumption, better housing, social, welfare and cultural facilities for the local community and maintain the productive and social infrastructure. It can thereby raise the prestige of the enterprise and its community and attract skilled workers and specialists. In short, the tendency to the maximisation of costs is not an economic irrationality, it is merely the view of the exploiting class of the tendency for the enterprise to expand the production of things for its own benefit: it is a drain on the surplus to the benefit of the needs of the direct producers, a subversion of the system of surplus appropriation.

The resistance of lower levels of the system to the appropriation of a surplus from above was the basis of the 'production pact' between soviet workers and managers,[1] an expression of the fact that, while individual workers and line managers had opposing interests in the everyday struggle to meet the plan, they had a common interest in maximising supplies, minimising plan targets and keeping plan overfulfilment within limits, which would permit the earning of bonuses without risking an excessive ratcheting of the plan. Within the soviet system this commonality of interest in thwarting the system ran all the way from the bottom to the top. The soviet enthusiasm for the crudest version of Taylorism is a reflection of this contradiction at the heart of the system: one way of trying to check such collusion was the systematic application of the 'scientific organisation of labour', the ideal being for scientifically determined technical norms to be applied to every task in every workplace in the country.

---

[1] Simon Clarke and Peter Fairbrother, 'Trade unions and the working class', in Simon Clarke *et al.*, *What About the Workers?*, p. 99.

Such a mechanistic approach to the organisation of labour could not possibly work, for obvious and well-known reasons,[1] so the 'scientific organisation of labour' was supplemented (or even displaced) by more direct intervention to drive workers to ever greater efforts, that intervention in the late soviet period becoming the responsibility of the trade union. Stakhanovism, shock work, counter-plans, socialist competition, production conferences, unpaid working Saturdays (*subbotniki*), campaigns to encourage invention and innovation, the distribution of honours and awards were all the responsibility of the trade union, which was supposed constantly to exhort the workers to greater efforts, even if such activities had little impact. On the one hand, they were regarded with scepticism or derision by the majority of workers – production conferences, which had been reintroduced in the 1950s, were dominated by engineers and specialists rather than ordinary workers.[2] On the other hand, management resisted any attempts by the trade union to interfere in the management of production, which were likely to prove disruptive and to undermine the authority of line managers.

The limited capacity of the planning system and of the apparatuses of local and municipal government meant that industrial enterprises were given responsibility not only for the production of their assigned outputs, but also for the physical and social reproduction of the labour force. Enterprises constructed housing for their workforce, often built the roads and amenities for their surrounding district, constructed and ran social, cultural, health, educational and sporting facilities for their employees and their families and, in the case of larger enterprises, for their local communities. The enterprise was also assigned other responsibilities to the local community, such as providing voluntary labour to clean the streets, particularly after the spring thaw, repairing and maintaining local roads and community facilities and providing labour for agricultural work, particularly at harvest time. This raft of obligations imposed on the enterprise was one reason why soviet enterprises maintained much larger labour forces and appeared grossly overmanned in comparison with their capitalist equivalents. On the one hand, some of this expenditure can be considered as a form of collective payment in kind to the labour force, providing some compensation for relatively low wages. On the other hand, however, it nevertheless imposed a considerable financial burden on many Russian enterprises once they had to make their own way in the market economy.

The large social, cultural and welfare apparatus attached to the soviet enterprise did not only have an economic significance. It was an indicator of the much greater centrality of the soviet enterprise in the lives of its employees than

---

[1] Richard Edwards, *Contested Terrain: The Transformation of the Workplace in the Twentieth Century*, New York: Basic Books, 1979; Paul Thompson, *The Nature of Work: An Introduction to Debates on the Labour Process*, London: Macmillan, 1983; Vladimir Andrle, *Workers in Stalin's Russia*, New York: St Martin's Press, 1988; William G. Rosenberg and Lewis H. Siegelbaum (eds), *Social Dimensions of Soviet Industrialisation*, Bloomington: Indiana University Press, 1993.

[2] Blair Ruble, *Soviet Trade Unions: Their Development in the 1970s*, Cambridge: Cambridge University Press, 1981, Chapter Five.

is normally the case with its capitalist equivalent. When we consider the extremely cramped living conditions and the very limited provision of social and cultural facilities outside the workplace, it is understandable that many people considered their place of work to be their 'second home', which provided the focus for much of their social and cultural life. This is expressed in the conception of the soviet enterprise as a 'labour collective', a social organisation whose function is not only the production of goods according to the directives of the plan, but also the social reproduction of the workforce and, indeed, of the local community. This conception was manifested in the iconography of the soviet enterprise, whose achievements were measured not simply by its honours and awards and the growing volume of its production but by the size, education and skill composition of the labour force, the number of houses built, kindergartens supported and the scale of its cultural and sporting facilities.

This ideological representation of the soviet enterprise was one in which production was the means to increase the technological, cultural and educational level and material well-being of the labour collective. It was in the name of the labour collective that the administration ruled the enterprise and pressed its interests against higher authorities, and it was in the name of the labour collective that individual workers were subjected to managerial authority. It was the labour collective which was made responsible not only for production activity but also for the everyday behaviour and moral character of its members. This was not simply an ideological mystification. The members of a brigade, a shop or an enterprise, workers and managers alike, really did have a common interest in the struggle over the appropriation and redistribution of the surplus. The director really did represent the interests of the labour collective in the battle for the plan, the shop chief in negotiating the targets for the shop, the foreman in seeking to achieve slack norms for their workers. Once the plans, targets and norms were set, these defined the determinate limits of the exploitation of the labour collective, within which limits it could subordinate the process and the results of production to its own needs; the resources which remained at the disposal of the enterprise could be devoted to meeting the needs of the collective: to building new housing, sports and cultural facilities and so on, while the workers could rest once the plan tasks were completed. The shop chief or enterprise director really could pose as the paternalistic guardian of 'his' labour collective, a pose expressed in a variety of powerful symbolic representations; the director was expected periodically to 'go to the people', touring his shops and greeting veteran workers by name. He (rarely she) was expected to be accessible, holding regular 'surgeries' to which employees could, at least in principle, bring any problem, even personal ones, to the attention of the director. He was expected to live modestly, in the same conditions as the mass of his workers. The good director was not soft, since the success of the enterprise depended on the discipline of the labour collective, but he was expected to be 'firm but fair'.

The concept of the labour collective is central to an understanding of the system of 'authoritarian paternalism' which defined the distinctive forms of soviet management. Paternalism within the soviet enterprise was much more than a management practice, but was embedded in a wider paternalistic structure under the domination of the state, just as the labour collective of the enterprise was only a part of the working class in whose name the state ruled. Thus the content of paternalism consists not only in the additional benefits selectively provided by the enterprise to its employees, but also in the fundamental guarantees of employment and a minimum subsistence provided by the Party-state to all its citizens, guarantees which were fulfilled through the enterprise. It was this guarantee that appeared to be the basis of the social stability of the soviet system and, as such, was monitored and administered by state bodies which had a degree of independence from enterprise management, in particular the trade union and Party committees.[1] With the collapse of the wider soviet political system and the disappearance of the guarantees that it rhetorically endorsed, the security of the labour collective assumed an even greater importance for many of its members, as an island of stability in a world of chaos and disorder.

Soviet economic growth was primarily based on extensive investment, with production capacity being added by the construction of new plants, while it was very rare for outdated plants to be closed down. Instead an outdated plant would eventually be scheduled for reconstruction, usually on the same site and often in the same buildings. In the meantime, the maintenance and upgrading of plant and equipment were often patchy because enterprise directors and line managers were reluctant to take plant and equipment out of service for maintenance, repair or upgrading for fear of undermining the achievement of their monthly plan targets. For the same reason, new capacity tended to be installed alongside the old, which would often be kept in operation or in reserve to facilitate the achievement of plan targets, particularly because the centralised allocation of new equipment meant that the latter was often incompatible with existing equipment or inappropriate to the needs of the enterprise.

Although the last decades of the Soviet Union saw an increasing importance attached to the production of consumer goods for the mass of the population, the planning system was based on clearly defined priorities which gave the lion's share of resources to heavy industry and the military-industrial complex. This was expressed in higher levels of investment, priority access to advanced technology, better training facilities, higher wages, better access to housing and much more developed social and welfare apparatuses. The priority sectors could attract and retain a high-skilled labour force and maintain relatively high levels of labour discipline, while the industries producing for the consumer market generally had to hire anybody they could find to work in poor working

---

[1] On enterprise paternalism see Petr Bizyukov, 'The mechanism of paternalistic management of the enterprise: the limits of paternalism' and Samara Research Group, 'Paternalism: our understanding', both in Simon Clarke (ed.), *Management and Industry in Russia: Formal and Informal Relations in the Russian Industrial Enterprise*, Cheltenham: Edward Elgar, 1995; and Vladimir Ilyin, 'Social contradictions and conflicts in Russian state enterprises in the transition period', in Simon Clarke (ed.), *Conflict and Change in the Russian Industrial Enterprise*, Cheltenham: Edward Elgar, 1996.

conditions with low levels of labour discipline. This was one reason for the notoriously low quality of the output of the consumer goods industries, and why the production of consumer durables, for example, was largely diverted to military-industrial enterprises.

The centrality of the control of supplies to the control of the system and the inability of the administrative-command system of economic management to ensure the timely delivery of appropriate supplies led to a strong tendency towards autarky at every level of the system. Each ministry tried to ensure as far as possible that it had facilities to provide its enterprises with the parts and raw materials that they needed to achieve their plan targets and favoured large integrated plants over more specialised facilities. To this end there was a regular tendency in soviet times to organise and reorganise production associations and integrated production complexes, often including research and design institutes, experimental production complexes and training establishments as well as the various stages of the production process, to facilitate the co-ordination of production units. The dismantling of these production associations and complexes in the privatisation process in the early 1990s played a major part in promoting the disintegration of the Russian economy and the disconnection of training and research and development from production, while creating the space for new commercial and financial intermediaries to get a stranglehold on the dissociated enterprises and recreate these links by forming new corporate structures.

In order to reduce its vulnerability to the uncertainties of supply, each enterprise in the soviet system similarly sought to acquire the ability to produce necessary components for production and spare parts for plant and equipment for itself. This led to a proliferation of small and inefficient sections and workshops and seriously compromised the quality of the product and of maintenance and repairs carried out with non-standard parts.

Despite their best efforts, enterprises could never even approach self-sufficiency. The main barriers to the achievement of the enterprise plan were the constant shortages of appropriate equipment, parts, raw materials and labour. The enterprise's entitlements to labour and supplies were negotiated as part of the negotiation of the plan, but it was always a problem to secure the implementation of these entitlements. This underlay many of the negative features of the soviet system.[1] Production would be at a standstill while the enterprise awaited the delivery of necessary parts or materials, to be followed by days of 'storming' as the enterprise worked at breakneck pace to meet the monthly plan.

The overriding need to achieve plan targets meant that enterprises had to accept delivery of sub-standard supplies. The uneven pace of production, inadequate maintenance of plant and equipment and sub-standard supplies meant that product quality was sacrificed to the need to achieve plan targets at all costs, leading to the notorious unevenness in the quality of soviet products.

---

[1] Joseph S. Berliner, *Factory and Manager in the USSR*, Cambridge, MA: Harvard University Press, 1957.

Deficiencies in the system of supply also underpinned the tendency to hoarding that was characteristic of the soviet industrial enterprise. Enterprises would accumulate vast stocks of metal, timber, building materials, machinery, parts and raw materials, often stored in inappropriate conditions, not only to ensure the security of supply, but also to barter with other enterprises for other necessary items or services. Many enterprises owed their survival through the 1990s to their ability to produce parts and components or their possession of large reserve stocks of components and materials which they could not afford to buy on the market.[1]

Although in principle enterprises were assigned deliveries of the supplies that they required in order to meet their production plans, in practice they had to take various steps to expedite these deliveries and to obtain additional parts and materials to facilitate their operations. In general, enterprises would supply and be supplied by the same partners year after year, so that long-term relationships would be built up in which informal personal ties reinforced formal business relations. These relations could be lubricated by exchanges of favours, gifts and bribes to expedite deliveries. Many large enterprises retained agents, 'pushers' (*tolkachi*), to represent their interests in securing supplies, arranging barter deals and so on. They could also call on local Party officials to use their own connections to bribe, persuade or pressure suppliers to meet their obligations. These networks of connections which lubricated the flow of goods and services in the soviet system provided the infrastructure around which market relations could be rapidly constructed to fill the gaps left by the collapse of the administrative-command system.

Technological legacies

The driving force of the accumulation of capital is the constant transformation of the productive forces. The soviet system, by contrast, was notorious for its inherent barriers to innovation. While there was substantial investment in research and development, and striking technological achievements in military and space technology, there was a significant gap between scientific achievements and their practical implementation and there was substantial resistance to the incorporation of new technologies in production. Enterprise directors were reluctant to introduce new technologies because the innovation process was disruptive of existing production, impeding the achievement of plan targets, because of likely teething problems with the introduction of the new technology and the likelihood of having to achieve higher plan targets once the innovation had been introduced. As noted above, innovation therefore tended to take the form of piecemeal additions to existing plant within the existing production framework, additions to production capacity built alongside existing plant, or, much more rarely, total reconstruction with the closure of the

---

[1] One of our case-study enterprises, MetZ3, a high-tech engineering enterprise, in 2004 was still producing from stocks of materials that had been accumulated before the collapse of the soviet system.

enterprise for the period of reconstruction. One result was that some enterprises, which had been commissioned or reconstructed relatively recently, entered the market economy with relatively modern plant and equipment, while others found themselves having to compete while producing old-fashioned designs with a worn-out stock of outdated plant and machinery.

There was no system of investment planning within enterprises because investment was assigned centrally, against future plan deliveries. The enterprise might make its own proposals for investment projects to modernise or expand capacity. The cost of such projects for the enterprise would be the increase in plan deliveries that might be anticipated, the benefits of such projects would consist in the possibility of thereby obtaining additional allocations of labour and raw materials and perhaps an increase in subsidiary funds and in the prestige of the enterprise. An internal source of innovations to which considerable importance was attached (at least ideologically) was the activity of 'rationalisers and innovators' who would earn honours and bonuses for making proposals which could increase efficiency by economising on labour and resources. The advantage for the enterprise of such innovations was that they were not immediately associated with increased plan deliveries, so could benefit the enterprise directly.

Soviet enterprises were established by decision of the central authorities to produce according to the directives of the plan. Such decisions were taken not on the basis of purely economic criteria, but on the basis of pragmatic bureaucratic and strategic political considerations. There was a tendency for central ministries to sponsor the construction of gigantic plants, partly because of a single-minded belief in economies of scale, partly for reasons of national prestige and partly because it was easier for the central authorities to manage a small number of large plants. This notorious tendency to gigantism was not universal. There was also a tendency to proliferate the construction of relatively small enterprises in low-prestige branches such as food processing, construction materials and light industry to supply their local regional or municipal markets, partly for the convenience of planning and partly because of the inadequate transport and distribution infrastructure.[1] The location of plants was also

---

[1] For example, the McKinsey report on the Russian confectionery industry found that in 1997 more than three-quarters of capacity and 80 per cent of employment was in 914 plants which were below the minimum efficient size because they were too small to install automated processing and packaging. Moreover, the small plants were no more specialised than were the eleven large plants which were above the minimum efficient size. Indeed, the small plants were too small (on average only 6 per cent of the size of US plants) to be economical even if they specialised (McKinsey Global Institute, *Unlocking Economic Growth in Russia*, Moscow: McKinsey & Co. Inc., 1999, Confectionery, p. 4). Similarly, 57 per cent of capacity in the dairy industry was in plants which were below the minimum efficient size for a western dairy plant, again because they were below the scale required for the installation of automated packaging (ibid., Dairy, pp. 4–5). Even the steel industry had many small plants, employing almost a third of the production workforce, well below the current efficient scale, using outdated technology, most of which were established before World War II, with some dating back to the nineteenth century (ibid., Steel, p. 7).

determined by strategic considerations of national defence, which motivated the location of heavy industry in Siberia, and by lobbying by major cities and regions to host prestigious developments. This immediately implied that many enterprises were disadvantaged by their size or their location once they had to compete in a market economy.

Soviet technology was developed on the basis of soviet resource endowments and without reference to the cost constraints which have structured western technology. While such technologies were viable, if wasteful, within the soviet planning system, with the incorporation of Russia into the world capitalist economy Russian producers had to start to produce according to world standards and to pay for their resources at something approaching world market prices. A number of aspects of soviet technology increased the difficulties of adjustment faced by soviet enterprises.

By international standards, soviet technology was extremely energy intensive, which was partly a reflection of resource endowments, partly a reflection of climatic conditions, but also a reflection of the absence of effective cost accounting. Very little attention was paid to the insulation of buildings or to the development and application of energy-saving technologies. For many Russian enterprises this factor alone meant that, if they retained their inherited technology and had to pay for their energy at world market prices, it would be impossible for them to cover their labour and material costs, let alone make a profit, however well managed they might be. According to former Russian Minister of the Economy Evgeny Yasin, all Russian industry, except the energy sector, is 'value subtracting',[1] which would imply that Russia would be better off if it closed down all of its industry and lived solely on the proceeds of the export of oil, gas and electricity. At the time of Yasin's interview it looked very much as though this was what global capital, through the world market economy, had in store for Russia.

Soviet technology was marked by a similar tendency to use more metal than its capitalist equivalent, partly as a reflection of resource endowments and partly to build in reserve strength to compensate for possible design and construction faults. This not only increased the cost of production, but also meant that many of its products were much heavier than their western equivalents, increasing transport costs and, for motorised equipment, the power and size of engines required and, correspondingly, energy consumed.

Soviet technology was marked by a relatively limited use of waste to make by-products, which reduced the earning potential of soviet enterprises but also contributed to problems of waste disposal and environmental degradation. There was little effective environmental regulation to restrict harmful emissions and correspondingly little development and application of environmentally friendly technology, which further contributed to the degradation of the health of the urban population. Attempts to strengthen environmental regulation in post-

---

[1] Interview with Ariel Cohen, 'What Russia must do to recover from its economic crisis?', Heritage Foundation Backgrounder #1296, 18 June, 1999. Available <http://www.heritage.org/Research/RussiaandEurasia/BG1296.cfm> (last accessed 27 May 2006).

soviet Russia to conform to minimal international standards threatened many enterprises with closure or prohibitively expensive investment to control emissions.

Soviet investment priorities also determined the following distinctive characteristics of Russian enterprises, by international standards.

Investment and technological development tended to be concentrated in 'main production', those areas which contributed directly to the manufacture of the final product, because it was felt that such investment would contribute directly to the fulfilment of the production plan. 'Auxiliary production', which includes maintenance and repair, quality control, materials handling and so on, received much less investment, so that these areas were relatively labour intensive. Maintenance and repair were reliant on the skills and experience of highly skilled workers, who were often provided with limited diagnostic and testing equipment; quality control often depended on physical measurement and visual inspection, where a modern capitalist enterprise would use electronic instrumentation or automated testing equipment; materials handling relied on an army of unskilled, undisciplined, low-paid workers, who could also be deployed to do communal and agricultural work when the enterprise was called on to supply labour for these purposes.

As we have seen, there was a very low rate of replacement of redundant plant and equipment in the soviet economy, despite the fact that defects in construction, uneven loading as stoppages alternated with storming, inadequate maintenance and piecemeal repair meant that much equipment was unreliable, suffering frequent breakdowns and rapid depreciation. These features of the technical division of labour also implied a distinctive social division of labour, based on a heavy reliance on a core of loyal, highly motivated, skilled and experienced workers, alongside a large pool of unskilled manual labourers. Typically, once a factory was established it would continue to use its original technology and equipment for an extended period of time. Tried and tested machines would be patched up and kept in service long after they would have been scrapped by a capitalist enterprise facing competitive pressure.[1] The prevalence of antiquated equipment meant that the factory was very reliant on skilled and experienced workers, who could keep the equipment in service long past its retirement date. If new machines were acquired they would be incorporated into the old production system. This frequently led to problems of incompatibility, which would often have to be resolved by customising but also degrading the new technology to make it compatible with the old.[2] Similarly, the introduction of new technology into inadequate premises often led to problems

---

[1] However, this was also a practice characteristic of British industry while it remained dominated by competition among relatively small enterprises which were protected from international competition by their privileged access to imperial markets (see, for example, William Lazonick, 'Industrial relations and technical change: the case of the self-acting mule', *Cambridge Journal of Economics* 3, 1979: 231–62).

[2] One coal mine we visited in the 1990s had a special department, called the 'equipment modernisation department', whose task was to modify (degrade) imported equipment to work in Russian conditions.

of reliability as a result, for example, of uneven floors or excessive levels of dust. The old machines would often not be scrapped, but would be kept in operation or would be set aside as a reserve in case of breakdown or emergencies. New shops might be built alongside the old to produce new or complementary products. This kind of piecemeal modernisation has been identified as a major factor underlying the failure of the soviet economy to take full advantage of technological progress.[1] Eventually, after twenty or thirty or seventy years, the factory might be reconstructed, with completely new facilities replacing or being built alongside the old.

The result of the piecemeal character of soviet innovation and investment was that every factory and every shop had a unique technology which was a legacy of its past and which bore the mark of the creative ingenuity of its workforce. This 'untechnological character of soviet production' was a fundamental barrier to any rational system of production planning or production management since only those in direct contact with the technology could possibly know its capacities and its potential.[2] This also put an enormous premium on the acquired skills of the labour force and line managers.

Management structure

The enterprise was charged with achieving a whole series of plan indicators which were repeatedly modified as the central authorities sought to induce enterprises to increase productivity, improve quality and achieve a wide range of economic and social goals, but the pre-eminent obligation of the enterprise was always to achieve its production plan for gross output (*val*). This determined the substantial bonuses of senior managers and the status and future prospects of the enterprise. All the structures and practices of management were oriented to this goal.

The interests of management at every level of the system, from the ministry in Moscow down to the brigade on the shop floor, were contradictory. On the one hand, the manager sought to minimise the demands imposed and maximise the resources obtained from above. On the other hand, once the resource entitlements and plan targets had been defined, the manager had to ensure that those resources were actually obtained and those targets achieved. Thus the administration of the enterprise was primarily concerned, on the one hand, with securing supplies of raw materials and equipment from partner enterprises and recruiting sufficient labour of an appropriate quality to be able to maintain production and, on the other hand, with transmitting the demands of the plan to the production units which made up the enterprise.

The traditional management structure of the soviet enterprise was a strictly hierarchical system of functional management under the overall control of the

[1] Robert C. Allen, *Farm to Factory: A Reinterpretation of the Soviet Industrial Revolution*, Princeton, NJ and Oxford: Princeton University Press, 2003, Chapter Ten.
[2] Sergei Alasheev, 'On a particular kind of love and the specificity of soviet production', in Simon Clarke (ed.) *Management and Industry in Russia*.

general director. This management system was adopted during the period of Stalinist industrialisation as the most advanced western practice of the inter-war years, alongside the introduction of advanced western technology, following the soviet interpretation of the principles of the 'scientific management' of Taylorism and Fordism, and in its essentials remained unchanged throughout the soviet period. Although this 'U-Form' of functional management was soon superseded in the western capitalist countries by the multidivisional 'M-Form',[1] it remained well adapted to the single-minded pursuit of the obligation to fulfil the gross output plan and was entirely consistent with the strictly authoritarian hierarchical political system in which it was embedded.

There was a functional division of labour within the management structure, in which production was absolutely dominant. Below the general director of the enterprise would be a number of deputies and heads of departments and services, who would be directly subordinate to the general director and would in turn be responsible for their particular spheres of activity. The role of all the services and departments was to support production: the whole management structure revolved around production, expressing the priority of achieving the production plan at any cost.

The job of the general director was to supervise, and take ultimate responsibility for, the performance of all his subordinates and to manage the external relations of the enterprise, negotiating the plan with the managing body, the ministry or the production association, consulting with the relevant supervisory Party bodies, negotiating with local authorities and inspectorates. The process of defending the plan involved long-drawn-out negotiations with the managing body, which for larger enterprises was in Moscow; in these the director would be supported by senior specialists and the trade union president. Once the plan was set, the priority of the director was to ensure that the enterprise obtained the equipment, raw materials and labour power that it needed, and this could involve extensive negotiation with state supply organisations, supplier enterprises and local and regional political bodies. In all of these negotiations, the political standing and network of contacts of the general director could play a decisive role. The general director was the link in the hierarchical chain connecting the enterprise with the higher authorities. His responsibility in relation to the higher authorities was to deliver the plan. In relation to the enterprise, he represented its interests by minimising plan targets and maximising the resources it obtained. This involved securing a favourable plan, negotiating deliveries of supplies, obtaining additional social development funds and minimising penalties for failures.

Within the enterprise, the general director headed a three-level hierarchical management structure with a functional division of labour between the principal functional divisions, each headed by a senior manager who was strictly responsible to the general director for their area of responsibility. Within each division would be a number of functional subdivisions each headed by a chief responsible for the particular tasks of that subdivision. The management

[1] Alfred D. Chandler, *Strategy and Structure*. Cambridge, MA: MIT Press, 1962.

structure was authoritarian and highly centralised, with flows of information converging on the general director and control emanating from the general director.

The general director was responsible for the fate of the enterprise and took full credit for its success. The ideal soviet general director was somebody who had worked his way up the traditional career ladder within that particular enterprise, or at least a similar enterprise in the same industry, knowing the technology and the production process inside out. The general director kept firm control of the enterprise, demanding that subordinates carry out their duties effectively, giving credit and apportioning blame where it was due. The general director would be accessible to all the employees of the enterprise. The director would normally have a designated time when any employee could visit their office with a request or a grievance. The director would regularly walk around the territory of the enterprise and visit the production shops, knowing many of the older workers and middle managers and greeting them by name. If any problems arose which held up production, the director would be liable to turn up in person and take things in hand. The ideal general director would be the subject of stories of legendary achievements and enjoyed the loyalty and even the affection of his employees, symbolising the enterprise and the achievements of its labour collective.

The production director (sometimes combined with the post of chief engineer) was the first deputy of the general director and was responsible for directing and co-ordinating the work of the main production shops. The chiefs of all the 'main' production shops, responsible for producing final products, were directly subordinate to the production director and were responsible for their shops achieving their daily, monthly and annual plan targets.

All of the auxiliary services revolved around and were subordinate to production, both in their authority, pay and status and in their everyday functioning. The chief mechanic was responsible for the auxiliary production shops, whose chiefs were responsible for the installation, servicing, maintenance and repair of the plant and equipment of the main production shops and other auxiliary services such as internal transport and materials handling. The chief power engineer was responsible for maintaining supplies of gas, electricity and water. The auxiliary production shops were subordinate to the main production shops and the staff of the former had lower pay and status than the latter, even if they had higher levels of skill.

The work of the other services and departments of the enterprise administration was mostly routine. The sales and supply department was responsible for ensuring that supplies were delivered to the enterprise in time, and for organising deliveries to customers according to the plan schedule, but very often would be overridden by the general director or the shop chiefs, who had the connections and authority to secure scarce supplies that the head of the supply department lacked, and often its function was no more than to process orders and record shipments and deliveries. The planning-economic department was responsible for checking the consistency and achievability of production plans to support negotiations with the managing body over the annual plan and for disaggregating the plans to provide monthly, weekly and daily targets for the various shops and departments. The department of labour and wages recorded information about working hours and performance and calculated wages according to set formulas. Normsetters followed routine procedures to calculate the 'scientific' production norms against which piece-rates were calculated. The personnel department simply maintained the staff records and recorded personnel movements, disciplinary sanctions and so on. The chief bookkeeper's department kept the financial accounts of the enterprise to ensure that spending was in line with that authorised by the plan and reported to the higher authorities. But all of these functions were essentially record-keeping and reporting functions. The task of these services was not to ensure that production management was constrained by the availability of personnel, supplies or financial resources, but to ensure that production proceeded as smoothly as possible. In the event of over-spending, for example, the chief bookkeeper would not have the authority to intervene, but could at best draw the attention of the general director to the problem. The departments which were formally concerned with such record-keeping had very little authority within the enterprise.

This system of management was embodied in the traditional management structure, but it was also embedded in the training, salaries and social status of the various management specialisms, in everyday management practices and procedures, in the career progression of managers and in the corporate culture of the enterprise.

Production management was unequivocally the leading branch of management and engineering qualifications and production experience were essential for career advance. The typical career path of the older generation of enterprise directors started on the shop floor and proceeded up the steps of the production ladder, to foreman, shift foreman, section chief, shop chief, chief engineer, production director to general director, with engineering qualifications having been acquired on the way. The younger generation of enterprise directors would have acquired their engineering qualifications before starting work as a foreman and then advancing up the career ladder. Those without engineering qualifications could never hope to advance beyond the position of department head, unless they pursued a parallel Party career.

The result was that the educational and professional background of the overwhelming majority of top managers was in engineering and they rarely if ever had any kind of training in management skills, especially the skills of personnel management or in methods of economic or financial analysis. Moreover, this ensured the dominance of a technocratic management ideology which did not attach any importance either to economic considerations or to the role of the 'human factor'. The primary qualification for a manager was to be a 'good specialist' who knew production inside-out. Production management was a predominantly male occupation and enterprise directors were predominantly male except in 'women's industries' such as textiles and food processing, although even in these industries auxiliary production shops and chief mechanics were predominantly male. Economists (including accountants, wage specialists and normsetters), supply staff and personnel managers were predominantly female, which both expressed and reinforced their subordinate status in the management hierarchy and the perception that their jobs required the stereotypically female qualities of care, responsibility and diligence rather than the exercise of judgement, decisiveness and authority.

The formal management structure of the soviet enterprise was predicated on the smooth functioning of the enterprise, with everything being carried out in accordance with the (scientifically developed) plans and routinely monitored and reported. In practice, of course, things very rarely went according to plan. Production had to be carried out in accordance with the demands of the plan in an environment of acute shortages of labour, parts and materials, with undisciplined workers and unreliable equipment. The supply department had to track down the parts and materials needed to maintain production, negotiate their release and organise their delivery. Shop chiefs and foremen had to spend all day scurrying around to make sure that their workers had the tools, parts and materials that they needed, that the workers were at work, reasonably sober and doing their assigned jobs, and that faulty machines were repaired as quickly as possible. The formal structures of hierarchical control and the functional division of management were far too rigid to be able to respond to the constantly changing demands of production.

Disruptions to supply, shortages of labour, breakdowns of machinery or a lack of coordination could all disrupt the smooth running of production and in this case the priority was not to follow bureaucratic procedures, but to overcome the problem as rapidly as possible. Managers at all levels would use their own judgement and exploit their informal connections to achieve their designated tasks as quickly and simply as possible. Behind the formal management structure, depicted with precise lines of authority in organisation charts, was an informal structure of connections, competencies, reputations and personal authority based on personal relationships built up over many years of working together, in which the real jobs that people did often bore very little relation to their formal responsibilities. In reality, management processes were very *ad hoc* and personalised, with personality playing an important role. Despite the strictly authoritarian character of the formal hierarchy, managers were known for their 'democratic' or their 'authoritarian' styles of management and there was a great deal of negotiation and wheeling and dealing involved in resolving issues in the informal structure of management. As one senior manager in a bakery said to us regarding the informal resolution of problems: '*Everyone has worked here a long time, everyone knows everyone else, so why create bureaucratic barriers between one another?*' (**KhBK1**).

The importance of the informal management structure meant that it was very difficult to change the formal structure. Job descriptions might be modified, new posts created and old posts abolished, lines of responsibility and authority might be redrawn, departments might be amalgamated or dismembered, but in practice the same people would tend to continue to do the same things in the same ways, simply by-passing new structures and ignoring new procedures, so long as they were able to achieve the required result of delivering the plan.

Corresponding to this informal structure, alongside the formal system of recording and reporting there was an informal system of communication and information flows in the soviet enterprise which was centred on frequent meetings to assign tasks, co-ordinate work, discuss problems and report on outcomes at all levels. There would also be regular monthly meetings devoted to particular topics: 'the quality day', 'the day of raw materials' and so on. There was little formalisation of procedures or documentation of the decisions of such meetings so they provided a system of centralised hierarchical control of the informal channels of information flows and decision-making. In a large enterprise, factory-wide meetings might be conducted over the factory intercom, with the heads of shops and departments reporting in turn, for example, and the general director making comments and issuing instructions. The general director would typically hold a meeting with the heads of departments and services at the beginning of every week. The general director would also make regular tours of the enterprise to see for himself what was going on, and these tours provided an opportunity for informal lobbying and decision-making.

Department heads would normally hold a meeting with their staff every day, passing on relevant information from above. The shop chief would have a meeting at the beginning and the end of the day with the foremen and section heads, to discuss the daily tasks and to report on their fulfilment and any problems arising. The foremen and/or brigadiers would meet with the workers at the start of the shift to assign tasks for the day and administer any reprimands arising from production failures or disciplinary violations. Shop chiefs, who were the focal point of all the activity, could easily find themselves spending half or more of their working day in meetings resolving problems and discussing and co-ordinating this and that.

Production management and the disciplinary regime

The production shops were the heart of the soviet enterprise, served by all other departments, since the fulfilment of the plan depended ultimately on them. It was the responsibility of middle and line managers – shop chiefs, section heads and foremen – to organise and manage production in order to deliver the plan at the end of every month.

Shop chiefs, although the core of the enterprise, did not normally participate in strategic decision-making, although they could make representations regarding the production capacities of their shops and the resources required to achieve particular levels of output, which would feed in to the negotiations of the enterprise with the planning authorities, and which would inform the monthly allocation of plan tasks and resources to the shops. The shop chiefs, whose bonuses (unlike those of the workers) depended directly on plan fulfilment, had an interest in pressing for plan tasks which they could be sure to fulfil, so the representations of the shop chief expressed the limits to the degree of exploitation to which the labour force could be subjected. Thus the relationship between superior and subordinate typical of the soviet system of planning was reproduced at shop level, the shop chiefs representing the interests of the shop as a whole in their relations with superior levels and those of the system in their relations with the shop.

Soviet industrialisation took place in the 1930s in the context of an acute shortage of experienced engineers and managers, reinforced by repeated purges and the promotion of experienced cadres to higher positions, so that workers, driven on by threats and exhortations, were encouraged to display initiative and were assigned a high degree of responsibility for the management of production and accomplishment of production tasks. With the routinisation of the system in the post-war period, in a parody of Taylorism, the organisation of production was put on an increasingly formalised 'scientific' foundation. The staffing levels and particular skills required to operate a specific production facility were determined 'scientifically' and embodied in the staffing and production norms associated with the installation of such facilities and applied by the enterprise's specialists. The ability of a worker to operate a particular piece of equipment would be acquired and certified through an authorised training programme and certification renewed through regular attestation. According to the late soviet Labour Code workers could not even be transferred from one job to another against their will. The result was that on paper the shop had a very rigid division of labour with very narrow occupational specialisation and so, formally, it had very limited flexibility. In reality, of course, such a rigid organisation of production could not function in the best of conditions, but in soviet conditions it was an absurdity.

In fact, the high degree of autonomy of shop floor workers persisted throughout the soviet period as the uneven delivery and variable quality of supplies, the unreliability of equipment and persistent shortages of suitably qualified labour meant that the continuity of production continued to depend to a considerable degree on their initiative and ingenuity. The main tasks of shop chiefs and even foremen were accordingly to chase supplies, recruit and retain labour, resolve conflicts between shops, sections and brigades, fix breakdowns and monitor performance in relation to targets, so that the direct production workers were largely left to get on with production as best they could, with very little managerial intervention, and were generally expected to overcome problems themselves. Soviet workers had retained a high level of control over production, much of which capitalist workers had lost in bitter struggles,[1] not because they had won a battle to retain or to seize control from the management, but because they had been given a high degree of responsibility for ensuring that they achieved the tasks assigned to them.

Day-to-day responsibility for the supervision of production was in the hands of the foreman or the elected brigade leader, but in practice production management was based on understandings and informal negotiation, typically

[1] William Lazonick, *Organisation and Technology in Capitalist Development*, Cheltenham and Brookfield, VT: Edward Elgar, 1992; David Noble, *America by Design: Science, Technology, and the Rise of Corporate Capitalism*, Oxford: Oxford University Press, 1979; Katherine Stone, 'The origins of job structures in the steel industry', *Review of Radical Political Economics* 6(2), Summer 1974: 113–73.

on a personal and individual basis, between line managers, brigadiers and workers.[1] Formally, the payment system ensured that workers had an interest in completing their assigned production tasks, but fulfilling the plan often required workers to do much more than simply to fulfil their own tasks. Labour shortages meant that line managers had few negative sanctions to press recalcitrant workers into line, so they had to use the limited positive levers at their disposal to induce workers to co-operate. These included the ability to allocate workers to more or less well-paying work, the ability to pay small bonuses from the foreman's or shop chief's fund, the ability to authorise paid or unpaid leave, turning a blind eye to poor time-keeping and other disciplinary violations and discretionary scheduling of holidays and allocation of social and welfare benefits.

The fact that soviet workers had a high degree of control over the way in which they produced does not mean that they had power: the limits of their autonomy were set by the norms and targets imposed on them and embodied in the incentives and penalties built into the payment system. Workers were willing to accept the authority of the foreman and shop chief, within the limits imposed on him or her from above. A good chief defended the shop in bargaining for plan targets and resource allocation, secured supplies, did not seek to drive the workers above the demands of the plan in order to advance him or herself, and was fair in the distribution of penalties and rewards. Workers would then identify with their chief in competition with other shops and in struggles with the administration. If things were not going so well, if supplies were short, norms unfulfilled, bonuses lost, the workers would blame their shop chief. Workers attributed their relative good or bad fortune to the personality of the chief, and restricted any collective expressions of their grievances to complaints against this or that individual. There was therefore a high degree of collusion by the workers in their own exploitation, and class conflict was displaced and diffused into individual and sectional conflicts within the hierarchical structure.

Workers had to show a great deal of initiative to overcome the regular dislocation of production through breakdowns, defective parts and materials or the absence of supplies, and often had to work all hours in the regular 'storming' at the end of the month. This made it impossible for management to impose its will on the workers by purely repressive means. Although labour shortages and the demands of the plan apparently put a great deal of power in the hands of the production workers, they did not, in general, exercise this power to resist the demands made on them by their line managers, although in *extremis* they might show their strength by deliberately failing to meet the plan,[2] but their expectations of steadily improving living standards as compensation for their

---

[1] Sergei Alasheev, 'Informal relations in the process of production', Simon Clarke, 'Informal relations in the soviet system of production', and Pavel Romanov, 'Middle management in industrial production in the transition to the market', all in Simon Clarke (ed.), *Management and Industry in Russia.*

[2] Marina Kiblitskaya, 'We didn't make the plan', in Simon Clarke (ed.) *Management and Industry in Russia.*

effort and commitment were filtered up through the system through the representations of managers to successively higher authorities for improved resource allocations.

Not all workers were ready to show the dedication and commitment of those in the front line in the struggle for the plan. To achieve its plan targets, the soviet enterprise relied very heavily on a core of production workers and line managers who were reliable, skilled, enterprising and flexible (the elite of whom would be recruited into the Party), whose efforts kept the whole system going. These people often worked extremely hard and enjoyed high status, relatively good pay and extensive privileges. The strategic significance of this grouping was not determined simply by its technical role in production, but rather by the fact that production was organised socially around this crucial stratum.

Recruitment into this stratum of the labour force was a matter not just of technical training, the quality of which was, in general, low, but also of passing through a series of filters in which the workers' 'moral' and 'ideological' qualities would have been evaluated in addition to their technical skills. Once recruited into this stratum a worker was relatively secure, so long as he (or occasionally she) continued to toe the line.

This core stratum of relatively skilled workers formed a bridge between workers and management – they were better paid than all but the most senior managers, in some cases even earning more than the general director, and some could expect to progress into management as shop chief, chief engineer, general director and even higher. They had access through their Party membership and trade union activity to senior management and to the processes of enterprise decision-making. Their position within the hierarchical status and pay structure of the enterprise underpinned their 'activism' and their identification with the productive tasks imposed on them.

Labour discipline in the Stalinist period was backed up by draconian legislation that prescribed a term in the *gulag* for lateness or absenteeism, and where failure to achieve plan targets could lead to a sentence for sabotage, although the rigorous application of such penalties would have condemned virtually the whole working class to the *gulag*. In the post-Stalin period, by comparison, soviet managers had very limited disciplinary powers. Workers could only be dismissed 'under article' for theft, drunkenness at work or persistent absenteeism, and even then only with the approval of the trade union committee. This was not because of the soft liberalism of the soviet regime, but because the basis of the disciplinary system was re-education and rehabilitation. To dismiss a recalcitrant worker was to throw him or her onto the streets, beyond the supervision of a labour collective, into a life of parasitism, so it was the responsibility of the collective to rehabilitate the worker through moral pressure and, in the case of alcoholism, medical treatment. Moreover, the increasingly acute labour shortage meant that managers were reluctant to dismiss even the most derelict of workers when there was no prospect of finding another so that, within limits, even theft and drunkenness at work were often tolerated. Labour discipline was considerably stricter in the most privileged enterprises, notably in the military-industrial complex and heavy industry, which paid the highest wages and provided the best housing, social and welfare facilities, where drinking at work would be confined, at worst, to loaders and unskilled labourers. But in the least privileged and lowest-paying industries, such as light industry, food processing and, above all, the production of beer, wines and spirits, drinking at work would be rampant.

Low levels of labour discipline was one reason for the low, or uneven, standards of quality in soviet production, but probably not as significant a factor as unreliable machinery and equipment, the uneven rhythm of production and low-quality parts and raw materials. The Soviet Union had a highly developed system of state quality standards against which products should be tested and certified and extensive systems of quality control within the production process, which were even taken as a model when capitalist countries began to develop systems of quality certification. On the one hand, workers and line managers were in general responsible for identifying faults and monitoring the quality of their own production. On the other hand, the technical control department (OTK) had its own laboratories and testing equipment and monitored the production process and the final product. The fact that this system could work is demonstrated by the high quality standards that were maintained in the military-industrial complex. Soviet televisions and radios may have been unreliable, but soviet spacecraft flew and soviet aeroplanes stayed in the air. The problem was that, outside the military-industrial complex, the overriding importance of achieving the gross output plan meant that producers had no option but to accept defective components and had a very strong incentive to issue defective products in their turn, while consumers had no choice but to take what they were offered.

Personnel management

As a corollary of the technocratic management ideology, personnel management, let alone human resource management, did not exist as a professional specialism or as a functional division of the soviet enterprise. The 'personnel department' (*otdel kadrov*) was responsible for routine registration and record-keeping and carried out some organisational work, for example placing advertisements for vacancies or organising training courses, but played little or no substantive role in the management of personnel. The functions of personnel management were diffused through the enterprise.

The trade union was responsible for reinforcing labour motivation. Under the collective agreements signed in industrial enterprises, the trade union committed the labour force to dedicate itself to achieving its plan targets in exchange for the regular payment of wages, 'social protection' and the provision of various social and welfare benefits to be paid for out of enterprise and/or trade union funds. The trade union was responsible for organising 'socialist competition', under which shops and brigades competed to outdo one another in the overfulfilment of production plans, and encouraged the activity of 'rationalisers and innovators'. The trade union organised regular 'mass-cultural' events to celebrate such anniversaries as New Year, International Women's Day (8 March), May Day, professional holidays and so on, and organised sporting events and various forms of communal rest and recreation, all of which were supposed to encourage enterprise patriotism and the spirit of collectivism.

The department of labour and wages (OTiZ) was responsible for administering the wage and incentive systems. Wage rates were dictated by centrally fixed tariff scales, together with regional and industry coefficients, additional payment for work in harmful conditions and so on. Production norms for the calculation of piece-rate payments were established by the normsetters on the basis of formalised criteria and procedures, the ideal being to apply 'scientifically' calculated norms which did not provide any scope for discretion. Bonuses were determined by the fulfilment and overfulfilment of norms, but in practice were consolidated into normal pay since the failure to fulfil norms was most commonly not the fault of the workers in question but the result of breakdowns of machinery, disruption of supply or interruptions in the production process. In practice the wage system rarely functioned as an instrument of personnel management.

The direct personnel management functions – hiring and firing, induction and initial training, probation, discipline, punishment and reward, selection for promotion, assignment for training – were carried out by department heads and line managers, even though the latter had no qualifications or training in personnel management. Formalised procedures, where they existed, were largely irrelevant. Personnel management was carried out, as noted above, through informal relations rather than formal procedures, and the style of personnel management depended very much on the personality of the line manager. Some shop chiefs would be noted for their democratic participatory management style, while others would have a reputation for a strict authoritarian style of management. As far as their subordinates were concerned, managers were judged by the results they achieved and their authority depended on their ability to maintain the smooth running of the shop, so that workers could maintain a regular work rhythm and earn their regular bonuses.

The personnel department had little involvement in training. Training was conducted according to training plans handed down to the enterprise, with the training being provided by specialised training establishments. Employees were generally selected for training by their line managers, and the personnel department rarely did any more than handle the relevant paperwork. In principle workers had to undergo additional training every time equipment was modified or a new piece of equipment was installed, but this was often a mere formality. Employees were supposed to undergo regular attestation, to check that they were competent to carry out their duties, but for most occupations this was equally a formality.

Payment systems and social policy

The traditional payment system was one in which direct production workers were paid on a piece-rate system, while auxiliary workers, managers, specialists and office staff were paid on time-rates or salaries. Job rates and salary scales, together with a wide range of coefficients and supplementary payments, were laid down centrally so that in principle the enterprise had very little discretion in the payment of wages.

Until the end of the 1970s piece-rates were predominantly individual, but at the end of the 1970s the 'brigade system' of labour was introduced and many workers were paid a collective piece rate, with the wages of individual brigade members being adjusted according to their 'coefficient of labour participation' (KTU). The KTU for each member of the brigade was normally determined by the elected brigadier, sometimes endorsed by a meeting of the brigade, but in practice wages were almost always divided equally within the brigade. The authorities constantly railed against such 'levelling' tendencies, which undermined the principle of payment according to individual responsibility and results, but levelling expressed the strong egalitarian values of soviet workers and was an effective means of ensuring collective responsibility. However, this egalitarianism was only a very limited expression of workers' solidarity – brigades would be very selective about whom they would admit and would try to get rid of poorly performing members, so as to increase the earnings of the brigade as a whole, rather than distribute wages unequally.

Egalitarianism was also reflected in the fact that wage differentials in the soviet system were not very large, so that there were limited possibilities of achieving higher incomes through promotion. Workers were ranked on a system of six grades, but progression through the grades was pretty standardised. Nevertheless, the possibilities of promotion depended on the occupation as well as the passage of time. Main production, which directly delivered the plan, had much higher status than auxiliary production, which merely serviced main production, and workers in main production earned significantly more than workers in auxiliary production services, such as fitters, mechanics and electricians. Foremen, who were generally on the bottom rung of a career in production management, usually earned significantly less than skilled workers, and an experienced skilled worker would often earn as much as a shop chief.

Throughout the soviet period the authorities searched for the ideal piece-rate payment system, in the belief that a rational payment system based on 'scientific' norms, which rewarded workers for their individual efforts, would provide the appropriate incentives to raise productivity. Such a conception rested on the soviet (and very unMarxist) ideological belief that the failures of the soviet system could not be systemic, but were the result of individual failings, and that barriers could be overcome by individual effort. Needless to say, the soviet system suffered from all the familiar disadvantages of piece-rate payment systems and the provision of individual incentives was never sufficient to overcome the deficiencies of the soviet system of production management. Piece-rate payment systems presuppose that the principal determinant of output is the effort and diligence of individual workers, but in the soviet system the main barrier to plan fulfilment was not the negligence of workers, but failures of co-ordination, disruption of supply and breakdowns of machinery. In such circumstances, with a rigid piece-rate payment system, workers would often lose earnings through no fault of their own. In order to maintain the loyalty and commitment of the workers on whom they depended, line managers had to manipulate the payment system to ensure that their workers had a guaranteed income, even if they failed to meet their norms.

Far from providing an automatic means of motivating workers, the piece-rate payment system was only one of a series of levers which line managers could use to secure the commitment of the workers on whom the achievement of production plans depended. Another very important lever was the right of line managers to allocate work, so that favoured workers could be allocated to the best-paying jobs, assigned to the best and most reliable machines or given additional work which attracted supplementary payments. Line managers could also use their discretion to ignore or cover up disciplinary violations, such as lateness, absenteeism or even occasional drunkenness or theft, when committed by loyal and reliable workers. Line managers could similarly give priority to favoured workers in responding to requests for leave or when drawing up holiday rotas and could favour them in making recommendations to increase their grade. Finally, line managers, often in collusion with the shop trade union chief, could favour the most reliable workers in the allocation of various social and welfare benefits, while recalcitrant workers could be penalised by denial of benefits or demotion in the housing queue.

Overall, the soviet system of production management was almost the antithesis of the Taylorist system of scientific management that it nominally espoused. Production management was an almost entirely discretionary art in which the line manager had to use a wide range of incentives and levers of influence to secure the loyalty and commitment of the workers in the struggle to achieve the monthly production plan in the face of all the difficulties and problems that they might confront. The result was that in every factory there was a status hierarchy of production shops and in every shop there was a finely graded hierarchy of workers, with privileges and penalties being administered on a personal and individual basis at the discretion of line managers. This had the effect of atomising workers and undermining their solidarity at every level. The introduction of the brigade system in the late soviet period established a basis for solidarity at the micro-level, while intensifying fragmentation by encouraging competition between brigades, each of which struggled for its narrow 'brigade interest'.

As noted above, the soviet enterprise took responsibility for the social reproduction of the labour force not simply through the payment of wages, but also through its social and welfare policy. Social policy was targeted at the labour collective, with enterprise provision or sponsorship of housing, health care, kindergartens, education, sport and leisure facilities, cultural events, sanatoria, holidays and so on, provided not only for workers and their families, but also for pensioners of the enterprise and often, in the case of large enterprises, for the local community. From the late 1970s enterprises increasingly provided subsidised consumer goods, food and clothing, and distributed land for allotments. Thus a large part of the reproduction needs of the worker could not be freely bought with the worker's wage, but could only be secured through the distribution channels of the enterprise. This system of distribution played a very important role in the allocation and regulation of labour within the system of production, allowing the strategically important enterprises to attract and retain scarce skilled labour and providing a powerful lever of managerial influence over the labour force.

The role of the trade union

Soviet trade unions were constitutionally under the leadership of the Communist Party and their function, assigned to them by Lenin, was to serve as the 'transmission belt between the Communist Party and the masses'.[1] In the enterprise, this prescribed their 'dual function' of implementing the Party's policies at the same time as representing the interests of the labour collective. However, the interests of the labour collective were not to be defined self-consciously by the workers themselves, they were rather the 'objective interests' of the labour collective, as part of the working class, as determined by the Party and embodied in laws, regulations, decrees and resolutions whose observance the trade union was expected to monitor. In practice, this meant that the trade unions were responsible, on the one hand, for encouraging the workers to ever greater productive efforts in order to fulfil and overfulfil the plan and, on the other hand, for administering most of the social and welfare policy of the enterprise, as well as the payment of state social insurance benefits, such as sick pay and maternity benefits.[2]

The trade unions were very unsuccessful in their attempts to carry out their thankless task of encouraging the growth of production, which acquired an increasingly ritualistic quality as the unions concentrated instead on the more fulfilling work of administering the social and welfare facilities of the enterprise, such as sanatoria, kindergartens, sporting and holiday facilities, and distributing housing, material assistance, holiday vouchers and other social insurance and welfare benefits to their members. These benefits were financed by the enterprise, directly or through its social insurance contributions, sealing the dependence of the trade union on management, but their provision was much the most important role of the unions for their members, absorbed the bulk of union resources and took up the overwhelming part of the time of union officers.

---

[1] V. Lenin, 'Draft theses on the role and functions of the trade unions under the new economic policy', in *The Essentials of Lenin*, London: Lawrence and Wishart, 1947 [1922], p. 766.

[2] For a fuller account of Russian trade unions see Simon Clarke and Sarah Ashwin, *Russian Trade Unions and Industrial Relations in Transition*, Basingstoke and New York: Palgrave, 2002.

Just as with management-dispensed benefits, the benefits provided by the union to its members varied considerably between enterprises, regions and branches of production, with the most generous benefits being provided by large enterprises in the priority branches of production and in the large cities. The inequality of provision is a clear indicator of the subordination of such provision to the priorities of production rather than to the needs of the workers. The distribution of benefits within the enterprise was similarly closely bound up with the role of the union in stimulating higher productivity and improving labour discipline: the trade unions' involvement in service and leisure provision was a source of patronage and control, with allocation being tied to length of service and disciplinary record, rather than an extended frontier in collective representation.

Social and welfare provision was as much to do with the moral and spiritual as the physical health of workers and their families and as much to do with surveillance and control as liberation from the burdens of work. Trade union volunteers would visit the sick not only to provide comfort and encourage a rapid recovery, but also to ensure a rapid return to work and to weed out malingerers. Kindergartens not only enabled both parents to work full time, but also ensured the proper moulding of a socialist personality in the most impressionable years. Children would be sent to trade union-run camps during the school holidays not just to give them a good time and some healthy fresh air and exercise, but also to educate them in the socialist spirit, rather than let them hang around the streets. Similarly for their parents, a holiday at an enterprise resort gave them a well-earned rest, but it was also another celebration of the collective: the priority of the collective was exemplified by the fact that it was often very difficult for husband and wife to go on holiday together. The organisation of sporting and cultural events, the distribution of New Year presents and the celebration of state and professional holidays were similarly means of 'raising the cultural level' of the labour force and affirming the identity of the collective. Many trade union workers still view their social and welfare activity in such traditional moral terms: not just as handing out a few miserly benefits but as elevating the moral and spiritual tone of society as a whole.

While members valued the benefits they received from the trade union, such provision did not increase the prestige of the trade union in the eyes of its members since it was always marked by its qualitative and quantitative inadequacy. The role of the trade union was to ration the distribution of scarce resources, and it was always suspected, not unjustly, of favouring not only exemplary workers and those in most need, but also senior managers, trade union officers and their friends and relatives.

During the late soviet period the rights and obligations of trade union members were codified in collective agreements which were drawn up jointly and signed between the management and the trade union of industrial enterprises. The terms of the collective agreement were mostly standardised, thus there was little scope for local variation, except in the areas of housing and social and welfare provision, and so there was little or no scope for bargaining between management and the trade union. In the collective agreement the workers undertook the obligations imposed on the enterprise by the annual plan to achieve planned production targets, to economise in the use of energy and materials, to minimise waste, to observe labour discipline and to engage in socialist competition and in rationalisation and innovation initiatives, in exchange for which the management undertook to pay wages and bonuses according to the centrally determined tariff scales and norms and to provide health, housing, social and welfare provision in accordance with the enterprise's social development plan, using both centrally allocated funds and the enterprise's own residual resources. In essence, the collective agreement expressed the obligation of the labour collective to subordinate itself to the achievement of the economic and social objectives of the Party-state.

In the event of conflict between workers and management, the trade union might make representations on behalf of the workers, for example regarding unsatisfactory working conditions or the quality of food in the canteen, and the union might defend individual workers in such matters as the miscalculation of wages or pension entitlement, or even in individual cases of manifest injustice. Workers would appeal to the trade union for support over social and welfare problems that they might have, for example with housing, health care or the payment of social benefits, and even with personal problems in their marriages or their relations with the neighbours, but it was rare for workers to turn to the trade union with any work-based grievances that they might have. As a rule workers with such grievances would appeal in the first instance to their line manager and, if the line manager was the object of the grievance, to a more senior manager, and it would be the relevant manager who would take responsibility for resolving the grievance, either by making representations to senior management on the workers' behalf or by seeking to mollify them. Conflicts were, therefore, normally resolved on an informal basis within the management structure.

The trade union was not seen by its members (who included all employees, from cleaners to the general director) as representative of the workers in opposition to management, but as the representative of the labour collective as a whole, expressing the unity of the enterprise in the face of the common tasks of fulfilling the production plan and building the radiant socialist future. The trade union was the social and welfare department of the enterprise administration, responsible for managing social and welfare provision for the labour collective and for building and maintaining the socialist 'corporate culture'.

Corporate culture

It has already been noted that the soviet enterprise was not simply a unit of production. It was the fundamental unit of soviet society, taking responsibility for the physical, moral, educational, social and cultural reproduction of the labour force as a labour collective. This conception of the enterprise as a labour collective was deeply embedded in the 'corporate culture' of the soviet enterprise, sponsored by the Communist Party and the trade union, expressed in the iconography of the enterprise, realised through social, welfare and cultural programmes, and celebrated on special occasions throughout the year.

The corporate culture of the soviet enterprise can be characterised as one of 'authoritarian paternalism' and 'alienated collectivism'. There was no ambiguity about the authoritarian character of the soviet system, but the legitimacy of authoritarian management depended not on the imperatives of building socialism, but on regular expressions of the care and concern of management for its subordinates, expressed in cultural events, in social and welfare provision and in individual expressions of the personal concern of managers for their subordinates in informal relations. Even ordinary employees expected to be able to take work or personal problems to the general director, either during his regular tours of the shops and offices or at set times at which he would be available in his office.

The collectivism of the enterprise was celebrated in its symbols and slogans and in corporate celebrations, but this was not a self-organised collectivism of a collectivity whose members determined their own aspirations and the means for realising those aspirations. The collectivism was purely symbolic, it was embodied in the physical apparatus of the enterprise and its social and welfare facilities and it was personalised in the authority of the general director. It was an 'alienated' collectivism in the sense that its members identified with the collective not as a means of their own self-expression but as an overarching force to which they were subordinate.[1]

The official ideology imposed by the Communist Party centred on the contribution of the work of the labour collective to the building of socialism and this was embodied in statues, posters and slogans, in the honours and awards listed on honour boards and bestowed on workers for heroic labour achievements, in the respect for labour veterans and pensioners of the enterprise, and in the speeches and ceremonies at public celebrations. Even those who might be sceptical of the achievements of the soviet system as a whole could take pride in the achievements of the labour collective in production and in the social sphere and could share in the values of enterprise loyalty, patriotism and collectivism that motivated their efforts day after day.

Social structure of the enterprise

Despite the limited differentiation of pay and the ideological emphasis on collectivism, the soviet labour collective was marked by a clearly defined status hierarchy within which pay levels were a sign of status rather than a means of acquiring it, just as it was status rather than money that was the prime means of acquiring a wide range of goods and services. There was a clear division between managers and specialists (the administration), on the one hand, and

---

[1] Simon Clarke (ed.), *Labour Relations in Transition,* Cheltenham: Edward Elgar, 1996, p. 6; Sarah Ashwin, *Russian Workers: The Anatomy of Patience*, Manchester: Manchester University Press, 1999.

workers, on the other, manifested in marked differences in dress (suits versus overalls) and working conditions (quiet clean offices versus noisy and dirty production facilities). There was also a clear division between 'productive' and 'unproductive' employees, the former being those engaged in main production who were responsible for delivering the plan, the latter those servicing main production, which was expressed in marked differences in pay and status. Among the 'unproductive' employees, the office workers, mostly women engaged in routine clerical work, held the lowest status and were often regarded by production workers with barely disguised contempt.[1]

The traditional management structure had three layers. At the top would be the senior management team consisting of the general director and the key deputies, middle management would comprise department heads and shop chiefs and line management consisted of foremen and section heads. 'Engineering and technical workers' (ITR) consisted of specialists attached to shops and to central management departments.

On the shop floor, apart from the distinction between those working in main and auxiliary subdivisions, there was a marked difference between skilled and unskilled workers and, among the workers, between those loyal and committed workers with long service, the '*kadrovyi*' workers who constituted the core of the labour collective and on whom the manageability of the collective and the fulfilment of the plan depended, and the remainder who had not attained that status. At the bottom of the hierarchy were the general labourers, who were usually characterised by poor labour discipline and high labour turnover, and the 'junior service personnel' (MOP), mostly female storekeepers, cleaners and so on.

[1] Irina Kozina and Vadim Borisov, 'The changing status of workers in the enterprise', in Simon Clarke (ed.) *Conflict and Change*.

4 The soviet enterprise in the transition crisis

The soviet system collapsed around the soviet enterprise, radically transforming the environment within which the enterprise functioned without having any immediate impact on the internal structures and practices of the enterprise. The disintegration of the soviet system was at the same time the process of subordination of the Russian economy to the global accumulation of capital through its integration into the capitalist world market. The Russian enterprise had to find ways of surviving in this new environment, on the basis of its inherited social and material resources.[1]

As we have seen, the Soviet Union was never completely disconnected from the capitalist world market, but for most of the period of its existence, the relationship to the world market was one of 'managed integration'. The Soviet Union had always accessed the world market as a means of overcoming its own deficiencies, but the state monopoly of foreign trade insulated the domestic from the world economy. The ending of the state monopoly of foreign trade and gradual relaxation of restrictions on access to the world market in the late 1980s provided opportunities for those with the appropriate connections to make enormous profits by buying at low state-controlled domestic prices while selling for hard currency at world market prices. As the sphere of market transactions expanded within the Soviet Union, as well as in its foreign trade, a dual economy emerged in which enterprises increasingly clamoured for the opportunity to sell their output at market prices, while still paying domestic state prices for their labour power and material and energy inputs. This situation was clearly unsustainable, leading to massive suppressed inflation, so that by the end of 1991 market prices were escalating, the rouble was rapidly depreciating on the black market and almost nothing was available at state prices. The liberalisation of wages in late 1991 and of prices at the beginning of 1992 was no more than the inevitable recognition that the state had lost control of the

---

[1] For an account of the restructuring of management and labour relations in the transition crisis see Simon Clarke (ed.) *Management and Industry in Russia*; *Conflict and Change in the Russian Industrial Enterprise*; *The Russian Enterprise in Transition* and *Labour Relations in Transition*, Cheltenham: Edward Elgar, 1996. See also Guy Standing, *Russian Unemployment and Enterprise Restructuring: Reviving Dead Souls*, Houndmills: Macmillan, 1996.

economy and that economic relationships were now ruled by the market. The enormous 'monetary overhang' of rouble savings meant that adjustment to world market prices was not the relatively smooth process that the neo-liberal reformers had anticipated, but was accompanied by hyperinflation, with consumer prices increasing by 2,600 per cent in 1992. As domestic prices rose to world market levels, the opportunities for enterprises to profit from access to the market, which had looked so enticing in the late 1980s, had suddenly disappeared for all but those trading in natural resources. Meanwhile, the dislocation created by the collapse of the administrative-command system and the disintegration of the Soviet Union meant that galloping inflation was accompanied by deepening recession.

The collapse of the administrative-command system left enterprises in an uncertain legal position. Apart from the small number of enterprises which had been privatised or leased to the labour collective before the collapse of the Soviet Union, enterprises and organisations were still nominally owned by the state, even though the state had lost most of its levers of control over enterprises and in practice enterprise management had almost complete discretion in how they managed the enterprise and disposed of its resources. The authority of enterprise managers was by no means unconstrained. They had no clear juridical rights and the legitimacy of their position depended very much on maintaining the support of the management team and the labour force as a whole.

Following the collapse of the administrative-command system, it was imperative that the effective independence of the enterprise should be recognised juridically by enterprises being constituted as independent juridical and accounting units. Such a 'corporatisation' of the enterprise was quite consistent with continued state ownership, in the form of a state shareholding, but in fact the priority of the Russian government was to privatise the vast majority of state enterprises as quickly as possible, to undermine the possibility of a return to the old system and to give state enterprise directors a stake in capitalist development. The privatisation scheme that was adopted effectively transferred ownership of the majority of state enterprises to the labour collective free of charge. 'Privatisation to the labour collective' was by no means a victory of labour over capital, but rather a reflection of the fact that in most cases, as subsequent developments showed only too clearly, the enterprise was worthless and only the 'labour collectives' could be induced to take these liabilities off the hands of the state. In practice, collective ownership of the enterprise implied management control and over time share ownership in many enterprises was more or less rapidly concentrated in the hands of senior management. However, share ownership, even when shares were distributed free of charge, was rarely a route to prosperity. The majority of enterprises struggled to make any profits at all through the 1990s, and even most of those which were profitable did not pay dividends, devoting any surplus funds to investment in maintenance and repair and, occasionally, modernisation and re-equipment. Owner-managers rarely augmented their income directly from dividends, which would have to be shared with minority shareholders, but were more likely to do so by paying themselves generous salaries and by having an interest in commercial intermediaries through which the enterprise bought its materials and sold its products.

The reforms of the period of perestroika had given enterprises progressively more independence, but the resulting breakdown of co-ordination meant that they found themselves having to rely on their own resources in an increasingly chaotic environment. The dismantling of production complexes in the course of privatisation meant that the economy was now dominated by small independent firms which had to renegotiate their relationships with suppliers and customers. The priority of directors in the wake of the breakdown of the soviet system was to continue trading with traditional partners and to find new markets and new sources of supply, the latter often requiring the intervention of new commercial intermediaries who could use their control of markets to exert a stranglehold on the enterprise. Hyperinflation devalued the monetary savings of the population, but also the working capital of enterprises. These enterprises found themselves without money to pay for raw materials and intermediate products so that commercial transactions were based on the rapid accumulation of inter-enterprise debt, while the shortage of cash made it increasingly difficult for them to pay wages. New banks mushroomed to provide credit for industrial enterprises, initially at interest rates which turned out to be below the rate of inflation, but as inflation continued, interest rates rose and indebtedness increased, giving the banks enormous leverage over their dependent borrowers. Pressure on enterprise finances was further increased as supplier enterprises became increasingly reluctant further to extend credit and as the government insisted that enterprises should pay their tax and social insurance contributions in cash, with punitive fines imposed for late payment. The result was the increasing use of barter in inter-enterprise transactions, the development of increasingly complex barter chains and growing delays in the payment of wages. The preference for maintaining relationships with traditional partners and the growth of barter meant that tight networks predominated in inter-enterprise relations as the basis of a conservative survival strategy that strongly inhibited competition.

The disintegration and eventual collapse of the soviet system provided enormous opportunities for commercial intermediaries, particularly those dealing in commodities which could be exported, above all raw and processed raw materials such as oil, coal, chemicals and metals, and for financial intermediaries which could finance such deals. Some of these intermediaries were developed by traders who had operated, legally or illegally, within the interstices of the soviet system, some were devolved out of former state supply and banking organisations, some were set up by individuals, such as KGB officers, Komsomol officials and customs officers, who had good connections from soviet times, and some were set up by senior enterprise managers or their close relatives to profit from supplying and selling the products of their own enterprises. The staggering profits made by these intermediaries depended on maintaining control of supplies and supplier enterprises. During the early 1990s there were bloody struggles for control of privatised metallurgical enterprises, while the middle 1990s saw the 'loans for shares' deals, through which Yeltsin gave away the major oil companies at knock-down prices to those who backed his 1996 re-election campaign. The key to making profits in the 1990s was not ownership but control. Control could be exerted through majority ownership, but it could also be exerted through debt, through corruption or through the threat of violence.

External investments were almost entirely made for the purpose of gaining control of supplies, so that even in the lucrative export sectors there was almost no externally funded productive investment. Enterprises had to make use of their own limited funds for investment, some of which involved the piecemeal acquisition of equipment to make new products, but most of which was for basic maintenance and repair.

The priority of enterprise directors in the transition to a market economy was not the maximisation of profits, which only attracted the interest of the tax authorities and criminal structures, but 'survival', the reproduction of the enterprise as a social organisation, the 'preservation of the labour collective', which was the basis of the power and status of the director. This priority was reinforced by the expectations of the labour force carried over from the soviet period, for whom the legitimacy of the director's position did not derive from any property rights, but from the director's ability to preserve the jobs and wages of the labour force. This priority was further reinforced by privatisation to the labour collective and by pressure from local authorities, which depended on a functioning enterprise to provide jobs for the local population, to provide tax revenues for the local authority and, in many cases, to contribute to the maintenance of the local housing, transport, social and welfare infrastructure.

A prime requirement of survival for the enterprise in the demonetised transitional economy was to secure a source of 'live money' to generate a positive cash flow. Enterprises had obtained their plant and stocks effectively free of charge through the privatisation process, so their costs were only for materials, labour and fuel, and the growth of barter and inter-enterprise debt meant that the main need for cash, as in soviet times, was to pay wages. State orders, which had been the mainstay of the soviet system, became the last resort because it became almost impossible to force state bodies to settle their accounts. One immediate source of 'live money' was leasing or selling part of the premises of the enterprise and selling off stocks of materials. Enterprises in the traditionally low-status branches of light industry and food processing now found themselves in a privileged position because they were able to sell their products for cash and so pay wages. Enterprises which produced for consumer markets established their own networks of sales outlets, which was the only way to ensure that the sales revenue flowed back to the enterprise. Enterprises producing machinery and intermediate products faced a collapse in orders and often sought to use their existing labour, equipment and raw material stocks to produce consumer goods. Military-industrial enterprises had always been involved in the subsidiary production of consumer durables, and in many cases this now became their production priority. In many cases shop chiefs and even foremen were given responsibility for re-profiling production and chasing up orders for their shops to bring in some money to pay wages. Technological limitations and market instability meant that most such innovations involved custom-building or short production runs, often with inappropriate technology and raw materials, resulting in low-quality outputs. The lack of funds for investment meant that the enterprise depended on the skills and initiative of the workforce to keep archaic machinery in operation and to identify new products which could be made with the existing equipment and available parts and materials, so reinforcing the traditionally chaotic system of production management. Meanwhile, new private enterprises sprang up, the most successful being those which could identify an unfilled niche in the market.

New private enterprises had a big advantage during the late perestroika period, while state enterprises were still restricted by price and wage controls, which they by-passed by hiving off production units into 'co-operatives' and by using new private enterprises as intermediaries. During the early 1990s new private enterprises found their niche predominantly in trade, catering and consumer services. During the later 1990s there was a growth of new private enterprises providing business services, particularly in security, but also providing business consultancy, research and development, accounting and marketing services. The only productive sector in which new private enterprises made significant headway was in information technology. Although the reformers pinned great hopes on the growth of the new private sector, most new private enterprises remained small, with a very high failure rate, serving local markets. New private enterprises in the twin capitals of Moscow and Saint Petersburg had big advantages and were much better placed to expand their coverage by developing regional networks, absorbing local competitors.

Between 1992 and 1998 the Russian economy was marked by a steady decline. The collapse of investment left the engineering and construction industries facing a massive decline in orders. The military-industrial complex, even where it retained government orders, was hit hard by the failure of the government to pay for those orders. Consumer goods industries suffered from growing import competition, as consumers were seduced by the novelty of imported goods and inflation in the face of a stable exchange rate eroded the competitive advantage of domestic producers. Companies looked for new products and new markets which would enable them to keep working, but even the most enterprising could do little more than slow the decline. Only the exporters of raw and processed materials flourished, as the continuing decline of domestic demand freed fuels, metals and chemicals for sale on the world market.

In the face of tightening financial constraints there was rarely any money for new investment, while declining markets meant that enterprises worked at reduced capacity, which resulted in declining productivity. Enterprises were forced to cut costs by the threat of insolvency, but this meant that cost-cutting was not achieved by any planned reorganisation or re-equipment but by deterioration in the living standards and working conditions of employees. Enterprise directors under financial pressure were only too happy to abide by government instructions to divest themselves of the bulk of their responsibilities for the provision of housing and health, social and welfare facilities, which were transferred to municipal authorities which had neither the financial nor the administrative capacity to maintain them. The most effective economy measures were short-time working and temporary plant closures, which saved on wage and especially energy costs, and the non-payment of wages, taxes and suppliers.

Enterprises made little effort to reduce costs by reducing their labour force, despite falling production, primarily because they always lived in the hope of recovery, in which case they would need their skilled and experienced workers once more, while wages, even when they were paid, made up only a small proportion of costs. On the other hand, as wages were eroded in the face of inflation, and increasingly were not paid at all, more and more employees left declining enterprises in the hope of finding better opportunities elsewhere. Some of those who left were pensioners, but most were younger and middle-aged employees, particularly those with marketable skills, who had the best prospects of finding work elsewhere, or even setting up in business on their own. The result was that employment did tend to fall in line with the fall of production, though with some lag,[1] and those who left were those skilled younger employees the enterprise could least afford to lose. As the best workers left for jobs elsewhere those who remained were required to fill the gaps, leading to an intensification of labour and increased flexibility in the use of labour, often in defiance of labour legislation. In general such measures were accepted by the workers as the price of keeping their jobs, at least so long as they could be persuaded that management had no alternative. When the workers lost confidence in their director, their response was the traditional one of demanding the director's replacement, the great hope being to attract a new wealthy owner who would pay wages and make the investments necessary to secure their future prosperity.

In the attempt to hold on to valued employees many enterprises found ways of paying them wages or allowing them to earn on the side. Many workers on piece-rates were switched to time-wages, to ensure that they could keep earning even when production was at a standstill. Some would be found earning opportunities, whether it be maintenance and repair or even simply cleaning up the factory. Others would be allowed to use the equipment of the enterprise, and often even its parts and raw materials, to undertake jobs on the side, individually or collectively, for outside customers.

The collapse of the soviet system transformed the environment within which the enterprise operated and sought to reproduce itself, but it did not have any immediate impact on the internal structures, practices and resources at the disposal of management, although it did introduce tensions within the management apparatus and some change in the balance of power between different branches of management. The transition to a market economy raised the significance of those parts of the management apparatus which were responsible for managing the external relationships of the enterprise, removing or downgrading those branches of management which had been central to the administrative control of the enterprise, and expanding the commercial and

---

[1] Simon Clarke, *The Formation of a Labour Market in Russia*, Cheltenham: Edward Elgar, 1999, p. 298.

financial branches of management which play the leading role in the adjustment to changing market conditions. Typically this restructuring was associated with a dualistic management structure. The day-to-day management of productive activity remained under the control of the production director, chief engineer and shop chiefs, who were oriented to the preservation and reinforcement of traditional authoritarian management structures. Meanwhile the management of the shareholding company was dominated by the economic and financial branches of management, oriented to commercial and financial activity, which were the branches of management most heavily involved in parallel structures, through which some tended to follow what economists politely call a 'rent-seeking' strategy. Alongside this restructuring of the management hierarchy there was a substantial widening of pay differentials in favour of management as a whole, and within management in favour of the strategic senior managers, despite the fact that this violated the deeply held 'egalitarian' values of the workers who supposedly still owned the majority of enterprises.[1]

The keys to the survival of a Russian enterprise during the 1990s were not any internal reforms that the management might undertake, so much as the external connections that could be developed, through which the enterprise could negotiate access to materials, could find markets for its products and could find sources of outside finance and support from government authorities. A successful general director or senior manager was one who had good connections, probably built up as a result of working in the industry, if not in that enterprise, for many years. Even those enterprises which had some cash would be reluctant to use it for buying supplies, except at a very substantial discount, but suppliers were increasingly reluctant to supply against credit, which was most unlikely ever to be repaid, so securing supplies became increasingly a matter of arranging barter deals. If the enterprise produced a final product, then it might be able to barter its product directly for supplies, but more often barter deals required the establishment of very complex networks of multilateral trading handled by commercial intermediaries.

There was little point in negotiating barter arrangements to secure supplies if the enterprise was not able to sell or barter what it produced. Gradually enterprises began to adapt production to the limits of the market, although they would try to keep production at a break-even level and press the sales department to sell sufficient items at least to cover costs. Sometimes, particularly in continuous process production, they would produce steadily until the warehouses were full, and then close down for a period until the stocks were cleared. Such uneven production rhythms were very disruptive, not least because after a stoppage many of the key workers would not return, so it became more usual to try to adjust the rhythm of production to the rhythm of sales.

Enterprises had no experience of having to sell their products. Managers had grown up in a shortage economy, when almost anything that they delivered,

---

[1] Simon Clarke and Veronika Kabalina, 'Privatisation and the struggle for control of the enterprise in Russia', in David Lane (ed.) *Russia in Transition*, London: Longman, 1995.

whatever the quality, would be accepted. Sales had been very much the junior partner in the sales and supply department, since supply had traditionally been the barrier to soviet production. With the transition to a market economy being followed almost immediately by the collapse of the market, enterprises suddenly had to find ways of selling their products. Qualified, let alone experienced, sales managers were few and far between, and nobody knew how to assess the skills of a sales specialist in the first place, so sales usually continued to be the responsibility of the traditional sales and supply department. The retail sector was very undeveloped, with a large proportion of trade being carried out in open-air markets and kiosks and small retail outlets. There were very few wholesalers, and those that did exist were generally concerned to establish and defend a monopoly position, by whatever means might be necessary, rather than to serve as commercial agents. Thus sales were generally handled directly by sales agents, with line managers, foremen and even ordinary workers often being sent off to explore sales possibilities on commission. Many enterprises set up sales outlets on the factory premises and this often developed into a chain of shops selling the factory's products.[1] It became common for enterprises to pay their workers in kind, either with the products of the factory or with products obtained through barter, which the workers themselves would try to sell on the streets.

Many enterprise managers and workers showed enormous ingenuity in attempting to overcome the difficulties that they faced in trying to secure the survival of the enterprise through the transition crisis. However, the decline was inexorable as the reformers heralded the new dawn each year, only to see incomes, output, employment and investment fall year by year. Restrictive monetary policies, which were supposed to combat inflation and drive out unprofitable producers, simply intensified competition on domestic markets by driving up the exchange rate and promoted the continuing demonetisation of the economy. Enterprises received some relief from the fact that domestic energy prices continued to be far below world levels, but the scope for government to bail out loss-making enterprises with subsidies was steadily declining. The sum of unpaid wages grew steadily, and the length of wage delays grew ever longer. The proportion of transactions based on barter and of settlements through money surrogates continued to increase as the realm of money became more and more limited. Inter-enterprise debt and enterprise debts for the payment of taxes and social insurance payments mounted. Barter transactions, non-monetary settlements and accumulating debt made it possible for many insolvent enterprises to continue to show a book profit, but the number who reported losses continued to mount, the majority of all enterprises being loss-making by 1996. The demonetisation of the economy and the complicated web of transactions and obligations made it almost impossible to evaluate the real financial situation of any enterprise. This was compounded by the fact that the

---

[1] A 1997 survey of 682 Russian firms found that 22 per cent had established their own retail network (Simeon Djankov, 'Enterprise restructuring In Russia', in Harry G. Broadman (ed.) *Russian Enterprise Reform: Policies to Further the Transition*, Washington, DC: World Bank, Discussion Paper No. 400, 1998, p. 131).

bankruptcy procedures made it almost impossible for an enterprise to be declared bankrupt against its director's will, so that rather than going into liquidation the most unsuccessful enterprises merely continued their steady decline. In this period the bankruptcy procedure turned out to be a means of saving enterprises from bankruptcy, as they would transfer all their assets to a new company and then liquidate the shell of the old company, now consisting of little more than the enterprise's liabilities.

Russian capitalism on the eve of default

GDP at constant prices was halved between 1990 and 1998, while both agricultural and industrial production fell by slightly more than half. Even those sectors which should have flourished with the transition to a market economy declined: the production of fuels, with the world market at its feet, fell by one-third. Retail trade turnover fell by almost 20 per cent, food processing fell in line with the rest of industry, while light industry, the Cinderella of the soviet system, was decimated by falling living standards and foreign competition, its output declining by more than 80 per cent.

The collapse of production was accompanied by the collapse of investment, which was most dramatic in the years of disintegration of the soviet system, when gross fixed investment fell by half in just two years, and by a further half in the next three years, before settling at one-fifth of its historic level. The result is reflected in the ageing of industrial plant. The average age of industrial plant and equipment in the late soviet period was about nine years, but by 1999 it had increased to over eighteen years, with less than 4 per cent being under five years old and about two-thirds having been installed even before the beginning of perestroika in 1985.

Far from being regenerated by the transition to a market economy, the Russian economy was still capitalising on the deteriorating legacy of the past. Despite the huge profits being made from the export of oil, gas and metals, almost no investment was being made by the oil and gas and metallurgical companies which supplied the new banking-centred corporate structures of the oligarchs so that, as noted above, the production of fuels was declining, existing reserves were being rapidly depleted and the exploitation of new reserves postponed because of the lack of investment. Oil extraction fell by a third between 1990 and 1998, although the number employed in the industry more than doubled. In 1998 the rate of fixed investment as a proportion of output in the oil industry was only one-third of the 1985 level.

The collapse of the economy was reflected in the decline in employment and wages. Total employment fell by over 20 per cent, with employment in industry falling by 40 per cent, construction by 44 per cent, and science by 54 per cent, while employment in credit and finance increased by 80 per cent from a very small base. Employment in public administration increased by the same proportion, creating five times as many new jobs as credit and finance – so much for the transition to a market economy – while employment in trade and catering, the one branch dominated by new private enterprises, increased by two-thirds (despite the decline in the turnover of retail trade).

Real wages collapsed in the three bursts of inflation in 1992, 1995 and again in the wake of the August 1998 crisis. By the end of 1998 average real wages had fallen to one-third of their 1990 level, although this gives a somewhat misleading impression, since the increased money wages of the late Gorbachev period could not be utilised as there was so little to buy. Two-thirds of all wage earners earned less than twice the subsistence minimum, in other words they did not earn enough to support one dependant. The fall in wages was associated with a dramatic increase in wage inequality, from a Gini coefficient of 0.24 in the soviet period to a coefficient of 0.48 after 1992, generating Latin American levels of inequality. Moreover, this increase in inequality does not primarily reflect an increase in class inequality, although that is very striking in every large Russian city. Half the inequality is accounted for by differences in wages between different workplaces, so that a cleaner in a prosperous bank could earn more than the director of a declining industrial enterprise.[1]

Alongside the devastation of the productive economy and the pauperisation of the Russian population, the small group of oligarchs and the companies they controlled accumulated staggering fortunes almost overnight. But where did their fortunes come from? The first fortunes were made through commercial and financial intermediation. Traders were able to make enormous fortunes by exploiting the differences between Russian and world market prices in the period of perestroika and the first years of reform. If they could monopolise the trade by obtaining exclusive licences and permits, or by using threats and force against potential competitors, their profits could be all the greater. As privatisation got under way, they were able to consolidate their control of the market by acquiring a controlling interest in the supplier companies. This could be achieved, as it was in metallurgy, by buying up the shares that had initially been allocated to workers and managers. The most dramatic fortunes were acquired through the notorious 'loans for shares' auctions in 1996, when most oil companies were sold off to insiders at derisory prices. But in all these cases, the oligarchs made their profits not by investing in the modernisation and development of production facilities in the oil and metallurgy industries but from their commercial intermediation, usually selling at low prices to their own offshore companies in which they sheltered the profits. Where the oligarchs did invest and expand their fortunes domestically, it was not in productive investment but in the commercial banks that they controlled and through which they managed their commercial activity, which made the bulk of their profits from speculation in foreign exchange and the government debt. Moreover, a large proportion of the assets of the new commercial banks in the early 1990s, which they lent to the government at exorbitant rates of interest and through which they financed the 'loans for shares' deals, was in fact the government's own money, because the commercial banks were given the commission to collect taxes and customs revenues on behalf of the government.

[1] Simon Clarke, 'Market and institutional determinants of wage differentiation in Russia', *Industrial and Labor Relations Review* 55(4), July 2002: 628–48.

The 1990s was the period which Michael Burawoy characterised as 'merchant capitalism',[1] in which capital is accumulated through intermediary activities, without any significant involvement or investment in production. This represents the purely formal subsumption of labour under capital that was discussed in Chapter 1. The vast majority of Russian enterprises struggled to survive in the face of intense domestic and foreign competition, with minimal investment and earning little or no profits, using inherited plant and equipment and retaining the traditional soviet social organisation of production, while the bulk of the surplus was appropriated by monopolistic and at best semi-criminal commercial intermediaries. Enterprises cut costs not by revolutionising production methods but by reducing real wages and intensifying labour, and they stayed in business by defaulting on their payments to suppliers and to their own employees. Internally Russian enterprises and organisations continued to function much as they had in the soviet period, with little change in their management structures and practices and with an orientation to survival rather than to the maximisation of profit. Although the vast majority of enterprises had been privatised, the majority were worthless as capitalist property, making almost no productive investment and making almost no profit. In 1998 enterprises and organisations as a whole recorded a net loss amounting to 4.3 per cent of GDP. While the taxation of company profits in 1998 amounted to 1.3 per cent of GDP, total dividends paid out amounted to only 0.3 per cent of GDP. Meanwhile, by 1998 the cost of servicing government debt had risen to 4 per cent of GDP, much of which was paid to Russian banks, and capital flight was running at $20–25 billion per year, more than 5 per cent of GDP and five times as much as gross inward foreign direct investment.

Foreign capitalists were showing no more enthusiasm for investing productively in Russia than were their Russian counterparts. Foreign direct investment in Russia lagged behind that in Poland and was at about the level of FDI in Hungary or the Czech Republic, amounting between 1994 and 1998 to an average of about $3 billion per annum, although it increased sharply in 1997, with total foreign investment peaking at just over $12 billion (some of this would have been repatriated capital outflows) before collapsing again after the 1998 default. Only 2.2 per cent of the derisory amount of total fixed investment in 1998 was due to foreign investors, almost double the level of the previous year, with a further 4 per cent being due to Russian investors with foreign partners. In 1998 19 per cent of foreign investment went into oil and metallurgy, 13 per cent into the food processing industry and 30 per cent into trade and catering, commerce and finance with only a trivial amount in the remaining industrial branches.

Although the soviet form of surplus appropriation might have had some characteristics in common with that of feudalism, most particularly in the dissociation of production from the appropriation of a surplus, the soviet economy was not a feudal economy based on subsistence farming, but a complex industrial economy. Following the collapse of the soviet system, the surplus that had been appropriated by the state was now appropriated by the new

---

[1] Burawoy and Krotov, 'The soviet transition from socialism to capitalism'.

Russian capitalists and their foreign partners, but this appropriation now took place not through an administrative-command system of economic management, but through market mechanisms. The administrative-command system had provided a bureaucratic apparatus that could seek to reconcile the appropriation of a surplus with the expanded reproduction of the system, but the new forms of surplus appropriation based on 'merchant capitalism' lacked any mechanisms that could secure the reproduction of the system of production and so did nothing to regenerate the Russian industrial base to enable Russian industrial capital to compete on the world market..

The extent to which Russian industrial capital lagged behind its global competitors was charted by a report prepared in 1998–9 by the McKinsey Global Institute, a research group within the McKinsey Company. This was based on the findings of case studies of ten varied sectors of the Russian economy: steel, cement, oil, confectionery, the dairy industry, food retailing, general retailing, computer software, housing construction and hotels. The performance of Russian firms in these industries was benchmarked against 'best global practice' in the same sectors to identify the extent to which the productivity of Russian firms lagged behind best practice and, most importantly, the principal reasons for this lag. The results of the research were striking and, in some respects, surprising.[1]

The McKinsey researchers found that labour productivity in Russian enterprises was extremely low in comparison with their US equivalents, with an average of only 17 per cent of US productivity levels, ranging from 7 per cent in cement to 38 per cent in computer software. Moreover, the productivity of assets inherited from the soviet period had fallen by about half as a result of low capacity working and about one-quarter of all industrial capacity was in sub-scale or obsolete plant. There had been minimal new investment since 1992, even in industries such as oil and consumer goods which should have considerable potential, and new assets introduced since 1992 were also very unproductive, at below one-third of US levels, primarily because they were below efficient scale or undercapitalised.

The three main reasons for low labour productivity identified by the McKinsey researchers were the retention of labour despite low-capacity working; failure to adopt modern management practices, in particular poor quality control, lack of marketing and sales skills, lack of effective profit incentives and the absence of team-working; and failure to take advantage of profitable investment opportunities to upgrade existing plant, particularly to improve quality and energy efficiency, and to develop new assets.

The McKinsey researchers explained Russia's poor economic performance primarily by the failure to close down inefficient and unprofitable plants, which meant that even the more efficient plants were working well below capacity and so were not able to make a profit. They put considerable weight in their explanation for the failure to close unprofitable plants on continued subsidisation of unprofitable manufacturing enterprises by regional authorities, primarily by toleration of the accumulation of debt for tax and energy payments,

---

[1] McKinsey Global Institute, *Unlocking Economic Growth in Russia, op. cit.*

and the protection of inefficient local companies through tax breaks, privileged access to contracts, licences and permits and the lax enforcement of regulations. They argued that the protection of inefficient producers was partly a result of misguided attempts to preserve jobs and partly a result of corruption, although it should be noted that such protection was perfectly rational for local authorities and local communities in the face of a macroeconomic crash, unless the federal government was willing to compensate them for the loss of jobs and local revenue. In comparison with the preservation of excess capacity, they found that other factors often cited, such as poor corporate governance, inadequate legal enforcement, lack of labour mobility and transport bottlenecks had already been largely overcome and so were not such significant barriers to growth.

The McKinsey researchers concluded that Russia had considerable growth potential once market distortions were removed, with considerable potential for the reactivation of viable idle capacity, the most promising growth sectors being export-oriented investment in the oil industry and import-substituting growth of light manufacturing, driven by foreign direct investment which could provide the necessary finance and introduce best-practice technology and management methods. The McKinsey study was carried out on the eve of the recovery which followed the 1998 crash and which soon mopped up much of the excess capacity that the McKinsey researchers had identified as the principal cause of the poor performance of Russian industry. In the rest of this book we will consider to what extent the recovery has enabled Russian capitalism to unlock its potential by transforming its management methods.

After the crash – the Russian boom

The steady decline of the real economy through the 1990s could not be sustained indefinitely. Plant and equipment was deteriorating rapidly without the resources for modernisation and replacement, or even for proper maintenance and repair, while the ageing industrial and agricultural labour force was losing its skills and, with extended stoppages and short-time working, the work ethic inherited from soviet society was being eroded. There is nothing unusual about integration into global capitalism leading to the destruction of indigenous productive resources and the pauperisation of the mass of the population, but new investment was increasingly urgently required in the modernisation and re-equipment of the extractive industries, oil, gas and metallurgy, if global capital was to continue to be able to pump out Russia's natural resources. The opportunities for profit from the extraction and primary processing of natural resources were so enormous that investors would eventually be found who would be ready and able to overcome any barriers presented by corruption and criminality.

In fact the environment was transformed by the 1998 default and devaluation and the subsequent steady rise in the world price of fuels, metals and other mineral resources. After regularly hailing the 'coming Russian boom' with every publication of unfavourable economic indicators,[1] most liberal commentators proclaimed the 1998 default a disaster which would seriously postpone the anticipated Russian recovery. The liberal economists proved wrong yet again, as the Russian economy seemed to turn the corner in the wake of the default, with steady GDP growth in each succeeding year.

There were three factors which fuelled the Russian boom, when it eventually came. First, the increase in the world market prices of oil, gas and metals gave a substantial and continuing boost to the Russian terms of trade, its balance of international payments and the government budget. Second, the sharp devaluation, which was not initially compensated by increased money wages, gave domestic producers a substantial competitive boost on domestic and, in some cases, export markets and attracted foreign companies which had begun to supply the domestic market to explore opportunities for direct investment in Russian production facilities. Third, the decisive factor in sustaining the boom was that the investment environment was radically changed. By 2002 the benefits of devaluation had been largely neutralised by domestic price and wage inflation, while most domestic excess capacity, which McKinsey had identified as the biggest drag on the Russian economy, had been mopped up, so that sustained growth would depend on new investment. The 1998 financial crisis hit the banks very hard and led to a sharp reduction in the possibilities of profiting from financial operations, so that the dominant bank-centred financial-industrial groups had to turn their attention to other, more secure, ways of making money.[2] Most of the leading domestic players had managed to extricate themselves from their over-commitment to the banking system before the crisis struck, leaving foreign investors to carry the heaviest losses, and had transferred the centre of their operations from banks to broader holding companies, the largest of which were built around fuel, energy and metallurgy enterprises. The loss of opportunities to profit by financial speculation and the transformed prospects for domestic investment led to a substantial reorientation of Russian holding companies towards domestic productive investment. At the same time, the introduction of a new bankruptcy law in 1998 made it very easy for creditors to use the law to acquire even solvent enterprises at very favourable prices.[3] As a result, following the 1998 crisis, Russian capital moved into production on a large scale as holding companies purchased industrial enterprises, often at knock-down prices, through share purchases, debt–equity swaps or the

[1] Richard Layard and John Parker, *The Coming Russian Boom: A Guide to New Markets and Politics*, New York: The Free Press, 1996.

[2] Evgeny Novitskiy, *Corporate Business: Core of Russian Economy*, 25 June 2002. <http://www.rencap.com/eng/research/morningmonitors/PDF/01abe3f2-24a7-4af3-9749-7e2cbef42ec3.pdf> (last accessed 27 May 2006).

[3] Carsten Sprenger, *Ownership and Corporate Governance in Russian Industry: a Survey*, EBRD Working Paper 70: 30, 2002. The bankruptcy law was revised again in 2002 to make it much more difficult for outsiders to gain control, but by this time the holding companies had been able to use the 1998 law to take their pick of acquisitions (David M. Woodruff, *The End of 'Primitive Capitalist Accumulation'? The New Bankruptcy Law and the Political Assertiveness of Russian Big Business*, PONARS Policy Memo No. 274: 4, 2002).

bankruptcy procedure. Moreover, by contrast to the period before the default, the holding companies began to invest and to intervene directly in the management of many of their subsidiary enterprises.[1] This has led to a sharply increased concentration of ownership, particularly in the 'strategic' sub-sectors in which Russian corporations have been most active – oil and raw materials, automobiles and chemicals. In other sectors Russia continues to be marked by low levels of ownership concentration and, even if the plants are large by international standards, the firms tend to be small.[2]

The 1998 default and devaluation and the subsequent sustained economic recovery transformed the environment in which Russian enterprises were struggling to survive. Markets were now expanding, the pressure of foreign competition was eased, bank credit was more accessible so that sales could expand and wages could begin to be paid. Not every enterprise was equally well placed to benefit from the macroeconomic recovery. All enterprises had suffered from the economic decline of the 1990s, but some had much more favourable conditions for recovery than did others. All enterprises were stocked with ageing plant and equipment, but some enterprises had been built or reconstructed in the 1980s, while others had not undergone reconstruction since the 1950s or 1960s. The extractive industries enjoyed enormous advantages in the world market because of Russia's favourable resource endowment, while other industries, such as light industry, did not have the technology to compete with advanced capitalist producers nor, despite their pitifully low wages, could they compete with low-wage producers in Turkey and China. Some enterprises enjoyed very favourable locations, with good transport links and convenient access to their sources of supply and/or their markets, while others were in extremely unfavourable locations, remote from supplies and markets, their location having been selected for strategic or political reasons. Some enterprises had very cramped premises, which imposed considerable costs for storage and materials handling, while others had expansive well-laid-out premises. Some enterprises owned land and buildings in prime locations, which they could rent or sell to finance their operations, while others were on derelict sites in remote urban districts. Some enterprises had a well-developed and maintained urban infrastructure, making the district an attractive place to live and work, other enterprises were located in run-down districts with poor municipal services which they were called on to repair and maintain. Some enterprises had significant support from local, regional or federal authorities, while others faced significant bureaucratic obstructions (a contrast that was particularly marked between regions with different political regimes, but that would also mark local enterprises in comparison with those expanding from other regions). Enterprises

[1] Guriev and Rachinsky found that by 2002 firms controlled by oligarchs were outperforming other domestically owned firms and were not lagging far behind foreign-owned firms (Sergei Guriev and Andrei Rachinsky, *Ownership Concentration in Russian Industry*, Moscow: Centre for Economic and Financial Research, Working Paper 45, 2004).

[2] *From Transition to Development: A Country Economic Memorandum for the Russian Federation*, Washington, DC: World Bank, Report No. 32308-RU, March 2005.

based in Moscow and Saint Petersburg gained significant advantages from their immediate access to the much more developed market infrastructure and international connections of the twin capitals, having access to professional business consultants, well-trained specialists, financial markets, marketing resources and transport hubs so that they could more easily service the national and export markets.

Against all of these objective factors it is difficult to say how much difference management can make. It is unlikely that even the best management could overcome an accumulation of such disadvantages, while even bad management might prosper in an advantageous situation. We therefore have to be cautious in seeking the secret of the success of our case-study enterprises in their management practices, or in assuming that in selecting successful enterprises for study we will necessarily find examples of the best management. Nevertheless, our case studies provide us with a considerable variety of enterprises in a range of industrial sectors. Every enterprise has its own unique history, and each is fascinating in itself, but together they offer a cross-section which allows us to develop some generalisations about the character and extent of management restructuring in contemporary Russian enterprises. In the next chapter we will look at the corporate management structures and practices which have been adopted in successful Russian enterprises. One of the findings of this review is that there has been much more substantial reform in the management of the external relations of the enterprise than in its internal practices. In following chapters we will therefore look more closely at production and personnel management and the reform of wage and payment systems, before drawing some final conclusion.

5 The corporate management of Russian enterprises

Soviet management confronts the market

The soviet system of management may have been adequate to the task confronting the soviet enterprise of delivering the plan at all costs, but it is not well adapted to the management of an enterprise operating in a market environment, which must have management systems through which production can be subordinated to the constraints of the market and expenditure kept within the limits of receipts. The quality and design of the product has to correspond to the demands of the market and the production costs must be limited to the revenues that the sale of the product can secure and generate a surplus to fund new investment. This implies fundamental changes in the management structure, management systems of information and control and the status of different management functions.

The adaptation of management structures to the constraints of profitability in the developed capitalist countries took place over a long period of time and often involved significant conflict within management, as some managers resisted changes which eroded their status and authority, while others saw change as an opportunity to advance their personal and professional careers. These conflicts involved not only professional and personal interests, but also articulated differences in the understanding of the role and character of the enterprise. Engineers may see the key to success as lying in technical excellence, marketing specialists see it in the design and promotion of products, accountants put a premium on the accounting and control of costs, personnel managers on good training, employment practices and working conditions. The outcomes of these conflicts differ according to the different constraints and opportunities facing different companies and industries and also according to the different institutions and cultures of different countries, so there is no single model of best practice to which post-soviet enterprises could adapt. Nevertheless, competitive pressures should ensure that only those companies that manage to adopt management structures and practices appropriate to a market economy will survive and prosper. This means that internal management conflicts in the longer run are subordinated to these dominant imperatives and particular specialisms achieve prominence by demonstrating their capacity to meet these imperatives.[1] Rivalry between individual managers and management specialisms therefore takes place within the framework of strategic objectives defined by top management, while senior managers distinguish themselves by embracing this viewpoint.[2]

The traditional management structure of the soviet enterprise is particularly inadequate to the demands of a market economy in at least three respects.

First, the overwhelming dominance of production management and engineering priorities over economic and financial constraints imposed by the market is unsustainable in a market economy. This dominance was brutally challenged in Russia by the experience of the 1990s, when most companies faced a collapse in the demand for their products and were unable to cover even their tax obligations and their current spending on raw materials and wages from their current revenues, while only limited credit was available at a very high cost. Even the most stubborn production director had to recognise that in the capitalist world there can be no production without a market. Senior managers may recognise the urgency of subordinating production to the constraints of marketing and finance, but even when this has been recognised at the level of senior management it has to be transmitted to the management of the production shops so it involves radical changes both in the horizontal relationships within the senior management team, and in the vertical relations between senior and middle or line management. We will consider the former aspect in this chapter, and discuss the problem of middle management in more detail in later chapters.

Second, the hierarchical functional management structure is not an effective form of management in an environment which requires adaptability, flexibility and the exercise of initiative at lower levels. This was already the case in the soviet enterprise, where the inflexibility of the official management structure was compensated by the network of informal practices, but such informal practices were still subordinate to the unequivocal goal, imposed through the management hierarchy, of fulfilling the plan. Such a functional management structure had been typical of western capitalist enterprises in the nineteenth and early twentieth centuries, from which the Soviet Union adopted it in the 1920s and 1930s, but in the west it had increasingly been replaced by a divisional structure from the 1930s onwards. The divisional structure has many advantages over the functional structure, particularly in large and complex enterprises. First, it facilitates the decentralisation of management, the devolution of decision-making and the flattening of management structures which is essential to the co-ordination of a large and complex organisation. Second, it is necessary for proper cost accounting, by making it possible to allocate expenditure to appropriate cost-centres and so to achieve a greater degree of transparency in

[1] Peter Armstrong, 'Management labour process and agency', *Work, Employment and Society* 3(3), 1989: 307–22, and 'Contradiction and social dynamics in the capitalist agency relationship', *Accounting, Organizations and Society* 16(1), 1991: 1–25.

[2] Tony J. Watson, *In Search of Management: Culture, Chaos and Control in Managerial Work*, London: Routledge, 1994.

tracking costs. As we will see later, the overwhelming majority of our case-study enterprises have retained the traditional functional system of soviet management. Large holding companies have introduced divisional structures, but these merely involve the allocation of subsidiary enterprises to the appropriate product division, without any radical change in the management structure of the subsidiary. Some companies have espoused more collegial forms of management in theory, but in practice this has not involved any significant devolution of power, with the director retaining the last word. Some companies have flattened or delayered their management structures by removing one link in the hierarchical chain, but this has usually been the result of a substantial decline in production and employment and an aspiration to economise on staff salaries rather than representing a significant change in management structure. Foreign-owned companies have changed their management structures more radically than most Russian-owned companies, but even here the changes are not deep-rooted and traditional practices still prevail.

Third, the soviet management system was marked by a sustained neglect of personnel management. It has become a commonplace in advanced capitalism that 'people are our most important resource' and a great deal of effort and expense is put into personnel selection and training, career development and 'human resource management'. Although the Soviet Union was supposed to be a 'workers' state', in the soviet system the personnel were simply regarded as a part of the means of production and personnel management was essentially a bureaucratic task of allocating personnel to workplaces, regularly testing them, certifying them and assigning them for training, just like any other pieces of equipment. Once they had been assigned to their workplaces, it was the responsibility of foremen and shop chiefs, who had been selected for their technical rather than their personnel management skills, to keep them working, with the resources at their disposal. Just as they would give their machines a regular kick and an occasional drop of oil, so too the workers would be kept at work and encouraged to meet the plan targets with the administration of fairly crude punishments and rewards to reinforce informal personal relations of loyalty and dependence. Personnel management was essentially a subordinate part of production management. The adoption of more enlightened and effective systems of personnel management, in both their 'soft' developmental and their 'hard' disciplinary aspects, therefore depends on the transformation of production management and the development of new priorities in production.

In this chapter we will concentrate on the changes that have taken place at the top level of management, in the structure of corporate management, in response to the transition to a market economy. In examining the changes that have taken place in the corporate management of Russian enterprises, it is useful to distinguish between three types of enterprise, which differ in the extent to which they are compelled to adapt to the market environment. The management objectives of enterprises which have been acquired by holding companies are dictated from above, by the holding company, and the enterprise management has little choice but to subordinate the enterprise to the achievement of those objectives. In independent enterprises the management has a greater degree of freedom to determine its objectives, within the limits of the market, particularly where the enterprise is owned by insiders, although this freedom will still be constrained by external pressures from government and business partners and by internal pressures from management and the workforce. Owners are likely to have much more freedom to determine the objectives of a new private enterprise, which they have built up by investing their own resources, than the owners of former state enterprises, which have been acquired through more or less dubious processes of privatisation and redistribution of property, where the attempt to assert the rights of ownership suffers from a lack of legitimacy.

Insider-controlled privatised enterprises

The management structure of insider-controlled former soviet enterprises has changed little since soviet times. During the 1990s the main priority of almost every enterprise was day-to-day survival and there was very little space or opportunity to undertake any radical changes in the management structure. The privatisation process exposed the vulnerability of enterprise directors and made it essential for them to try to maintain the cohesiveness of the senior management team. The majority of Russian enterprises were privatised to their own management and employees, but there was often a subsequent redistribution of shares, the outcome of which was unpredictable. Workers had little interest in keeping their shares, which usually neither paid dividends nor gave them any degree of control. In many cases outside investors showed an interest in buying up shares, which was obviously a potential threat to the status of the existing management, who equally sought to buy up shares in order to consolidate their own position in the enterprise. However, unless or until the enterprise director could accumulate a controlling interest in their enterprise, their position would always be vulnerable. This was not a situation in which the enterprise director could afford to risk opening up divisions within the senior management team or between management and the labour force by undertaking any radical redistribution of authority and responsibility. On the contrary, enterprise directors had to secure their position by representing themselves as the paternalistic guardian of the labour collective in its struggle to survive in a hostile world.[1]

During the 1990s, outside investors were able to gain control of an increasing number of privatised enterprises by buying shares from existing employees, buying residual tranches of shares sold by the state at privatisation auctions, acquiring the assets of the enterprise to redeem debts, through the bankruptcy procedure or through various forms of force and fraud. Those enterprises which were able to keep their independence tended to be those which enjoyed some special protection or which offered little prospect of quick profits for a new owner. Of the thirteen insider-controlled enterprises which we studied, seven

---

[1] Simon Clarke and Veronika Kabalina, 'Privatisation and the struggle for control of the enterprise in Russia', in David Lane (ed.) *Russia in Transition*, London: Longman, 1995.

worked in two of the most depressed industrial sectors in the Russian economy in the 1990s, construction and construction materials and textiles and clothing (ST2, ST3, SM4, SM5, ShF1, TF1, FNP1); one was a bakery (KhBK1), an industry which is unattractive to investors because it is still subject to local government regulation and price controls; two retained their independence because they serviced only one or two clients, who accounted for over 80 per cent of their turnover and acted as their patrons (KhZ3, ET2); one is a large engineering enterprise which is formally still majority state-owned, although in practice completely controlled by its management (MZ8), one is a closed company in which no shareholder can own more than 1 per cent of the shares (MZ4), and one was a small rubber factory rescued from dereliction by outsiders who bought in to it and took the top management positions (KhZ4).

The precise shareholdings of the owners of insider-controlled enterprises are a closely guarded secret, but it would appear that in at least three of the thirteen that we studied the general director alone held a controlling interest, in one share ownership was spread through the labour force and in the remainder the controlling interest was held by the senior management as a whole, sometimes with the support of retired manager shareholders. When these enterprises were first privatised to their own employees the Board of Directors usually tended to be composed of representatives of the main production departments, with perhaps the trade union president to represent the collective as a whole, but now the Boards of Directors are dominated by those senior managers who own the majority of shares.

Even if directors of privatised enterprises manage to acquire a controlling interest, they have nothing like the authority of the owner-director of a new private enterprise. Everybody knows that they did not acquire ownership of the enterprise by investing their own money, so ownership contributes little to managerial authority in relation to the other managers and the labour force as a whole. Such directors have to legitimate their position by the quality of their management and ability to meet the needs and aspirations of the management team and, beyond them, the labour force as a whole.

This is a very important factor in explaining the management ideology of independent privatised enterprises and their tendency to reproduce the traditional work ethic and corporate culture of the soviet enterprise. The declared aim of the top management is very rarely 'to make profits for our shareholders', but is nearly always to achieve economic success in order to secure the prosperity of the enterprise and its labour force, the 'labour collective'.

KhZ3 is a scientific research and design institute which was privatised in 1992 under the patronage of two giant enterprises, which together provide 90 per cent of its business and own almost half its shares, with the labour collective retaining the controlling interest. The general director explained how the enterprise had embraced the market economy, while remaining true to its traditions: *'Our main aim is to preserve the institute, that is, to preserve the scientific research and design work in the structure of the institute. Then* *our constitutional aim is to obtain the maximum profits, the interests of the labour collective, the shareholders'.*

KhZ3 is one of the few insider-controlled enterprises which pays dividends, albeit small, to its shareholders. Most insider-controlled enterprises prefer to retain profits within the enterprise.

'At the moment we have got many shareholders outside the factory. So the management is more interested in paying money for the 13th wage [the New Year bonus] *than in dividends. Because this is a collective, which works for results here, rather than for those people who have left us for a pension or have quit'* (chief economist, chairman of the Board of Directors, *SM4*). This was not an example of the so-called 'Yugoslav disease', in which worker-owned enterprises distribute all their profits in the form of wage bonuses, because SM4, like the other insider-controlled enterprises in our sample, pays around average wages and devotes most of its profits to investment.

The directors of insider-controlled enterprises are just as oriented to earning profits as are those of other enterprises: when asked to choose between profits, the pay and well-being of the labour collective, and the development of production capacity as the main aim of the enterprise, all the general directors of insider-controlled enterprises who responded to the question chose profits as their most important objective. However, several respondents insisted that economic and financial success is their priority because it is the only secure means to achieve the prosperity of the labour collective and local society. Thus, only one director agreed that an enterprise should reduce the number employed to improve its profits and prospects. The most important long-term aims of these enterprises were unequivocally to increase profits and production and to raise the quality of their products. But only two enterprises, both facing strong competition in the wider markets into which they were trying to expand, had the long-term aim of reducing costs.

  The directors of many of the enterprises in our sample which are still insider-controlled had been the directors of their enterprises in soviet times and had steered them through the crisis of the 1990s into the relative prosperity of the new century. In other cases, the original director had died, retired or been replaced, usually internally by another senior manager. The directors of these enterprises are on average much older than those of other enterprises that we studied, with much longer experience of working in their present post and at their present enterprise. All the directors had a technical educational and professional background, but at least three had taken management courses since 1990. Most of the rest of the senior management team was also made up of long-serving employees of the enterprise, particularly because their share ownership since the early 1990s had consolidated their attachment to the enterprise. Two-thirds of the senior managers in these enterprises owned shares and almost half of them had been working at the same enterprise since before perestroika began in 1985. One in five had even been appointed to their present post in soviet times. Even where younger people had been appointed to senior positions more recently, particularly in new specialisms such as marketing and finance requiring an economic rather than a technical background, the newcomers found it difficult to get into the inner circle since they were not co-owners of the enterprise and were rarely invited to join the Board of Directors. The senior management team at these enterprises tended, therefore, to be a cohesive group of like-minded people who were deeply rooted in the enterprise and the industry and had worked together for many years.

All of these enterprises retained from soviet times the traditional hierarchical and deeply authoritarian management systems which were embedded in the habits, values and personalities of the senior managers. However, the fact that the senior managers were so experienced and had worked together for so long meant that relations within the senior management team were often more collegial, although the general director would always have the final word. The paternalism towards the labour collective, which was the other side of soviet authoritarianism, also meant that the director and senior managers would be willing to consider suggestions and representations from any employees.

Corresponding to the retention of the traditional management structure and practices, the managers rooted in production usually carried the greatest weight in the senior management team, with the production director normally standing in for the general director in their absence. The production division was the dominant division in the majority of enterprises, but marketing was given at least equal weight with production in almost half these enterprises. Marketing is particularly likely to prevail where the product and production technology are unsophisticated, so that marketing is seen as the key to success, as exemplified by the case of a bakery.

> **KhBK1** is a bakery in which the director seems to have the controlling interest. Production management has been completely sidelined, and is now responsible only for baking bread and pastries. The post of production director involves little more than general record-keeping and is combined with that of chief of the main shop, who is paid significantly less than the finance and marketing directors. The chief of the second shop reports directly to the general director. The chief engineer is a newcomer, who has the status of deputy director, but in reality directs only the work of the auxiliary production services. The production managers are completely excluded from the strategic decision-making system – not one of them is a member of the Board of Directors, and they are not even included in the senior management team.

Although remaining very attached to traditional ways of doing things, the senior managers in these enterprises do not stand out as being markedly different in their managerial values from those in the other enterprises that we studied. Many of them have embraced the market economy with enthusiasm, because it has provided them with the opportunity to prove themselves as highly skilled specialists who are able to produce what the customer wants.

All of these enterprises had gone through very difficult times in the 1990s, with substantial reductions in production and employment, heavy debts and long delays in the payment of wages, in many cases working at 10 per cent of capacity or less in the depth of the crisis. In most cases there had been substantial employment reductions, but usually by natural wastage as people left for better opportunities elsewhere rather than through compulsory redundancies. Most of the enterprises had already managed to stabilise their situation before the recovery following the 1998 default, but in every case it was the improved macroeconomic situation that was decisive in enabling them to move forward.

The improved macroeconomic situation may have been necessary for the recovery of traditional enterprises, but it was by no means sufficient. Many traditional enterprises were not able to take advantage of the situation and continued to run up substantial losses even during the recovery, with around 40 per cent of all enterprises still being loss-making during the 2000s. Most of the successful insider-controlled enterprises that we have studied are characterised by a cohesive senior management team of experienced specialists led by a dynamic director, who have worked together for a long time. But they have also generally had other advantages as well. They may have inherited a relatively modern stock of equipment and well-located premises in good condition; they may have a monopoly in their local market or in highly specialised production (for example, *FNP1* had been the largest producer in the Soviet Union, with 70 per cent of the market; after the collapse of the Soviet Union *MZ4* was the only enterprise in Russia with its particular technology); they may be supplying enterprises in a booming sector, such as oil and gas or metallurgy; their director may have good political connections which give access to lucrative orders. Thus it has been the ability of the senior management team to take advantage of favourable circumstances to gain an increasing share of a growing market that has in most cases been decisive.

The turn to the market

Sales was the biggest headache which faced industrial enterprises following the collapse of the soviet system because they had been accustomed simply to making deliveries according to the plan, but now had to find their own customers. Distribution companies for various products had emerged out of the former soviet supply organisations and semi-legal intermediaries, but these were more akin to extortion rackets than competitive wholesale organisations, so most enterprises sought to set up their own trading networks. For those supplying intermediate products for other industries, the basis of their trading networks was their links with their traditional customers, reinforced and supplemented by the personal connections of the enterprise director and senior managers, but macroeconomic decline and competition from imports meant that traditional markets did not provide a sufficient basis for survival during the 1990s, nor for recovery in the new century.

Many managers explain the secret of their success in terms of their orientation to the market, and a strong market-oriented ideology is a feature of many of these enterprises. But their orientation to the market is severely constrained by the limited resources available to insider-controlled enterprises.[1] Insider-controlled enterprises are extremely cautious about looking for external sources of finance for their activity. This refusal is based on the experience of the 1990s, when many enterprises fell heavily into debt, were crippled by interest payments and in many cases bankrupted by their creditors and/or acquired by new owners using the lever of debt.

> *'I have been here since 1982, but I've never taken a single rouble of credit. You take from outsiders – you sell yourself. Mad rates of interest. I have never taken, and pray God, that I never will take it. Working capital is enough, sometimes we bite off a lot, but we manage'* (general director, **SM4**).

This means that insider-controlled enterprises lack the funds to carry out major investments to develop their product range, reduce their costs or improve the quality of the products. All thirteen of our insider-controlled enterprises reported that they relied primarily on their own retained earnings to finance their activities, only five of them made any use of bank credit, none had any state support and only two used any investment funds. Eight of them reported that they had external debts, but only one was for a loan, the remainder were arrears in the payment of federal and local taxes and payments to social insurance funds.

The lack of funds means that insider-controlled enterprises are largely constrained by the technology and equipment that they already have in place and rely heavily on the skills of the existing workforce. The first priority in making investments is in the maintenance and repair of the existing equipment.

> **SM4** makes reinforced concrete fabrications for the construction industry and has developed its product range with the existing equipment, using the skills of its own technologists and designers: *'Talk must begin not with the modernisation of production, but with what we have managed to preserve in conditions of perestroika. The machines are in excellent condition. We do not obtain new machines (only trivia), basically we maintain them. Our production capacity is in good condition'* (chief technologist). *'There are no aims to replace the equipment with new, if they are repaired in good time then they will work for twenty to thirty years. Our production is not the electronics industry'* (general director).

The second priority is usually to strengthen the independence of the enterprise by increasing the vertical integration of the production chain, introducing preparatory or finishing facilities, or power- and steam-generating facilities. This is particularly the case where the enterprise was originally part of a larger concern or association, which had provided these facilities in soviet times:

---

[1] According to the annual survey of business activity published by Goskomstat, about two-thirds of industrial organisations report a shortage of money as a factor limiting their business activity, as against around 40 per cent citing shortage of demand as a limitation.

TF1 is a clothing factory which in soviet times had been the head enterprise of a regional production association. In the crisis years of the 1990s it had closed a number of subsidiary sewing enterprises, but with recovery found it was having to contract out a third of its sewing work, which made it vulnerable to the sewing factories which had their own plans. In addition to buying three sewing factories to expand its own capacity, the enterprise has begun to build its own boiler house to achieve independence in the supply of steam for heating and processing.

ST2 is a specialised construction unit which had been part of a large trust. After privatisation the enterprise began to organise its own supply of gas, water and electricity and developed its own facilities to produce construction materials: plaster moulding, forging, reinforcing, joinery and painting, the sale of whose products is developing into a profitable sideline.

Where capacity is expanded this is often achieved by buying second-hand equipment from bankrupt enterprises elsewhere.

One of the few insider-controlled firms to have borrowed to finance investment is **KhZ4**, which was a small rubber goods factory which had expanded the production of rubber boots in an attempt to get into the consumer market in the early 1990s.[1] In deep crisis in the mid-1990s, a new senior management team decided to reorient the factory to the production of parts for the neighbouring auto factory, with which the head of security, later appointed as head of sales and supply, had good connections. The new management bought equipment to expand their product range from loss-making and ruined factories across Russia at very low prices or in exchange for automobiles which they had acquired as barter payment from the neighbouring auto factory. They also built new premises, their own stores building, new toilets, a canteen, a trade outlet and a garage and built up their own transport fleet. The enterprise has also bought a shop for the production of rubber mixes, which it is transferring from another factory.

However, the usual shortage of funds means that insider-controlled enterprises do not have the resources to undertake expensive marketing exercises, or even to hire skilled and experienced specialists in sales and marketing. Many were cautious about revealing how much they spent on sales and marketing, but of those who did report their spending, the majority estimated 1 per cent of the production cost or less, **TF1** estimated spending on sales and marketing as 5 per cent and **KhZ4** as 4 per cent of their production costs. Half the insider-controlled enterprises we studied had no marketing department or marketing director. In others the department retains its traditional name as the department

---

[1] This case is the exception that proves the rule, since the details of ownership were very secret. The new senior management team consisted of outsiders who seem to have bought their way into the enterprise, but dividend payments are trivial and the management structures are still very traditional.

of sales and supply, even if it carries out marketing functions. In KhZ4 the marketing specialist is called the 'engineer for supply, third category', although she is responsible for all the marketing functions. Even where there is somebody responsible for marketing, that person rarely has relevant qualifications or experience. Of the eight enterprises which have someone responsible for marketing, in five cases that person has worked at the enterprise for more than twenty years, and two of them are already pensioners. Of the newcomers, one had previously been a production manager and only one had previously worked in sales and marketing. All but one originally had technical, rather than marketing or economic, qualifications. Since 1990 one had taken a further degree in marketing and two had followed special courses in sales and marketing of up to three months. So most of those responsible for sales and marketing have a background in technology and production and only a handful have undergone even a short course in marketing.

The assignment of the sales and marketing role to a technical specialist is not necessarily inappropriate. It can be very helpful for somebody with a thorough understanding of the technical capacity of the enterprise to make contact with customers in order to identify marketable possibilities for the development of production.

At *MZ4* the chief technologist of the factory was transferred to head the new marketing service in 1992. The company is the only one in Russia which has the technical capacity to produce a particular range of industrial instruments, and the former chief technologist knows the regional, Russian and international markets well, so he is able to position his products on the market, assess the products of his competitors and feed back technical information to help to develop the product range.

ShF1, which produces clothing, sells some of its production through two local shops. The deputy general director for production, number two in the enterprise, left her job to become manager of one of the shops. Her new job does not so much involve selling as observing the customers and discussing the clothes with them. She is in the factory practically every day, discussing ways of improving the products with the designers and seamstresses, something which could not be done by an ordinary salesperson or marketing specialist, because they are not involved in garment production. The former deputy for production can even go into the production shops and find the workers to carry out a particular operation and introduce changes in their work. However, the effectiveness of her work was not matched by that of the sales department of the company, which still has an extremely traditional approach to sales.

In many insider-controlled enterprises, as we have seen, the director has been in post for twenty years or more and has a very extensive network of contacts (four of the thirteen considered that their business connections contributed to their market success). In companies producing intermediate products for sale to other enterprises, the director probably knows the market very well, because it was often the director's responsibility to maintain such relationships within the soviet system. In these cases it is quite common for the general director to take responsibility for getting orders for the enterprise and to see no point in spending money on marketing.

SM4 makes concrete fabrications for the construction industry. Not only does it not have a marketing department, it does not even have a sales department, just a supply department and a finished products store. The production department is responsible for sales and most sales contracts are lined up and negotiated by the general director through his extensive contacts in the construction industry. *'I have worked here as the chief for a long time, since 1982, I know the customers who can build. I go with my assistants and conclude an agreement. For now it works. I have this information'*. This conservative approach means that the enterprise focuses on maintaining long-term relationships with well-established partners, but the general director laments that *'while in the past there were plans, construction programmes; we knew which objects were in place. But now there are no orders'*. Despite the old methods of selling the products, the ideology of work with customers has changed. *'You must not overlook the customer, there is a market struggle'* (general director). The enterprise has therefore made efforts to ensure that they can attract and hold their customers by offering custom production, high quality, reliable delivery times and a good price.

This conservative approach limits the enterprise to its traditional markets. This can create problems if the enterprise has been diversifying its production and needs to move into new markets.

ST2 is a specialist construction firm that has no marketing department. The management position is that marketing is only necessary for large enterprises. They tried advertising in regional and national construction journals in the early 1990s, but this had no effect and they have not tried since. The search for orders is undertaken personally by the general director, who is convinced that it is the reputation of the firm for reliability in the completion of contracts that secures its orders. Moreover, he is only willing to sign contracts with people whom he knows or who have been recommended by his personal acquaintances and are trusted for their personal honesty and responsibility. However, the enterprise has expanded its production of construction materials well beyond its own production needs and urgently needs to expand its sales of these materials. The head of the production base noted their inadequate knowledge and experience of work in marketing and the need to develop this activity. Until recently a female economist worked at the enterprise with responsibility for the promotion of products (she organised participation in exhibitions, the preparation and distribution of advertising booklets, etc.), then she left and the post of economist-marketing specialist has been vacant ever since. However, at the top level of the enterprise the need for marketing activity is still not understood and the priority is to reduce management expenses, so it is most likely that the head of the production base will be given the job of selling his products. Meanwhile, the shortage of work has meant that the company has had to take on construction jobs for the regional and federal administration, which are always problematic because the government does not pay on time.

Other enterprises in the same industry have taken more active steps to develop their sales in the attempt to break out of their traditional markets.

SM5 has established a sales department and appointed three sales managers in the attempt to break out of their regional market. They have plans to establish a dealer network, but at the moment sales are organised by the sales managers through direct contacts.

Even where a marketing department has been introduced, in almost every case its main activity is routine processing of sales and there is little strategic intervention to develop the market for the products. In so far as marketing has been conducted, it has been a spasmodic, trial and error activity. Many enterprises set up their own sales networks to by-pass the existing intermediaries through the 1990s. Those serving the consumer market opened shops on their own premises and built up a network of shops and kiosks, those selling intermediate products tried to establish dealer networks and sought representatives in other regions, although such efforts rarely made more than a marginal impact on sales figures. In some cases the enterprise set up a separate subsidiary trading company to handle sales, which had tax advantages and provided some insurance for the parent company against succumbing to trading debts, itself an indication that such activities tended to be loss-making (although, of course, in some cases such a division was also a means of skimming off profits). Some made half-hearted attempts to advertise the products, but most were sceptical of the cost-effectiveness of advertising and confined themselves to advertising on billboards around the factory and more recently on the internet. Most of these initiatives seeking to expand the product market were ineffective and for most enterprises the bulk of sales continue to be through traditional channels.

Insider-controlled enterprises generally retain the traditional soviet management structure and practices articulating the traditional dominance of production. As far as the production management is concerned, the job of the sales and marketing department is to sell everything they produce at a price that will cover their costs and bring the enterprise some return to finance new investment. However, although there is often resentment at the inability of sales and marketing staff to sell enough to restore the enterprise to full capacity working, there has been a growing appreciation, at least at the level of senior management, that production has to adapt to the demands of the market. For most enterprises this means finding an appropriate balance between price and quality. In most spheres the Russian market is fragmented, with high-quality but high-priced imported goods at the top end of the market and low-quality low-priced goods flooding the bottom end, either imports from low-wage producers such as China and Turkey, or the products of small private and derelict state enterprises which cut costs by running up debts, paying low or no wages and avoiding taxes. Only five of the thirteen insider-controlled enterprises considered that they were price-competitive, but all thirteen believed that the quality of their products gave them a comparative advantage. Six thought that they had benefited from their flexibility or from diversifying their product range, and five that they had found a technological niche. Thus all of these competitive advantages relate to the organisation of the production process and its adaptation to the demands of the market. In most of these cases production management has the upper hand in negotiations with the sales and marketing departments about what will be produced. In a few cases, however, marketing had gained a more dominant position.

In addition to KhBK1 above (p. 71), a notable exception is *FNP1*, which is a fairly large enterprise with an advanced technological base, producing non-woven fabrics as intermediate products. It did not follow the fashion of the 1990s of moving in to consumer markets to generate cash flow, 'live money', but embraced the barter economy, which its sales specialists hailed at the time as '*a new and promising word in the world economy*', and followed the path of vertical integration, taking control of the production of its own raw materials, and diversifying its product range in response to the requirements of its traditional customers, in particular expanding sales to the relatively prosperous auto industry. In 1999 it sharply reversed its barter strategy and moved to direct monetary sales to its traditional partners. The general director, previously head of international economic relations, also adopted a policy of systematically raising the prestige and significance of sales and marketing in the enterprise, appointing a dynamic young marketing director, so that now sales plans determine both the volume of work and the range of production. The sales and marketing department has a real influence on increasing the flexibility of production and re-customising the equipment to fulfil the orders it has secured. Indeed, the appearance of representatives of the commercial service in the production shops was met with real anxiety, even among workers, because it signified that a new order had come and they were going to have to get down to the readjustment of the equipment to meet its demands. Nevertheless, even here sales prevail over marketing and traditional customers still take about 80 per cent of their production.

Overall, then, the internal management structure and practices of insider-controlled traditional enterprises have changed little since soviet times. Planning continues to be carried out in physical terms, using the traditional norms for calculating labour, materials and energy input. Half the enterprises had a budget to regulate spending and just over half had some kind of computer network, but in most cases where they existed, budgeting and information systems were pretty rudimentary. Control of spending in these enterprises was nearly always highly centralised, with production shops and service departments having no funds of their own. However, centralised control of finances was not a means to secure the effective control of costs since the budgets were merely a monetary expression of the plans drawn up in physical units, with monitoring of the use of labour and resources being in physical rather than in financial terms. The following are typical examples of the limited penetration of cost accounting and limited concern with the control of costs in these enterprises.

ST2 is a high-quality construction organisation. A budget for each project is drawn up on the basis of the established state norms for the use of labour, equipment and materials. There is no special system of control of expenditure in the enterprise and no discussion of the problem of reducing production costs. The spending of money and approval for the use of material resources is strictly centralised, with everything having to be signed off by the executive director.

MZ8 is a giant engineering enterprise with a very experienced team of senior managers, augmented by new staff in the key positions of economic management who have been brought in from banking structures. Nevertheless, the management systems are very traditional, based on hyper-control and almost military discipline, with an authoritarian style of management and paternalism in relation to the labour collective. The 'militarised' character of the system of production management has not changed at all and is based on a strict vertical hierarchy and strong centralisation of financial flows. The plan, established by the top management team for the year and for each month, is sent down to the subdivisions in terms of products and norm-hours; cost indicators are not used. The reduction of production costs is not articulated by management as a priority task and there is no special comprehensive programme for accounting and optimising expenditure at the enterprise: *'in the past, before perestroika, we didn't consider money'* (chief tool-making engineer). The general view that cost is not a consideration persists from soviet times among managers at all levels, who insist that it is not possible significantly to reduce production expenditures on such complex items: *'this is the military-industrial complex, and whether we like it or not, we have to maintain everything, even if it is off-stream. So in our production they hardly ever talk about expenditure . . . strict observance of the technological regime, strict demands on materials, and the strictest quality demands and so on. It is not possible to economise on this'* (acting production director). Nevertheless, they are now more actively oriented to saving water, heat and electricity, which are monitored by a special commission, and checks are often conducted incognito. They have begun to approach the material-technical supply of production more assiduously: *'Whereas in the past we got everything necessary for production without question, now the equipment and materials department tries to use up its reserves. If there is not the required kind of metal in the stores, they try to replace it with another type from those which they do have'* (shop chief). The planning-economic department and the security service of the enterprise are constantly involved in checking contracts so as to control the prices of raw materials, parts and equipment that are purchased.

The bakery **KhBK1** has a complete centralisation of management and no special system of control of expenditure. At the primary level everything looks pretty traditional: the chiefs of shops and functional subdivisions only refer to the norms: *'we have norms for the consumption of this or that raw material on different types of product: flour here, raisins, sugar and so on'* (shop chief). Nevertheless, there is apparently no system to control the observance of the norms or the quality of the product. For example, in reply to a compliment concerning the taste of the fruit-cakes produced by the shop at the end of her interview, the shop chief said: *'I say to the girls that they put an awful lot of raisins into them, probably they should put in less, I will tell them to put in fewer raisins'*. In the opinion of the chief economist the only possibility for reducing expenditure is through increasing production efficiency by increasing capacity. At the time of the research they were preparing the introduction of a budgeting system. The director got the idea of budgeting and introducing a corporate computer system on training courses. It is likely that for him this is more a matter of fashion than a deliberate economic calculation.

One of the few independent enterprises to use cost accounting is **MZ4**, but this is a legacy of the particular history of the enterprise in soviet times, rather than a reflection of its embracing the market economy. MZ4 was one of the pioneers of self-financing from 1982, even before the launch of perestroika, for which it served as a model, before being leased in 1991 and privatised to its labour collective in 1992. The enterprise has a long-established system of budgeting which identifies the financial returns to the various activities and sets strict limits to the spending of all subdivisions.

Traditional enterprises under outsider control

Enterprises which have come under outsider control constitute a heterogeneous group, corresponding to the diverse paths through which control fell to outsiders and the diverse interests of these outsiders. In the course of Russia's privatisation programme, most enterprises were privatised in the first instance to their labour collectives, but some shares were allocated in exchange for the privatisation vouchers which were distributed to the whole population, and other blocks of shares were kept in state hands and sold off later at auction. In principle, the bidders in most such share auctions had to guarantee to invest a certain amount in the development of the enterprise, but in practice such guarantees were not always honoured or enforced. In the first instance, outside shareholdings tended to be consolidated in the hands of the new commercial banks and investment funds which acquired a portfolio of enterprises in order to generate profits and shareholder value for the investment company, but in the conditions of the 1990s, when few enterprises made a profit and those with a controlling interest had no interest in paying out dividends to minority shareholders, outside shareholdings were worth very little if they did not give control. Once in control, profits could be extracted from an enterprise by a variety of routes, the most widely used being through trading companies through which all the purchases and sales of the enterprise could be channelled or through various kinds of sale and leaseback arrangements. These are the practices that Michael Burawoy characterised as 'merchant capitalism' and were the means by which the foundations were laid for many of the fortunes of the Russian oligarchs.

The theft of resources from former soviet enterprises was rampant in the 1990s, and insiders were by no means immune from the temptation to engage in such practices, but not all outside owners were interested only in extracting as much profit from their dubiously acquired assets in as short a time as possible. The recovery following the 1998 financial crisis opened up new possibilities for longer-term industrial investment, particularly in the extractive sectors and related industries. This launched a rapid wave of formation and consolidation of integrated industrial groups, which brought enterprises together at the regional and national levels into horizontal and/or vertical structures under the control of holding companies.

We will look at the forms of management characteristic of enterprises under the control of such holding companies in the next section, but in this section we will look briefly at some enterprises which are under the control of outsiders but which have not been absorbed into integrated holding companies. There are only six such enterprises in our sample,[1] probably because the vast majority of successful enterprises under outside control have already been absorbed into integrated holding companies, many of the remainder having already been squeezed dry by their outside owners. We cannot draw many conclusions from such a small number of disparate enterprises, but they do have some interesting features, so we will briefly outline the salient characteristics of each of them.

MZ5, created in 1961, was a producer of cranes, which had employed 1,300 people. It survived through the 1990s by using the equipment to make tools and parts and to do odd jobs. By 1998 there were only 250 people left and they had not been paid for eight months. In 1998 the then director persuaded the employee shareholders to sell 80 per cent of the shares to a Moscow investment company, whose identity is still a closely guarded secret, which immediately secured some orders for the enterprise. The director remained in post for a further three years, when he was replaced by an appointee of the owners, who died in 2002. On his death, the 25-year-old commercial director was appointed as the new general director. He quickly constructed a team of

---

[1] In two of the six, the controlling interest is owned by the state (LVZ1, KhDK1). The senior managers of two of the enterprises that we have classified as insider-controlled had bought their way in from outside (KhZ4, ET2).

similarly young senior managers with degrees in economics and previous experience in business, replacing the existing managers as they retired or moving them sideways. The production director had come to the factory as a security guard in 1998 and enjoyed accelerated promotion, as had the chief engineer, who had come as a foreman in 2000. The former general director was kept on in a newly created post as 'director for new technology'; the previous chief engineer has been retained as a designer, while the personnel manager is the only remnant of the old guard, having been in post since 1969. These new young managers were by no means the puppets of the owners (and they do not own any shares), but were using the opportunity to make their own careers (the general director also has his own unrelated business) and were critical of the lack of interest shown by the owners in the enterprise. The owners maintain strict financial control through the Board of Directors, which the general director attends by invitation, but had only made an insignificant initial investment and have left the management to run the enterprise as they chose. According to the new management, the owners neither helped nor hindered, but the enterprise had managed to recover by its own efforts, using its own funds and external credit, and was approaching full-capacity working with 450 employees. The company has not yet paid a dividend, residual profits being assigned to pay off debts.

The new management does not have the resources to invest in replacing the worn-out equipment, but is making considerable efforts to cut costs by rationalising the organisation of the production process, economising on energy (including installing their own gas-fired generator), buying in rather than producing some parts, and intensifying labour. They have also paid considerable attention to quality, especially in monitoring the quality of their supplies, and to meeting promised delivery dates.

SM1 is a decrepit small cement works with a captive local market. The enterprise went into prolonged decline through the 1990s, producing at less than 10 per cent capacity by the end of the decade, yet surprisingly it was the subject of a struggle for control, involving murders and kidnappings, before it was acquired by a mysterious group of investors through the bankruptcy procedure in 2002, the suggestion being that this was a criminal organisation seeking to legitimise its money. The new owners brought in a new team of senior managers whose background was in finance and marketing and who had little knowledge of the cement industry, made some initial investments in production, and separated the sales and supply functions out into a different company. Nevertheless, the new businessmen and the old production managers seem to work together reasonably harmoniously, because there has been a significant revival of production and the new owners claim to have secured financing from a local bank for substantial investments in the modernisation and diversification of production, in exchange for which the bank has been given a seat on the board. The changes at the top have brought a strict subordination of production to sales and finance, but production is still based on traditional methods using the labour force which remained in the depressed enterprise, which was basically made up of those too old or demoralised to have found another job. Line managers have been given the responsibility of ensuring the delivery of the required quantity and quality of production using their traditional methods, exploiting the loyalty of the old core workers who continue to work for low wages in appalling conditions. There is considerable tension within the senior management team, which it seems is related to questions of ownership, and between senior and middle management, because the former make unrealistic demands on the latter in the form of production plans which cannot be realised because of the ancient equipment and ageing labour force, but the new management cannot dismiss their line managers because they are irreplaceable.

KF1 is a confectionery factory that was established in 1892 and had a regional monopoly in soviet times, but experienced a severe decline in the 1990s in the face of intense competition from national confectionery brands, many under foreign ownership, which became a feature of the industry. By the end of the decade the factory, with no marketing strategy or sales channels, was producing at only 10 per cent capacity, making heavy losses and delaying the payment of wages, but it still employed 700 people and made 450 different products. The factory had been privatised in 1992 and a shareholding built up by a local voucher investment fund which took control of KF1 after being acquired by a larger financial-industrial group in 2002. It appointed a new general director, who sacked and replaced almost the entire management team in 2003, with personnel selection purportedly on the basis of management qualifications but also on ideological grounds and, most decisively, on the basis of personal connections, to provide a team of like-minded, market-oriented managers who could work well together. The new management team had no experience of the confectionary industry or knowledge of production, for which they relied on the production director who had been at the factory for thirty-seven years. The production director also played the key role in mediating between the new market-oriented management and the completely traditional soviet production structures and personnel: '*There is the head of production, for whom we pray to God that he has given us such a person. Well, we arrived, we did not understand anything, we could not help her with anything. Now we can already help her in some things. There are people who turned out well, who have managed to reconstruct themselves. Well, there are some who have not managed, but very few of them remain*' (personnel director).

The declared strategy of the new owner was not to make large investments, but to turn the company into a niche producer for the middle-class market, while using traditional skills to produce specialist products to order, and transferring production from the existing city centre site to new premises in the suburbs. The declared aim of the new owner for its companies is '*to increase their capitalisation*', but some suspicion about their intentions is aroused by the fact that their main line of business is in real estate and the existing premises on a very valuable site. Nevertheless, the initial results of the new regime were to stabilise the situation by cutting out loss-making production lines; introducing a marketing strategy, developing its own distribution network and working more closely with the retail shops; and making a concerted effort to improve quality. At the time of our study the new managers were beginning to replace the middle management and address the management of the production personnel which predominantly comprises women who have worked at the factory for a long time: *'It is a women's collective, compliant, submissive – psychology!!!'* (personnel director). *'Well, women, like, to start with, they grumble a little, grumble a little and all the same they do everything, they listen to everything and do all their tasks'* (foreman).

ET1 is an industrial giant in the electrical equipment industry which today employs about 5,000 people. A controlling interest in the company was acquired in 1995 by a local businessman, who is still chairman of the Board of Directors and all the purchases and sales of the company were channelled through trading companies controlled by the same interests. The company went through difficult times in the 1990s and was hit hard by the rise in metal prices following the 1998 crisis, but has grown rapidly since 1999 on the back of sales to oil and gas companies, the electricity supply industry and exports, with regular customers taking 70–80 per cent of their output. The majority (four out of seven) of members of the Board of Directors, which makes all strategic and financial decisions, are senior managers of the enterprise. The senior management team itself is made up of veterans of the factory, together with some new appointments in 'economic' positions. The general director has a technical background, but the day-to-day management of the factory is in practice more the responsibility of the commercial director.

In a typically Russian scheme, all the profits have been made by the associated trading companies, while ET1 has consistently reported small losses which have prevented it from declaring any dividends. As a local journalist observed, *'ET1 has good money, but they do not want to share it with minority shareholders'*. ET1 has extended its influence by buying up, and sometimes squeezing dry, producers of some of its raw materials, so that it has developed into a powerful, vertically integrated industrial group. However, the owners' interests have not been simply to extract quick profits from the company, they have also made substantial investments to make the company a world leader in its field. An investment programme launched in 1997 was frozen after the 1998 crisis, but resumed in 1999, with plans to spend at least $60 million by 2010. Despite their predominantly production background, the senior management team has a strong market-oriented ideology based on a commitment to quality, economy and meeting the needs of customers. However, this ideology has not penetrated lower levels of management, let alone the shop floor, and the ideology and practices of production management are still very traditional.

KhDK1 produces ice-cream and other frozen foods, but is still majority owned by the federal government because it was once part of a network of cold stores which constituted the strategic reserve and which turned to the production of frozen foods to make full use of their compressor capacity. In 1998 these companies were partially privatised almost overnight, with 49 per cent of the shares being transferred to the labour collective and the remainder being administered by the State Property Ministry. In this case all but ten of the shares assigned to the labour collective were rapidly bought up by local businessmen. The State Property Ministry has been very active in asserting its ownership rights, insisting (with the passive support of the minority shareholders) on paying out substantial dividends rather than allowing the management to invest, which drove the company to the verge of bankruptcy.

Not all the failures of the enterprise are due to its rapacious owner. Nearly all the senior management team are close to or beyond pension age and have worked there for thirty years or more. They recognise the importance of a market orientation and have invested their meagre profits not only in repairs but also in improving packaging and expanding the product range (as well as cutting costs by degrading the product). However, the whole enterprise is very traditional in its structure and practices and there is considerable tension between the production departments and the trade and commerce department. The producers criticise the trade department for failing to promote the products and only working with those customers who come to the factory on their own initiative: *'There are no sales, because of this production is reduced . . . The trade department is an old structure, they have only created their network of kiosks, shops and cafes. And that is all. But, you understand, that is a completely different approach. I am not in a position to judge but, of course, something must change there. Now they only work with their own network and whoever comes, we serve them . . . I do not know the details, it is their structure, but basically, of course, as a result of this we suffer'* (head of the ice-cream shop). As a result there is growing tension between the senior management, preoccupied with financial results, and the line managers and workers, who do not see any improvement in their conditions.

LVZ1 is a vodka factory which is owned by the regional administration. The factory employs 200 people and the tax on its products is an important source of revenue for the regional budget. For this reason, the regional administration had protected the factory from competition by assigning it a legally enforced quota of 50 per cent of vodka sales in the local market. Following a change in the regional leadership in 2002, this protection was withdrawn, exposing the company to stiff competition. A new general director was appointed from a factory owned by one of the big players in the Russian vodka market and he managed to maintain production at about 80 per cent capacity, partly by licensing one of the leading brands of his previous employer, but the factory still ran at a loss (there were rumours that he had been put in place by his previous employer in order to bankrupt the factory and transfer it to the previous employer's ownership). In 2004 he was replaced by yet another general director, this time with instructions to improve the economic situation of the company, who appointed a completely new management team. Although only working at 30 per cent capacity, the new management team claims to have brought some improvement in finances by privatising its network of sales outlets into a separate company (a profitable company, which happens to be owned by the general director of the factory); opening a wholesale warehouse to trade in the products of other companies; closing production of loss-making lines (low-alcohol cocktails, launched two years ago after the purchase of extremely expensive equipment, sufficient to supply 2 per cent of the entire Russian market, on the initiative of the regional ministry) and putting non-core production (confectionery) on a self-financing basis; improving quality and developing a new 'premium' brand; and cutting costs, partly through managerial redundancies ('*I do not touch production*'). The organisation and management of production remain completely traditional, except that the post of shop chief has been eliminated and foremen made directly responsible to the production director.

The position of this enterprise is almost certainly unviable in the longer term, unless the regional administration were (illegally) to reintroduce protection of the market, because the vodka market is completely dominated by big Russian and international companies, on the one hand, and bootleg producers, on the other.

It is often difficult to identify the interests and intentions of outside owners, because all business activity is conducted in the shadows, and there is a massive amount of suspicion of outside owners, fuelled by black propaganda spread by opponents and competitors. One key test of the owners' intentions is the extent to which they are willing to invest in the development of the enterprise, as opposed merely to making the most profitable use of the resources at their disposal. However, most outside owners which are not holding structures do not have the resources to invest, so outsider-owned independent enterprises tend to be intermediate between insider-controlled and holding company-owned enterprises. We will not consider outsider-owned enterprises as a distinct category any further, but in all of the subsequent discussion MZ5, KhDK1 and LVZ1 will be included with insider-controlled independent enterprises, because in these cases the outside owners do not intervene directly in the management of the enterprise, unlike SM1, KF1 and ET1 which we will include with integrated holding companies.

Corporate management in holding companies

The largest group of enterprises in our sample comprises those which are part of integrated holding structures. This is to be expected of a sample of successful enterprises, because we have seen from the cases already discussed that enterprises which remained independent have great difficulty in securing the funds to make the investments needed to maintain and modernise their capital stock, to raise quality and to introduce new products or to undertake effective marketing activities. Integration into a holding company, on the other hand, could provide an enterprise with access to the funds, technology, specialised skills and marketing and supply networks which are essential to success in an increasingly competitive environment. Although most insider-controlled enterprises jealously guard their independence, in some cases the management could see that integration into a holding company was the only way forward.

TF2 is a large textile and clothing enterprise, leased in 1991 and privatised to the labour collective in 1992, which has succeeded in preserving most of the features of its soviet past. The enterprise found itself in deep crisis in the 1990s, with production coming to a virtual standstill in 1999. At that point, the chief power engineer was elected general director and came to an arrangement with a horizontally integrated holding company that had emerged out of the former ministerial structures, which provided raw materials and took the cloth produced on commission. In 2001 the labour collective sold out to the holding company. The holding company is only interested in the enterprise as a source of cloth. It provides the enterprise with raw materials against contracted deliveries of cloth on terms set by the holding company, but has not provided any other support and otherwise does not interfere in the management of the enterprise, nor has a dividend ever been paid. The different phases of cloth production have been integrated into a single production process concentrated in one building and the remaining buildings sold off or rented out to pay off debts. In addition to its contracted deliveries to the holding company, the enterprise continues to make and sell clothing for its own account.

However, most of the enterprises which are integrated into holding companies were obviously attractive investment prospects which had already lost their independence in the mid-1990s, subject to the depredations of banks and trading companies, before being incorporated into holding structures as component parts of integrated production systems.

MetZ4 is a large non-ferrous metallurgical enterprise which was privatised to the labour collective in 1992 but by 1994 had fallen under the control of one of Russia's new commercial banks, which set up a scheme to siphon off tens of millions of dollars through an offshore trading company which handled all the company's sales. The enterprise, together with the trading scam, was sold on to a notorious foreign owner in 1997 because the bank's owner needed the money to finance his acquisition of a major oil company in a 'loans for shares' deal. However, in 1998 the company broke free of its foreign owner and was amalgamated with its principal customer, another metallurgical enterprise, to form a vertically integrated industrial group with cross-ownership, but controlled by the latter. The new industrial group has since raised substantial investment funding to turn it into one of the world's leading producers with a substantial export market.

In this case the enterprise had eventually become part of an integrated industrial production structure. However, by no means all holding companies have made this transition from 'merchant' to 'industrial' capitalism:

MZ6 designs and produces industrial gas installations. It fell into deep crisis in the 1990s, when employment fell from 700 to 200, with the research and design staff falling from 200 to 20 people. During this time, to handle its sales, it came to rely on a trading company, which was a subsidiary of a regional investment company, which thus got a stranglehold over the enterprise. The investment company, which had originated as a voucher investment fund in 1992, managed by these means to get control of this and a dozen other industrial enterprises in the region, which it formed into an industrial group supplying a common set of industrial customers in the power engineering, railway and oil and gas industries. A new 32-year-old general director was appointed by the holding company from its own staff, although the former general director was kept on as deputy and was given a position as Chairman of the Board of Directors, to provide a symbol of continuity with the old order. The holding company now handles all sales and logistics and has imposed a strict system of budgeting on the producing enterprises in order to extract more funds from them, a relationship which a senior manager compared to that between the ministry and the enterprise in soviet times: *'from there* [the ministry] *came something – the plan, a rough draft of the plan. Although the plan was drawn up at the factory . . . well, yes, on paper it was drawn up, it was tidied up there by agreement. They, of course, took 98 per cent of the plan products themselves and traded them themselves. And now* [the holding company] *trades. That is, the factory works, they trade. So in principle it works out just the same'.* Although the equipment of the enterprise is antiquated, the holding company has not made any new investment in production, but has concentrated on reducing employment and getting rid of non-core assets. It has transferred the production facilities to another of its industrial sites in order to integrate the production of the two enterprises and free up the very large territory of this enterprise, but this precludes any chance of the enterprise recovering its former glory because there is now no space to expand. All technical developments have been undertaken by the enterprise using its own skills and resources.

The relation between the holding company and its subsidiaries varies quite a lot from case to case. Some holding companies, particularly large companies in the fuel and energy and metallurgical industries, which are active in export markets, are building integrated industrial groups and investing heavily in their subsidiaries to expand production, reduce costs and meet international quality standards. At the other extreme are holding companies which have only a short-term perspective, do not invest in their subsidiaries and seek to extract as much profit from them in as short a time as possible. Since we have been specifically studying successful enterprises, and it is difficult to identify cases of pure extortion unequivocally until they have sucked the victim dry, we do not have any clear cases of the latter in our sample, but it should not be forgotten that across Russia as a whole the latter may be as typical as the companies we consider here.

We can roughly distinguish holding companies according to whether they are vertically integrated, acquiring enterprises which form part of a production chain, or horizontally integrated, seeking to establish a monopoly position in regional or federal markets. The distinction is significant because the interests of the parent are likely to be somewhat different in the two cases. Our sample includes twenty-three enterprises which are part of integrated holding companies, including the three outsider-controlled enterprises discussed in the previous section; of these eighteen are part of vertically integrated structures and five of horizontally integrated structures. Many of the vertically integrated structures are themselves part of wider horizontal groupings under the umbrella of a larger holding company or corporate group, which may comprise a number of relatively independent vertically and horizontally integrated holding companies.

Vertically integrated holding companies have developed particularly in the oil and gas and metallurgical sectors, where financial-industrial groups centred on oil, gas and metallurgical enterprises have acquired supplier and processing enterprises to establish integrated production chains, but they are also expanding in other sectors as the holding company seeks to strengthen the position of its existing subsidiaries in an economically and politically uncertain environment by securing control of its supplies and markets. In many cases the holding companies are reconstructing soviet-era production complexes and industrial structures which had been dismembered in the course of privatisation, often with the involvement of the personnel who controlled those structures in the last years of the Soviet Union. The concern of the vertically integrated holding company is to secure the reliable delivery of high-quality inputs and outputs at an economical price. This often requires substantial investment to modernise production facilities and ensure that products of the appropriate specifications can be produced, particularly in the case of production for export.

Horizontally integrated holding companies have developed particularly in sectors dominated by a relatively small number of large producers of a standardised product (in our cases, detergent, coal, cement, road-building, industrial pipes). The holding company's main concern is to establish dominance in regional or national markets and to cut costs by rationalising the operations of its subsidiaries. These objectives are achieved by concentrating production in the lowest-cost producers and by centralising management functions in the holding company, so that the subsidiaries are reduced to production platforms. Some horizontally integrated holding companies are export-oriented producers, and their priority objective is to secure control of supplies and ensure that quality meets world market standards.

There has always been a very close relationship between the emerging corporate structures and regional and federal government in Russia, to the extent that some commentators have seen a tendency to the integration of the two. Under Yeltsin the tendency was for the oligarchs effectively to privatise state powers, but under Putin this tendency has been reversed, and the power of the oligarchs harnessed to the enhancement of the power of the state. Some of the largest and most powerful holding companies, such as Gazprom, UES and Rosneft, in gas, electricity supply and oil respectively, are still majority state-owned and in some respects serve as instruments of state policy, but in their management structures and practices they are not significantly different from the fully private structures. Our case studies include enterprises controlled by such state-owned structures. Like their private counterparts, they are unequivocally capitalist structures oriented to maximising the profits that they can derive from their assets. Indeed, in some respects they may be considered to be at the leading edge of the development of capitalist corporate practice in Russia.

Finally, we might expect enterprises which have been acquired by foreign owners to impose a more radical restructuring. Foreign investors have various motives for buying Russian enterprises to export or to produce for the domestic market, rather than making greenfield investments,[1] but probably the most important are to buy the connections of an existing enterprise, to buy familiar Russian brand names to access the consumer market and to acquire a skilled labour force and, in some cases, advanced Russian technology. But whatever their motives, the foreign owners face the same challenge as do domestic holding companies, of reducing costs, increasing quality and establishing an effective sales and marketing network. Four of our case-study enterprises were wholly owned by foreign companies and two had a significant foreign shareholder (others had nominal foreign ownership, but these were just offshore investment vehicles for their Russian owners). We will consider the specific features of management restructuring in these foreign-owned companies later in the chapter.

In the rest of this section we will outline the common features of the restructuring of corporate management of enterprises which have been bought by holding companies, as they have emerged from our case studies, indicating differences corresponding to the character and objectives of the holding company, where these are significant. Although our findings are based on a relatively small number of case studies, rather than a representative sample of enterprises, the remarkable consistency across very different regions and industries gives us some confidence that these findings have more general significance.[2]

---

[1] There have been very few greenfield investments in Russia, perhaps reflecting the cautious approach of foreign investors. They have been largely confined to the oil and gas and mining industries (pipelines and new extraction facilities) and beverages (Coca-Cola, Pepsi-Cola and brewers expanding from initial brownfield investments). A new wave of greenfield investments is getting under way particularly around Saint Petersburg, where a Caterpillar plant opened in 2000, Ford opened a small plant assembling the Focus in 2002, and a Toyota plant was under construction in 2006. In the south, Nestlé opened an instant coffee plant in Krasnodar in 2005.

[2] The findings do not depart significantly from those reported on the basis of an earlier analysis of the first twelve case studies of enterprises which are integrated into holding structures (Simon Clarke, 'A very soviet form of capitalism? The management of holding companies in Russia', *Post-Communist Economies* 16(4), 2004: 405–22).

The first issue is the means by which the holding company maintains control of the subsidiary. In all of our case-study enterprises strategic decision-making is concentrated in the holding company and control of the subsidiary is achieved primarily through an annual business plan and associated budget. The subsidiary either has its own Board of Directors, which includes representatives of the holding company and senior managers of the subsidiary, or it is immediately subordinate to the Board of Directors of the holding company. In a minority of cases the general director is a member of the Board of Directors of the holding company, but in no case is the general director a significant shareholder. There is a clear demarcation of the functions of ownership and control.

The degree of freedom of the subsidiary varies, but in most cases the holding company does not interfere directly in the everyday management of the company, which is the responsibility of the general director, beyond regularly monitoring its performance, sometimes in considerable detail. Senior managers are well rewarded, but the penalties for failure can be sudden: the position of senior manager of the subsidiary of a Russian holding company is not a secure one. Many of our case-study enterprises have seen two or three changes of general director in less than ten years, and in many cases a new general director completely changes the senior management team to bring in 'his' people. The holding companies are often equally keen to ensure that directors of their enterprises will be loyal and appoint general directors from their own structures, although such outsiders can have difficulty working with local management. In some cases the holding company has its own representative in a supernumerary management position to work alongside the general director, with the authority to take or approve decisions on behalf of the holding company.

NKhZ2 is a relatively small petrochemicals company which is owned by a holding company based in another region. One of the owners of the holding company occupies the post of deputy general director for general questions. The position is a nominal one, there are no subdivisions subordinate to it and it does not even appear in the table of the management structure of the company. *'He stews with us in this cauldron, we are just very lucky, his office is right here. So there is not any distance here between the administration and the owner. In this sense we have a unique situation. If an acute problem arises, for example a shortage of money, with outgoings, everything is resolved very efficiently here and now. The owner is very accessible for us'* (head of the planning-economic service).

At *MZ1* the vice-president of the holding company comes to the enterprise every day (see below). At *ST1* the deputy director for production is one of the owners of the holding company, who was replaced as general director of ST1 after a conflict with the general director of the holding company, but is now well placed to watch over his successor. At *MZ2* there is a supernumerary post of 'executive director', which is filled by a representative of the minority foreign owner.

The degree to which holding companies intervene in the management of their subsidiaries varies quite considerably. We frequently heard from workers or middle managers that *'the director does not decide anything, everything is decided in the head office'*. The directors also recognise the limits of their authority:

> 'Activity is pretty strictly regulated both by the regulation about the general director and the charter, in which there is a section regarding the general director. I do not have the right to make decisions about every question, there are certain limitations on me' (general director, **MZ2**).

Nevertheless, enterprises owned by diversified investment companies usually retain a lot of their independence, as long as they meet the owner's financial targets, and this situation may continue even in integrated holding companies.

KhZ2 is a large chemical factory which was detached from a wider production complex for the purposes of its privatisation in 1992. The company worked at less than half capacity and made losses in the first half of the 1990s, but following the 1998 crisis more favourable market conditions enabled it to return to almost full capacity working. In 2001 the enterprise was incorporated into an integrated chemical company controlled by its largest shareholder, which is also its principal raw material supplier, so the factory is the final link in the production chain, selling 90 per cent of its product for export. The declared aim of the owners in forming the new company was to increase the efficiency of its enterprises so they could pay off their debts, and to get better control of the market. Senior managers of KhZ2 still have a majority on the Board of Directors, although there has been a tendency to replace them with representatives of the principal shareholder. The Board of Directors meets quarterly and decides strategic technical, financial and production questions, but business plans are drawn up by the management of the enterprise and submitted to the Board for approval, so the management has a great deal of discretion. The enterprise is itself responsible for financing its investment, already amounting to tens of millions of dollars, using its own retained profits and bank loans (it also received a low interest loan of $1 million from the regional administration). The senior managers have grown up in the factory, although the majority have had further training. In 2004 the general director resigned to take up a position in the regional administration and he was replaced by the commercial director.

The planning process in the enterprise is pretty traditional. The plan is drawn up by the planning-economic department, which gathers information from the commercial department (predicted volume of sales), production department (requirements for maintenance and repair and new equipment, according to the factory's technical re-equipment plan) and the finance department (the finance required for the planned actions). A budget for the year is drawn up on the basis of these plans, which is then reviewed and confirmed by the Board of Directors. On the basis of the approved budget a sales plan and investment plan for each subdivision are drawn up and thereafter income and expenditure are strictly monitored against the budget figures. Because it is continuous process production it is imperative to keep the equipment in good condition, so spending on repairs alone amounts to 4.7 per cent of total spending. *'The Board of Directors takes strategic decisions, but as far as preparation for the Board of Directors is concerned . . . [These are] our plans for re-equipment, modernisation, capital investment – these are things that they confirm and then come back to us as guides for action'* (chief engineer).

MZ1 was a major soviet producer of electrical equipment, with a significant research and design capacity and a highly skilled labour force, which was privatised in 1993. The factory had been established in 1943 and reconstruction planned in 1975 had been constantly postponed, so the premises of the factory were semi-derelict and the equipment was antiquated and worn out. The enterprise survived through the 1990s by taking on small orders but by 1998 was working at less than 10 per cent capacity and was burdened with debt. The enterprise had resisted attempts of its main competitor to buy it, but in 1998 a controlling interest was acquired by a group which was constructing a vertically integrated holding company in the electrical equipment industry. The general director took a position as deputy president of the holding company and the young head of sales and marketing was appointed general director in his place. All strategic and financial decisions, including the level of wages, are decided by the Board of Directors, but the general director is only given a general programme of activity and retains responsibility for all management functions. The enterprise itself remains absolutely traditional in its management structure and practices, with rigidly centralised finances and decision-making. There is no long-term planning, and even the monthly plan is subject to frequent revision in the light of sales. Even though the parent company has its own trading firm, most of the factory's sales, about 40 per cent of which are to long-term partners, go through the traditional channel of the factory's supply department. On the other hand, the holding company keeps close day-to-day control over the factory management because its vice-president, who had been the director of the factory for many years, comes to the factory virtually every day to participate in the morning and evening operational meetings and sometimes intervenes over the head of the director, as when he reinstated a shop chief who had been dismissed by the general director.

The incorporation of an enterprise into the structure of an integrated holding company usually leads to the centralisation of the functions of finance, sales and marketing and, in vertically integrated holding companies, supply in the holding company, with the corresponding services in the subsidiary largely reduced to their traditional roles of documentation, record-keeping and reporting. In some cases, personnel management functions are also subordinated to the personnel management department of the holding company. In most cases the subsidiary retains some capacity for independent decision-making in these areas, although all expenditure decisions require the approval of the holding company.

NKhZ1 was created in 2000 as an integrated production complex by reassembling parts of a large petrochemicals complex which had been dismembered through privatisation in 1992. The parts had not proved sustainable as independent companies, some of which were bankrupted in the late 1990s, and their assets were reassembled by a large vertically integrated holding company. NKhZ1 and KhZ2 above are both ultimately controlled by the same company, but through different holding structures with very different management practices. In this case the holding company's policy is that it should handle sales and supply and maintain strict financial control, while its subsidiaries should focus exclusively on production.

NKhZ1 is directly subordinate to the Board of Directors of the holding company, on which it is not represented. The senior managers are young, most with degrees in both technology and in economics, and were appointed by the holding company from other enterprises in the group. Their main strategic objective is to increase the value of the company. The Board does not interfere in current operations, but the general director can refer problems to the Board if necessary. *'I can request a meeting of the Board of Directors on any question, there is a discussion in Moscow and if the Board of Directors takes a decision, they call, they phone'* (general director). The holding company supplies the complex with raw materials, in return for which it is required to deliver a certain amount of products, with the prices set unilaterally by the holding company. *'We work on processing, so we have little relation with marketing. We have a plan and our task is to fulfil it fully and on time'* (commercial director). Investment plans are drawn up by the management and submitted to the Board for approval. Investment is financed directly by the subsidiary from its own profits and bank credit, supported by guarantees and additional financing from the holding company. The investment programme for 2000–5 was for $150 million to modernise and expand production facilities.

The annual business plan is drawn up by the economists in accordance with the programme of the holding company and submitted to the latter for approval. The production plan, which is a central part of the business plan, specifies how much of each product is to be delivered on what date and is, like its soviet equivalent, inviolable. The local managers can only influence the plan in the event that it is impossible to achieve in a particular month because, for example, repairs have been scheduled. The enterprise makes its own supplementary plan to use any spare capacity to make products for its own account, for which it has to find its own supplies and sales outlets. The overall plan is then disaggregated for the production shops and broken down into monthly and daily plans and it is fulfilled and monitored in exactly the same way as it was in soviet times. The only difference is that today there is a tighter daily control of expenditure against the norms given in the business plan, and a greater emphasis on quality.

This concentration of financial and commercial functions in the holding company reduces the subsidiary to a production platform, returning it to its traditional soviet function as a production-oriented labour collective. The planning process and the control systems put in place by the holding company are also strongly reminiscent of their soviet equivalents, with the relation between the holding company and the subsidiary being similar to the traditional relation between the enterprise and the ministry ('*by and large any holding structure today is a return to the usual ministerial interrelations. Just as in its time the ministry was the management company, so the holding company is now. The principal questions about the development of the enterprise are taken there*' (general director, *MZ1*)), although the quantitative physical indicators of the soviet planning system are supplemented by financial indicators which are equally rigorously enforced. Such indicators have the potential to force enterprise management to address cost issues, but as yet senior management tends to do so merely by restricting resources to line managers rather than by intervening in the organisation of production processes.

SM2 is a large cement factory which was modernised in the last years of the Soviet Union. It was privatised to the labour collective in 1992 but went into sharp decline, with growing arrears of unpaid wages. An investment company took control as unpaid workers sold off their shares, but the investment company had no expertise in the cement industry and by 1998 the enterprise was on the verge of bankruptcy. The former chief mechanic, who had worked there since 1960, was appointed general director and managed to stabilise the situation by scouring neighbouring regions for orders, but a whole new management team of young economists was brought in by the owners in 2001 to turn the enterprise round financially, leading to considerable friction between the new management team and the existing production-oriented staff. In 2003 the investment company sold the factory to a large cement holding company, which immediately closed the finance and commercial departments, which had been at the heart of the new management team, transferring sales and marketing functions to their own subsidiary trading company, and appointed one of its own staff, previously director of another of their cement factories, as 'executive director' of the factory. The production people were delighted to see the back of the 'independent experts' and the return of the factory to its traditional role as a production platform.

Under the previous owners, although business plans had to be approved by the owners and managers had to go to Moscow to defend the plan, they had a great deal of independence in all aspects of running the enterprise and were able to invest retained earnings, the owners only being interested in the capitalisation of the company. Under the new owners the factory is not simply given the task of producing as much cement as it can at the minimum possible cost, but is given detailed expenditure targets involving specific reductions in the cost of materials, energy and staffing which are assigned without any consultation, but which it is required to meet. Before, relations with the owners were mediated through the general director, but now the performance of each department is directly supervised from Moscow. None of these changes has had much impact at the level of the production shops, which have continued throughout to follow the instructions handed down to them in the traditional ways and regard this situation as perfectly natural.

The senior managers of many enterprises which have been acquired by holding companies have welcomed the reduction of their enterprise to its traditional function as a production platform, getting rid of the headaches associated with sales and marketing and finance. However, in other cases the holding company has had to tread more carefully in subordinating a formerly independent enterprise to its own interests.

MetZ3 is a giant metallurgical enterprise with a glorious soviet history, which was stripped of resources by new commercial intermediaries in the 1990s and eventually acquired out of bankruptcy by a major holding company in 1999. The new owners appointed a man who had worked his entire life at the factory as its general director and the senior management team consisted of similar factory veterans, all of whom knew the factory well and would be able to improve the production indicators while maintaining the stability of the enterprise. However, the owners required more radical changes and over the next two years reorganised the senior management, bringing in trusted and proven people from their own structures (some of whom had worked at this enterprise in the past) who would be willing to make more painful changes, reducing the number employed, selling off surplus assets, reducing investment spending and so on, which reflected a downgrading of the enterprise as the owners judged that the export of refined raw materials was more profitable than their further processing in Russia. This change, which was associated with a shift from a soft paternalistic to a strict autocratic management style, opened up significant conflict within the management apparatus of the enterprise, the opposition reflecting continuing pride in the traditions of the enterprise and the strong position of skilled workers and experienced managers in the local labour market such as the owners had not encountered in other enterprises under their control. Some senior managers endorsed the new autocratic style: '*Authoritarianism is a firmness of judgement, imposition of strict deadlines – managers must be like that*', '*Yes, strict, but that is how our mentality is in Russia. Well if you do not force them, they will not do things, and there is not enough of this. You have to encourage, to force*'. Other managers were critical of the new management style, but accepted the priorities imposed on the enterprise – '*To me the main thing is work, I must carry out the production process in any circumstances*' – while a significant section of management opposed the new general director, either overtly or, more often, informally with colleagues, '*in the corridors*'. Many recognised that the new general director was in the impossible position of trying to achieve targets imposed by the owners which could not be achieved with the resources put at his disposal. Eventually the Russian owners were very happy to sell out to a major foreign corporation.

Even though the subsidiary is wholly owned by the holding company, many of our respondents clearly thought of their enterprise as an independent subject, delivering its targets to the holding company in exchange for financial resources provided by the holding company, and distinguished between the resources of the holding company and the enterprise's 'own' resources, just as they would have done in soviet times. In some cases the enterprise was permitted to sell 'above plan' output on its own initiative and to use the revenues, with the approval of the holding company, for its own purposes.

ST1 is a road-building company which is part of a road construction holding company. Ninety per cent of its work involves work on state orders secured by the holding company, but it also works on the side using its facilities for its own benefit, not only in construction but also in things like car repair and even marketing consultancy.

KhBK2 is a bakery which started to make pasta in the 1970s. The bakery was privatised in 1992 and introduced its own brand of pasta, but did not develop the brand. The enterprise went through a deep crisis at the end of the 1990s, going through ten changes of general director. In 2000 it was bought by a grain and food-processing combine which had developed a leading brand of pasta. According to the present general director, who had previously headed bakeries in other regions and was appointed in 2001, the first two general directors appointed by the combine *'changed virtually nothing and this was a problem, the collective ate them up, absorbed them into itself'*. The present general director has been much more active, both in fulfilling the task set by the combine *'of stabilising the work of the enterprise, to put the organisation in order, to put the control of quality in order'* and in strengthening the bakery's own position.

The problem facing KhBK2 is that the combine is only interested in the factory as a supplier of pasta for its own brand, and even in this respect the enterprise takes second place to the combine's core pasta factory in another region. As the general director wryly noted, *'They have not invested anything . . . they did not play the leading role in obtaining the automatic packing machine, they will work for another five years, until the equipment is worn out'*. The factory produces pasta for the combine to order, against supplies of flour, but orders fluctuate and supplies are unreliable. *'Our task is only to fulfil the orders for production and delivery to the customers, who are also designated by the combine'* (commercial director). The factory is also permitted to produce pasta under its own, down-market, brand and the combine takes no interest in this, or in its relatively successful bakery business, which supplies local supermarkets and its own chain of five bread shops. The enterprise is free to develop these activities, as long as it meets the production plan of the combine and does not require an injection of resources.

However, there is in general very little leeway for such activity because the holding company keeps tight control of the allocation of resources and the expenditure of the subsidiary. This was the case with *NKhZ1*, which was permitted to use any spare capacity to produce for its own account, which could be between 5 and 15 per cent of various products. As we have seen in this case, the subsidiary prepares a business plan for the following year, with an associated and very detailed budget, which has to be defended in the holding company and, after appropriate amendment, is submitted to the Board of Directors for approval. The business plan will comprise the production plans and associated spending for labour, raw materials, maintenance and repair and auxiliary services for the following year, and will be accompanied by proposals for investment in new equipment, buildings and production facilities.

The planning process typically takes several months and involves all of the departments and services of the subsidiary. Planning is always driven by target sales figures for the following year. In vertically integrated holding companies these sales figures will usually be handed down by the holding company, since they correspond to the deliveries required by other enterprises in the production chain. In horizontally integrated holding companies there will be more interaction between the holding company and the subsidiary, since the holding company has its overall sales projections which it has to distribute across all of its production facilities, taking into account production costs.[1] Otherwise, the sales projections will be prepared by the marketing department, usually as a target increase in sales on the current year, following the soviet tradition of 'planning from the achieved level'. Where the holding company handles sales, projected product prices and, in vertically integrated companies, the key input prices will also be dictated by the holding company. In other companies product prices are determined through negotiation between the marketing and production departments, in the light of prevailing market prices and unit costs, with the general director having the final word if agreement cannot be reached.

The target sales figures determine the production plan, which will be passed to the shops and production departments which assess the plans against their production capacity, making allowances for downtime for maintenance or replacement of equipment,[2] and work out the corresponding requirements for labour and material inputs, maintenance and repair.

Investment planning is conducted along traditional soviet lines. Investment plans are based on proposals for re-equipment from the shops and from the technical specialists, dominated by demands for the piecemeal replacement of decrepit equipment and reconstruction of semi-derelict buildings, and are

---

[1] The case-study enterprises which are part of horizontally integrated complexes are all relatively low-cost producers so they are under pressure to produce to maximum capacity (or above). High-cost producers would expect to have lower production targets, but to be under strong pressure to cut costs or to face closure.

[2] Pressure from the holding company to increase production in expanding markets leads to pressure to minimise downtime, reproducing the traditional soviet neglect of maintenance and repair (Joseph S. Berliner, *The Innovation Decision in Soviet Industry*, Cambridge, MA: Massachusetts Institute of Technology Press, 1976).

reviewed and consolidated by the technical council before being defended in the holding company. Investment projects have to be substantiated economically, and in general only those which promise a very short payback period are approved. Somewhat surprisingly, more than a third of these companies did not have any formal system for the appraisal of the effectiveness of investment projects (nor did almost two-thirds of independent enterprises and more than 80 per cent of new private companies). More comprehensive reconstruction and larger investment projects are usually proposed by the holding company in accordance with its production needs. Maintenance and repair and smaller investment projects will usually be financed by the subsidiary from its own funds. Funding for large-scale investment may be provided by the holding company or the subsidiary enterprise may be required to raise a loan on its own account.

The consolidated plan and its associated budget are put together by the planning-economic department. If unit costs indicate that production is not profitable, the expenditure plans might be referred back to the shops to find some economies. The plan and budget are defended in detail with the holding company before they are submitted to the Board of Directors. The approved plan and budget then become the control document for the enterprise for the following year, with any modification requiring the approval of the holding company. The plan and budget will be adjusted regularly in the course of the year, on the initiative or with the approval of the holding company, in accordance with orders and achieved sales.

The main source of financing of the budget of the enterprise is the enterprise's own funds. This was the only source of funding in one-third of the case-study enterprises, while one-third also used bank credit and 40 per cent used investment funds, presumably sometimes from the parent company. Indeed, *UP1* reported that it relied entirely on the funds of its parent company. No enterprise reported any use of trade credit and only one, *SM1*, reported that it had any debts.

Expenditure in relation to the budget is very closely monitored, both within the subsidiary and by the holding company. Any overspending leads to an investigation and, usually, the punishment of those responsible, with the demand that the overspend should be recovered by subsequent savings. Any exceptional expenditure, for example in relation to unexpected breakdowns, must be approved by the holding company. This means that some familiar features of the shortage economy are reproduced, the shortage now being of money rather than of labour and supplies, so that the defects are in a sense self-inflicted, as the enterprise management decides how to ration its scarce funds. For example, at *LPZ2* the limited availability of funds to buy replacement parts means that essential maintenance is regularly postponed, with consequent problems of unreliability and deterioration of product quality.

Management structure and functions in the subsidiary

In most cases the general director is appointed by the holding company, usually from its own trusted staff, although in some cases the existing general director remains in place or is appointed from the existing management because of his (*all* are men in our case-study enterprises) detailed knowledge of the specific features of production and the characteristics of the enterprise. The other senior managers are more likely to be left in place or promoted internally, although about half the marketing and finance directors in our sample had been brought in from outside. Internal appointees had usually been working at the enterprise for many years, although many of them had only been promoted to their present posts relatively recently. Thus, half the heads of production, finance, personnel and labour and wages, but only a quarter of the marketing directors and one in six of the general directors had worked in the present enterprise for more than ten years, and only a handful of the latter had been in post for more than five years. The majority of senior managers in the enterprises studied were under 45 years old, although production directors tend to be older and marketing directors younger. This contrasts strongly with the demographic structure of the management of independent enterprises, whose senior managers are significantly older and have been at the same enterprise and in their current posts for much longer.

A repeated theme in these enterprises is the demand for high levels of professionalism and loyalty of the senior managers, with the latter quality being decisive. It is striking that of 112 senior managers for whom we have biographical details, only two finance managers, two heads of labour and wage departments and three personnel managers were appointed on a competitive basis, and not one of the key positions of general director, production director or marketing director was filled competitively. This is a strong indication of the extent to which loyalty and reliability are necessary requirements for filling senior positions in these companies.

The majority of general directors and almost all production directors have technical higher education. Only one-fifth of the general directors and none of the production directors had a degree in an economic discipline, although two-thirds of the general directors had taken management courses since 1990, the majority lasting less than a year. About a quarter of the marketing, finance and personnel directors had studied for a second degree since 1990 and more than one in ten of the senior managers interviewed had been abroad for periods of study. The appointment of people from outside to senior positions sometimes breeds resentment on the part of the existing managers, because it blocks their career paths and violates the tradition of appointing senior managers and specialists from within: 'our people', who have a detailed knowledge of and commitment to the enterprise and its traditions. This resentment is not expressed in any antagonism, so long as the new managers are recognised to be highly professional people and are willing to accommodate to the traditions of the enterprise.

In most cases there has been some management restructuring, sometimes initiated by the holding company, but in other cases on the initiative of a new general director. A common change at the level of top management is a move away from strictly hierarchical authoritarian management to a higher degree of consultation with colleagues and an emphasis on the collegiality of the senior management team, with horizontal flows of information between department heads and even a greater devolution of responsibility and authority to functional managers. We estimated that about one-third of the affiliates of holding companies still had a traditional authoritarian management system, about one-third had adopted a collegial system with collective decision-making, and about one-third had a 'democratic' system with some delegation of authority. A collegial style of management is more likely to be found in those enterprises with a strong technological base, where economic success depends on technological achievements. The 'democratic' delegation of authority is most likely to be found in the most 'westernised' enterprises, either those with a foreign owner or those whose senior managers have experience of working or studying abroad. However, the general director always has the ultimate authority, reinforced by his role as representative of the holding company in the enterprise, and there is always a heavy emphasis on loyalty, so collegiality and democracy are certainly constrained, and may often be more rhetorical than real.

Incorporation of the enterprise into an integrated holding company and the consequent centralisation of many management functions in the head office mean that the subsidiary is in many cases reduced to a production platform, meeting the production and financial targets laid down by the head office, a role very familiar from soviet times and very welcome to many Russian managers. One indication of the reinforcement of traditional priorities is the fact that when the directors of these enterprises were asked to identify their long-term aims, increasing the volume of production was the one most frequently selected, by eleven of the twelve respondents to this question, with eight selecting profits, five the minimisation of expenditure, four finding a market niche, three incomes and employment and only three quality, which had been chosen by three-quarters of the directors of independent enterprises, who ranked profits and increasing the volume of production about equally. Production remains the dominant division in almost half the enterprises, with marketing the dominant division in just over half, and the planning-economic and finance departments being dominant in the remaining three. We asked the key functional managers where they stood in the pay hierarchy. About half the production, finance and marketing directors found it difficult to say, but of those who did answer, the production directors were fairly confident that they earned as much as or more than the finance and marketing directors, only three out of forty-six thinking that they earned less and eleven thinking they were paid more or much more (in many cases the production director is the first deputy of the general director and stands in for the latter in his absence). Finance and marketing directors gave more varied answers, but on average thought that the different functional directors were paid about the same.

Where the enterprise retains responsibility for sales and marketing, the sales and marketing department tends to be the dominant branch in the senior management team, in accordance with the driving role of sales, which dictate production plans to the shops and production departments. Where sales and marketing are controlled by the holding company, the dominance of sales is expressed in the dominance of the holding company and the sales department of the subsidiary has a relatively lower status. However, in both independent enterprises and those which are part of holding structures, the balance of power between the marketing and production departments will also be influenced by the technology. In capital-intensive continuous-process production there are considerable economies of scale, while production stoppages impose substantial costs. In these enterprises the production departments are more likely to prevail, and the marketing department to accept selling prices and sales targets which can maintain full capacity operation. In the event of a sales shortfall the pressure will be on the marketing department to find ways of selling the surplus production and on the production departments to reduce costs. In industries where output can be changed more flexibly and with less loss, the production departments are more likely to have to work within expenditure and output parameters dictated by the sales and marketing departments.

The crane producer *MZ5* is exceptional in that the diversified holding company which owns the enterprise does not interfere in its management, and, despite the new young management team, production still dominates finance and marketing. The planning department draws up a budget each month on the basis of a particular production target and the available resources. The production target is based on sales contracts, but they produce additional cranes for stock, which have to be financed and sold. *'If there are no orders, we have to find additional monetary resources in order to make products, and the commercial department will then have the task of selling them, and in principle they will be sold'* (finance director). Sales *'drag themselves up'*: *'In selling the product the strategy is this: if production produces ten cranes, they have to be sold'* (head of the sales department). There is some collusion with competitors in price-setting, but if it is necessary to cut the price in order to achieve sales then they look for ways to cut costs accordingly.

The finance director is a pivotal figure, often appointed by the holding company, because he (or she: traditionally this was a women's job and the finance directors in half these companies are still women) is responsible for overseeing expenditure. The chief bookkeeper is also a very important figure because she is responsible for monitoring the legality of all transactions and the tax obligations to which they give rise.

The new foreign owners of the wood-processing enterprise, *LPZ2*, tried to remove the chief bookkeeper from the senior management team because they did not understand the high status that is traditionally attached to that position in a Russian enterprise and regarded her in western terms as no more than a clerical assistant. It took the best part of a year for the expatriate managers to understand why the local management repeatedly pressed them to clear all significant decisions with the chief bookkeeper.

Two-thirds of the subsidiaries of holding companies had budgetary systems and used the budget as a principal instrument of centralised management control. Most enterprises have introduced or are introducing computerised management information systems to provide real-time information to track expenditure and plan fulfilment. However, the possibilities of exerting financial control are still restricted by the limitations of appropriate information, the limited development of information systems and the predominance of functional over divisional management systems. This means that budgetary control is limited and remains quite crude, although it is much more highly developed than it is in independent enterprises, where, as noted above, the planning process still tends to be carried out in traditional physical units and only a minority of enterprises are beginning to develop systems of financial planning and accounting.

As noted above, the budget is usually drawn up by the enterprise as part of the planning process, using the traditional methods of calculating spending on the basis of production norms, and is then defended in the holding company, which may impose expenditure cuts. Spending is then closely monitored and any requests for additional spending have to be authorised by the holding company. In enterprises owned by diversified holding companies, or working on a processing basis, the holding company may merely impose overall financial constraints and leave the detail of the budget to the enterprise itself. In many enterprises managerial bonuses are dependent on keeping within the budget, with loss of bonus the typical penalty for unauthorised overspending and an additional bonus awarded for economies.

In some cases, particularly in foreign-owned enterprises, departments and shops are defined as cost-centres which have their own budgets, but in other cases the budget is centralised and production shops are not involved in any kind of financial accounting, but receive their plan indicators and norms for the use of labour and materials in the traditional way, in physical units. This range of practices is illustrated in the following cases.

The tool-making enterprise *MetZ1*, which has been owned by a large multinational company since 1994, has a very sophisticated system of financial planning and control, with a centralised budget and a large number of cost-centres. A section chief described the system: *'In my section there are five cost-centres. For each cost-centre expenditure is monitored: from the cost of the soap we use for washing our hands to the smallest parts that we buy to repair the machines. All this is planned through the budget. I know how many workers I have. The budget is calculated for each cost-centre and is concretised. If there is overspending in this cost-centre it immediately draws attention to itself. It may be only on one occasion – when there is an unpredicted increase in the volume of production. But, as a rule, I set it down, if I need $100 or $115, the accounting department adds its 5 per cent and there cannot be any global overspending here. . . . Everything is strictly controlled like that'.*

A controlling interest in the electrical equipment maker, *MZ1*, was acquired by a regional holding company in 1998. There is an absolute centralisation of strategic decision-making and monetary expenditure. The financial, planning-economic and marketing departments are integrated into the structure of the holding company and simply transmit decisions taken there. The financial service is mainly limited to accounting functions. The planning-economic service, by contrast to past years, does not participate in the real planning of production. It only sends down the plan, which has to be computed and sent to the shops in volume and product range, and the use of material resources has to be monitored and accounted for. There is no system of tracking and controlling expenditure in the enterprise. However, years of experience of production and the careful accounting of the use of resources which has existed since soviet times mean that this is not seen as a problem: *'We always know exactly what will turn out'* (director). The reduction of staff over the past 5–7 years has probably 'cleaned' the staff to the minimum. The head of the planning-economic department considers that the technological costs of production cannot be changed. In rare cases, increased expenditure leads to an analysis of the reasons – usually it is a result of a change in the cost of raw materials or the problem is rooted in the technology of production itself. The line managers do not even have material stimulation funds and have no access to financial information. They understand expenses only as wastage, which must not exceed the planned level of 2 per cent.

At the bread and pasta factory, *KhBK2*, information about expenditure is collected by the planning-economic department in order to calculate the production cost, but there is no systematic monitoring of expenditure. In the longer term there are plans to establish systematic monitoring of costs, not least because this is one of the standards of ISO 9000. However, at the moment this is done, in the words of the deputy general director for commerce, *'spontaneously – a problem arises and it is resolved'*.

Most subsidiaries of holding companies are under constant pressure to reduce costs. Because labour costs constitute only a small proportion of production costs, the first priority is usually to reduce energy and material costs. A substantial number of enterprises have constructed their own power and steam-generating facilities (eleven out of fifty-one enterprises of all types have built themselves a new boiler-house), insisting that such investments are very profitable because of the low domestic price of gas (although in most cases there had not been a systematic assessment of the cost-effectiveness of the innovation).

The metallurgical enterprise *MetZ4* is one of the largest consumers of electricity in the region, its cost amounting to about one-third of the cost of production. The enterprise traditionally enjoyed reduced rates, but when this privilege was cancelled in April 2001 it was decided to purchase turbogenerators to reduce dependence on the energy suppliers. The enterprise also sank its own wells to protect itself against increased tariffs for water supply.

The general director of the crane-builder *MZ5* has clubbed together with neighbouring enterprises to buy a gas generator to produce their own electricity, claiming that this would reduce the cost of electricity almost four-fold. The petrochemicals company *NKhZ1*, has installed a 5MW generator which, it claims, will reduce the cost of electricity almost three-fold.

This is not just a Russian idiosyncrasy. The foreign-owned detergent factory *KhZ1*, built its own boiler house in 2002, which it claims has cut the costs of supplying steam for production by half.

These measures promise to reduce not only costs but also the dependence of the enterprise on potentially powerful outside suppliers (the local authority or a neighbouring large enterprise in the case of the boiler house and Chubais's UES in the case of electricity generation). The same consideration lay behind the tendency through the 1990s for many enterprises to start to make their own parts and components, reinforcing the tendency to enterprise autarky which had been such a feature of the soviet system.

However, against such general tendencies to increasing autarky in some spheres, there has been an increase in devolving facilities and outsourcing in others. Most enterprises welcomed the opportunity to transfer their housing stock and much of their social and welfare apparatus to the municipalities in the 1990s, and some enterprises have similarly spun off their catering, transport, sporting, cultural and leisure facilities into independent self-financing enterprises. This often enables the enterprise to continue to use these facilities at much lower cost because their employees are no longer paid according to the pay scales of the parent enterprise, but will be paid at much lower rates. Some enterprises are even spinning off servicing, maintenance and repair, although they have to tread carefully in doing this, to be sure that they will still be able to receive quality services at an acceptable cost.

The petrochemicals company *NKhZ3* is seeking to reduce expenditure by devolving its auxiliary activities. *'Last year we removed from the enterprise a brick factory, catering combine, field service shop and section for repair of fittings, altogether 530 people. Only we did not have to get involved in redundancies, this is a normal process of structuring a business. People stayed in their jobs and did the same work, but now as part of a new service company'* (finance director). They are now planning to withdraw other service subdivisions from the structure of the enterprise. *'We are planning to withdraw the repair-mechanical service. This will happen in stages. First centralisation: in place of the corresponding services in each shop, we will create a single repair-mechanical shop for the enterprise. We will adjust this schema, we will assess the efficiency and when we see that everything is really working we will withdraw it from service. We must be confident that the repair-mechanical shop is in a condition to handle repairs of dynamic and technological equipment, that at the same time there is no loss of quality or efficiency and that such a schema is economically beneficial, only after this will the question of removing the repairers from service be resolved'* (general director).

Other areas in which the more progressive enterprises are typically seeking to reduce their costs are in more careful procurement decision-making, both to ensure that parts and materials are obtained at reasonable prices and to monitor cases of fraudulent invoicing, and through investment in energy-saving measures. Thus, while independent enterprises still put a premium on self-sufficiency, a small number of the case-study enterprises which are part of holding structures have begun to undertake a systematic evaluation of the relative cost of buying in parts and making them themselves, and in some cases have closed down their own production facilities.

There was a period in which **Metz4** had to produce practically all its parts for itself. Since 1998 there has been a constant analysis of the cost of production of parts in comparison with other producers. On the basis of this a decision has been taken to stop its own production and transfer to the purchase of parts.

However, the most progressive companies are not oriented so much to reducing expenditure as to increasing revenues, particularly where they have spare capacity and see full capacity working as the best way of reducing unit costs.

The management of the petrochemicals company **NKhZ1** sees the main method of reducing expenditure and increasing profitability to lie in increasing production. *'The volume of production immediately dictates the economic situation of the enterprise, and correspondingly, the very idea of full-capacity working, because even with an average loading we cannot avoid losses'* (head of the production planning department). The company is also planning to invest to increase profits by using its by-products more efficiently.

'When you begin to manage expenditure, you have the same expenses, you do not receive anything new with this. What we can save on this is kopeks compared to what we can earn. We do not set ourselves the task of reducing expenditure on petrol. Nobody needs that. We need to direct our efforts at receiving income, when you begin to concentrate on costs. . . . This is not that simple and needs a lot of time. If we divert some of our time to management costs, of course we will have an effect, but this will be an amount that we have diverted from earning money' (general director, **TK1**).

Thus the transition to a market economy and the rise of the holding company have led to substantial changes in management structures, on both the vertical and horizontal dimensions. On the vertical dimension there have been changes in the character of the management hierarchy. On the horizontal dimension there have been changes in the functional relationship between the previously dominant production divisions, on the one hand, and sales and marketing, on the other. In some of our case-study enterprises there has been a rationalisation of the management structure, with the combination of departments and centralisation of services to reduce the size of the management apparatus, but this has been a result not so much of a deliberate transformation of the management structure but more of the adaptation of the staffing and management of the enterprise to a substantial reduction in its output and/or its product range.

More radical management restructuring, however, is rare. Most of the holding companies themselves have divisional structures, with their subsidiary enterprises assigned to the appropriate product divisions, but in general the subsidiaries of holding companies themselves retain the traditional functional structure of management, with some reduction of management staff as a result of the centralisation of functions in the head office of the holding company.

The parent company of *MZ6* has established a divisional structure, with its subsidiary enterprises assigned to divisions corresponding to their principal customer. The holding company appointed a young member of its own staff as general director of MZ6, but it does not interfere in the management of its subsidiaries beyond demanding the delivery of products in accordance with the demands of the sales department of the holding company, within the limits of strict financial control.

The most dramatic changes in the vertical dimension of the management hierarchy take place when an enterprise is fully integrated into the structure of a holding company. When key management functions are centralised in the holding company, the relevant divisions in the subsidiary are reduced to executors of decisions taken elsewhere. In essence, the top level of the management hierarchy has been lopped off. This may be accompanied by a reduction of management levels and cutting of jobs in the subsidiary.

TK2 was the regional branch of a major national telecommunications company. Initially it had been relatively autonomous in its activity, although the head company tightened its control through the Board of Directors at the end of the 1990s and moved towards the formation of an integrated holding company. To this end, in 2002 it established an inter-regional company, of which TK2 became a regional subdivision. The top management of TK2 was transferred to another region, to provide the core staff of the inter-regional company, and there was a marked centralisation of management in the new company, with a common development strategy and uniform programmes for marketing, planning, investment, budgeting, introduction of innovations, personnel development and payment systems, with the management staff of TK2 now having the responsibility of carrying out decisions made elsewhere. Formally, the management staff of TK2 moved up a level as they were promoted to replace those who had moved, but in reality their functions had not changed. The number of managerial staff was reduced, corresponding to this curtailment of their responsibilities.

The new director appointed at **KhBK2** by the holding company replaced the entire senior management team and reduced the number of managerial posts from fifteen to eight by combining their functions. At **SM2**, integration into a holding company led to the abolition of the posts of finance, sales and marketing directors and the virtual liquidation of their departments, with the transfer of their functions to another subsidiary of the holding company.

A striking feature of even the most radical reforms of the management system is that they do not extend very far into the management of production or into personnel management. Almost three-quarters of enterprises which are part of holding companies have computerised management information systems, and in some cases these systems provide real-time information about production activity, but in the majority of cases the management of the production shops has only limited or no access to these systems. Even when the enterprise has a sophisticated system of financial accounting and control, the plan for the production shops will often be defined in physical units, without any financial targets or parameters, and the management of production itself is still the responsibility of line managers, carried out in the traditional ways. We will come back to a more detailed examination of production and personnel management in the following chapters, but first we will look briefly at the distinctive features of the corporate management of foreign-owned and new private enterprises.

The role of foreign ownership in changing management structures

Companies which come under foreign ownership, or which bring in western management consultants, are more likely to seek to transform their management structure away from the traditional soviet hierarchical system of management based on functional principles towards more 'modern' management structures. The models adopted are not uniform, but are based on the system of corporate management adopted by the holding company, and their implementation is often put in the hands of western management consultancies. These cases are sufficiently distinctive and interesting to describe them individually before drawing some overall conclusions. In the first three cases foreign companies are full owners or have a controlling interest.

MetZ1 was bought in 1994 by a major foreign multinational company which undertook a substantial investment programme. Voluntary quits and successive waves of redundancy saw the number employed fall from 1500 in 1988 to 260 in 2003. In 1998 the owners introduced a radical simplification of the management system, removing foremen and brigadiers from the management structure and introducing a 'client-oriented' approach which permits the by-passing of bureaucratic hierarchical structures in order to resolve questions. According to the head of the marketing department: *'What is good in our company is that here the vertical chains are quite short . . . When I first came here we had five or six hierarchical levels, which were absolutely impossible to understand. Now we have three hierarchical levels: workers, middle managers, chiefs. So a member of staff can go to the general director or to a middle manager. The head of a brigade or, let us say, a sector is in principle not distinguished in the hierarchy, he is paid more, admittedly, and has more authority, but he is a member of staff, that is he is on the same level and this does not prevent him from giving instructions to his subordinates and this does not prevent his subordinates from by-passing him and going directly to a higher manager. . . . That is, in our company to interact it is not necessary to go through the whole hierarchy. For effective interaction you must interact directly. We communicate between departments in any direction'.* The one exception to this possibility is in production, where all questions have to be referred upwards through the shop chief, although the latter tries to resolve everything within the shop: *'Production questions, or questions concerning workers personally, are considered within our section and, if necessary, I can go to the director for production, head of the planning department or the trade union. As for me, so far God has spared me and I have not faced a situation in which I have had to resolve a question with the general director. We try to resolve things ourselves, within the limits of the section; what is more the system works so that there is no need to replicate these small questions at a higher level. The director for production, of course, is informed about everything and can pass information on to the general or not, at his discretion'.* The foreign managers complain that their attempts to reform the structure of management are often thwarted by Russian bureaucratic and legal requirements, for example the demands of the State Technical Inspectorate. As the expatriate production director commented: *'It infuriates me as a manager, as a person who manages people that, according to Russian law, I cannot ever have that scheme of management of people . . . that I would like. . . . If there is something here called hierarchy, it is only thanks to Russian bureaucracy and the desire of the Russian state that we should be subordinated to some kind of letter of the law. Nevertheless, the tasks in MetZ1 are to have more equal relationships'.*

The detergent factory **KhZ1** has seen the most radical changes in management structure of any of our case-study enterprises. The controlling interest in KhZ1 was bought by a Russian bank in 1996 and sold on to a leading multinational company in the industry in 2001. The new owners incorporated KhZ1 into their Russian subsidiary as a structural subdivision within a divisional management structure. Although the management structure of the enterprise itself is still largely based on functional principles, it has been substantially reorganised by the new foreign owners to conform to their management model, with production subdivisions being combined, duplicate auxiliary structures eliminated and some functions of the auxiliary subdivisions (repairs, installation) being contracted out, resulting in a substantial reduction in the management apparatus and an overall halving of the number of employees. The top-level managers of the division are based several hundred miles away, at the headquarters of the group, and, apart from the personnel director, are expatriates. Their deputies, who are the Russian managers responsible for the various functional areas of activity on site, are responsible both to the top expatriate managers at the headquarters and to the local general director of the enterprise, but the latter can appeal directly to the Chairman of the Board of Directors of the main company in the event of a disagreement. The advantages of the management system introduced at KhZ1, supported by a comprehensive computerised management information system, were felt to be that it provided for flexible adaptation to a changing environment by making it possible to identify the degree of profitability of the work of various subdivisions and to plan accordingly. The disadvantage was seen as lying in the complexity of the system so that *'it is difficult to understand who is subordinate to whom'*, which gave rise to communication barriers and misunderstandings.

The new owners have introduced a decentralisation of the operational management of production, combined with a strict system of financial control through the budget, which is broken down into eighty-three cost-centres, for which twenty-three managers are assigned responsibility. This meant that the local managers felt that they had been reduced to functionaries, merely implementing decisions taken elsewhere. *'Whereas before I could say that I participated in planning, I influenced bonuses, I worked out the bonus regulations, now we do not deal with any of that. So our function in practice is just accounting and control'* (head of the department of labour and wages). Although the managers responsible for the various cost-centres participate in drawing up the annual budget, once it is approved any overspending has to be justified and strong measures are taken against managers who cannot justify an overspend, with dismissal the punishment for managers who consistently fail to control spending.

LPZ2 is a giant wood-processing enterprise which was built at the beginning of the 1960s and privatised to the labour collective in 1993. By 1996–7 it was on the brink of collapse, but has revived rapidly since 1998 and is now working at full capacity, exporting about half its output. Between 1998 and 2001 the company invested heavily in modernising its production facilities, with the investment being financed by foreign investment funds and minority shareholders. In 2002 a controlling interest was sold to a large foreign multinational company, to pre-empt its acquisition by a Russian predator. There were some doubts about the new owner's intentions, with some fearing that they merely wanted to run down and close a competitor (following the example of a large German company, which had been accused of plundering and bankrupting a Russian plant in which foreign banks had invested about

$200 million, before the German company had bought in to it at a knock-down price), and the former general director resigned in protest at their policies. Although they have not undertaken significant investments in the enterprise, they have maintained full-capacity working and introduced a substantial management restructuring, as recommended by a foreign consultancy company, to bring the management system into conformity with the company's global model. This has involved a de-layering of management, with only two levels (top and middle) and a matrix system of management organised around two functional subdivisions, 'management' and 'production', with the auxiliary production shops being assigned to the former. A number of subsidiary enterprises have been spun off from the main company, including most of the logging enterprises acquired during the 1990s, much of the social sphere (despite the resistance of local management), and the non-core production of plywood and toilet paper. The main marketing activity has also been hived off into a separate enterprise.

The new owners appointed their own (expatriate) people to senior management positions to oversee the management restructuring (only the deputy general director for social questions remains of the old team), but this led to chaos as the new managers had no experience of managing such a large integrated production facility and simply did not understand how it worked, so they were not in a position to take the necessary everyday decisions about the organisation and management of production. The owners had a low opinion of the local management so, rather than replacing the expatriates by promoting people internally, as a temporary solution they hired new senior managers from outside, Russians who had international business experience, the only remaining expatriate being the executive director, responsible for production. The longer-term solution to this problem was to set up a management training programme and form a management team out of local staff who would serve as deputies to the existing senior managers, with a view to replacing them in the longer term. The attempt to move away from the traditional hierarchical management structure was also of limited success because the middle managers preferred to do things in the traditional ways, agreeing things first with their superiors, rather than by-passing the hierarchy. In short, the new formal management structure was very soon subverted by a parallel informal structure, with its own powerbrokers and informal centres of authority, which enabled people to continue to do their jobs in the familiar and proven traditional ways.

The following three cases are enterprises in which there is significant foreign ownership and/or western management consultants have been influential.

MZ2 is an advanced specialised engineering enterprise which has an influential minority foreign owner who has made very substantial investments in the company. The foreign owner instigated the reorganisation of the management system and introduced a matrix system with four 'programmes' corresponding to the four main groups of products. The formerly soviet-style sales department was reconstituted as the 'sales management' subdivision, which headed up each of the programmes and began to take responsibility for all the basic production activity of the enterprise, co-ordinating the work of all the services at the enterprise, the idea being that expanding sales would pull production along behind. *'Our sales management was no longer a sales department, when the factory produced and their job was to decide where to send the stuff . . . They began to manage the factory. Any work began at the factory because the sales people had made a contract, where they had found a buyer and had agreed on a price . . . This is not sales, this is directing the programme of work'* (general director). This new management system was supplemented with a rigorous system of budgeting and financial control whose aim was to reduce expenditure as much as possible.

NKhZ3 is one of the largest petrochemicals complexes in Russia. It was corporatised in 1991 and in 1993 became a founder member of one of Russia's largest private oil companies which now has a significant share of foreign ownership. At the end of the 1980s and beginning of the 1990s the factory faced the real prospect of closure on ecological and economic grounds, but large-scale reconstruction began in 1993 under the direction of foreign consultants, focusing on improving the quality of the products to meet European standards. The enterprise offers a very interesting case of the modernisation of technology and management structures according to western models in a very traditional Russian enterprise. The senior management team is made up of veterans of the enterprise who had all grown up under the previous general director, who held the post from 1987 until his retirement in 2003. His replacement as general director, appointed to the post by the head company, was previously the deputy general director for production, a representative of the 'old team', who had been at the enterprise for his whole working life, having started as an engineer in 1977. The corporate culture of the enterprise is still very strongly production oriented. As the general director noted in an interview: *The previous director managed to make things so that people were devoted to production, felt themselves not "pawns in somebody else's game", but responsible for concrete matters as professionals and they began to trust the management. He always gave specialists freedom of action, did not concern himself with trivial matters. He took responsibility for the whole programme. That was how the collective, of which one could not but be proud, was formed'*. At the same time, the holding company is unequivocally oriented to the maximisation of profits, improving the quality of the product, and reducing costs.

The enterprise has been a test-bed for the holding company's project to modernise its management structures. Thus has involved the gradual introduction since 2001 of a 'process-oriented management structure' which *'will get away from the duplication of functions and increase efficiency and effectiveness. At the same time a certain number of specialists will be freed, but we have already calculated that they will all be employed in other parts of the enterprise'* (deputy director for supply and general questions). This system involves a de-layering of management, the delegation of authority, the assignment of responsibility for processes rather than individual functions and an orientation to cost-accounting and expenditure saving. The development of the new management system has been facilitated by the introduction of a comprehensive integrated management accounting system during 2003. The senior management team's commitment to production and the holding company's desire for profits have been reconciled by an investment programme amounting so far to about $400 million, which makes it possible to reduce costs and improve quality with the help of technological innovations, rather than merely by intensifying labour and tightening the disciplinary regime, as is the case in many other enterprises. There has been a significant reduction in the number employed at the enterprise, not through redundancy or at the expense of production personnel, but by an on-going cautious process of centralisation of the management of non-core auxiliary activities in order to spin them off into subsidiary enterprises.

MetZ3 is a giant metallurgical enterprise which was acquired by a large Russian holding company in 1999. The holding company began to develop a divisional management structure from 2002, under the influence of western management consultants, but a substantial restructuring of the management structure of MetZ3 has led to serious breakdowns of co-ordination and significant disruption because the new structure has not been defined in accordance with any clearly formulated strategic aims for the development of the enterprise nor has it assigned functional responsibilities sufficiently clearly and unambiguously. Management in MetZ3 continues to be functionally based and is still oriented in practice to the achievement of the production plan, leading to the use of inappropriate performance indicators for the various subdivisions. For example, responsibility for the organisation of quality control was removed from the shop chiefs and assigned to the quality department so that quality is now a secondary consideration for line managers, whose primary objective is to fulfil the production plan. At the same time, the job of the quality department is to identify faults, but the more successful they are in this the more they are penalised as production falls short of the plan targets. Similarly, as in soviet times, repairs and maintenance are postponed so as not to disrupt the production cycle.

On the basis of these cases, there is no doubt that enterprises with significant foreign ownership have introduced much more radical changes to their management systems than have Russian-owned enterprises. This is partly, of course, simply a result of their attempts to impose a uniform management system across all their subsidiaries, and it can lead to serious dislocation when the new management system fails to take sufficiently into account the values, habits and expectations of established managers and the existing management routines, as happened at *LPZ2*. This is not just a matter of ignorant foreigners failing to understand Russian reality or of stupid Russians resisting rational management practices, because much the same disruption and discontent could be observed at *MetZ3*, which at the time of our research was still Russian-owned. *MetZ1* and *KhZ1* have, like LPZ2, brought in expatriate senior managers to control all the key areas of management, but the expatriates seem to have established a satisfactory working relationship with their Russian colleagues. The real dividing line between the more successful and the less successful attempts to introduce radical reform of the management system seems to be between those reforms which were associated with the implementation of substantial investment programmes and those which were concerned to reduce costs by imposing stricter control of expenditure. Major investment in modernising and upgrading production facilities makes it possible to reconcile the commitment of traditional management to production and the aspiration of new owners to make profits and to introduce new management systems through which both can be achieved. In the cases of LPZ2 and MetZ3 there was a widespread suspicion that the new owners were not interested in investing in the core production capacity, but only in running down the productive assets in the interests of short-term profit. The new owners of LPZ2 even stinted on providing funds for essential maintenance and repair, while the new owners of MetZ3 made relatively small investments to diversify production rather than upgrading the core facilities.

Their proponents make great claims for the achievement of management reforms, but it is very difficult to say how radical and how effective these reforms have really been, because none has been in place for long, and in some cases they are only at the implementation stage. It is impossible to say whether the subversion of the new formal management structure by the reproduction of traditional management practices through informal relations is an exceptional outcome of a poorly implemented reform, or whether the deficiencies of that particular reform merely brought what is a more general process to light in this case. It is also important to note that many of these managerial reforms look more radical when set against the formal specification of the soviet management system, with its rigid hierarchy of authority and functional division of labour, because the soviet system never worked in the ways described by its organisational schemes. In practice the formal soviet hierarchy and managerial job specifications were constantly by-passed by informal relationships and *ad hoc* arrangements forged in the attempt to get things done, and ultimately to meet the production plan. The multiplicity of management meetings in the soviet enterprise constituted a parallel informal, de-layered, process-oriented management system in which reports would be presented and tasks allocated on the fly, according to the immediate needs and priorities within a framework defined by the ultimate objectives. To some extent the introduction of modern management methods, backed up by computerised communications and information systems, puts these practices on a more systematic footing and so such methods are not as alien to traditional practices as they might at first seem. Indeed, these more formalised management systems may leave something to be desired. It is interesting that at *MetZ1*, which is one of the most progressive foreign-owned enterprises we have studied, on the initiative of the Board of

Directors of the foreign parent company, the general director has resurrected the traditional weekly Monday meetings with the department heads at which he discusses the decisions of the Board of Directors, then the department heads have meetings with their departments and sections to discuss the issues in turn. Furthermore, this initiative was by no means unique:

> **KhZ1**, as we have seen, is part of a foreign-owned multinational corporation and is also managed through the traditional proliferation of meetings. The planning engineer holds a daily planning meeting with the sales department at which the daily production plan is confirmed or corrected. The heads of all production subdivisions and auxiliary services participate in daily operational meetings conducted by the deputy director for production. At these meetings questions of current work are discussed and the causes of problems (for example, departures from the production schedule) and the means of their resolution are identified. There is also a weekly meeting with the technical services at which the implementation of concrete projects is discussed (for example, co-ordination of the work of the technical services and production workers when machinery has to be replaced or repaired). There is also a weekly quality meeting at which heads of production divisions, shift chiefs and representatives of the quality service review the results of the analysis of product quality and enumerate the steps that have to be taken to eliminate any problems that have arisen.

Corporate management in the new private sector

Great hopes were placed in the new private sector in the early 1990s, as the source of the economic dynamism that would regenerate the Russian economy. These hopes were gradually dashed as the Russian economy continued its inexorable decline with no sign of the phoenix-like rise of a new private sector. Russian entrepreneurs complained of the bureaucratic and fiscal barriers and the degree of corruption they faced, and these complaints were echoed by western commentators as explanations for the very low level of development of small and medium enterprises in Russia, but small businessmen always complain about taxation and bureaucracy and the supposed low level of development of SMEs was actually a statistical artefact.[1] It was not that Russian small businesses were markedly less successful than those of other countries, but that the task they had been assigned, of regenerating a sophisticated industrial economy in a state of almost total collapse, was quite beyond them.

In looking at corporate management in the new private sector we are looking at those companies which have been built up by their owners, more or less from nothing, in the years since perestroika. Of course, the holding companies which control the Russian economy are also new private enterprises, but they have

---

[1] Stephen Batstone (ed.), *Russian SME Observatory Report 2001*, Moscow: Russian SME Resource Centre, 2002.

been built up through the acquisition, by fair means or foul, of traditional Russian enterprises and so fall out of our consideration in this section. The new private enterprises which we have researched are mostly quite small enterprises which have developed successfully since 1998, most being industrial enterprises or providing services to industry. Even amongst these enterprises it turns out that the larger ones have expanded by absorbing former state enterprises, buying up their premises and equipment and sometimes rehiring some of their workers.

MZ3 is typical of the new private enterprises on which hopes for the regeneration of the Russian industrial economy have been pinned, acquiring the premises and equipment of derelict traditional enterprises and putting them to profitable use in a new private company. It is one of a group of similar companies owned by eight private individuals, one of whom serves as general director of MZ3, although everyday management is in the hands of the executive director. The origins of the company lay in an auto parts company which had been created in 1985 and spun off from a larger enterprise. In the early 1990s the owners had undertaken various kinds of activity from the repair and sale of cars to the development of technical documentation and designs, before buying the present industrial premises and second-hand equipment in 1994 from large local engineering factories, from which they also drew their skilled workers, to establish themselves as a precision-engineering company. Through the 1990s the company continued to engage in various other activities, for example selling cars that it had received in barter payment and finishing and repairing cars in its own auto repair workshop, but with the recovery from the end of the 1990s it had abandoned these side activities to concentrate on precision engineering, making a specialised range of parts for the engineering industry at home and abroad. The specialist character of its products means that it has a limited market, but few competitors. The company has grown steadily, to employ 136 people, and is still expanding.

The owners and senior managers of the company had originally worked in large soviet enterprises, the company uses old technology in old premises, has drawn its labour force from traditional enterprises and production management is absolutely traditional. Although the company is oriented to profits, the character of its market means that everything is subordinate to production *'the most important is production, everyone works on it, both the commercial department and the designers'* (executive director). The production orientation of the management has enabled them to forge a common culture with the workers, based on the reproduction of a very traditional collectivist soviet work ethic and a promise, if not fully realised, of adequate pay. The novelty of the enterprise is that it is a small specialised company which can react flexibly and rapidly to a changing environment and it is this that has enabled it to survive while so many traditional enterprises have foundered. Its competitive advantage is that it can offer high quality at low prices, but this is not achieved through advanced technology and modern management methods, but through reliance on the traditional soviet work ethic of a skilled and experienced but ageing labour force.

We have not studied, and do not cover here, the bulk of new private enterprises, which are in trade and catering and other consumer and financial services. Most of the features of the management of new private enterprises in Russia are not specifically Russian, but mirror the experience of SMEs around the world. For this reason we will not explore these issues in depth here.

While in holding companies there has been a radical separation of ownership and control, in new private enterprises such a separation is very rare. The vast majority of new private enterprises are still owned and managed by their founders, who combine strategic and operational management and have more or less complete discretion in management decision-making.[1] The motivation of the owners of new private enterprises is varied, but while most of those in trade and catering are no doubt oriented primarily to making money, an additional motive of many owners of productive enterprises who went into business at the beginning of the 1990s was the pursuit of self-realisation. This is particularly the case of those who set up companies to provide advanced technology goods and services, who had often worked previously in universities or research institutes and who established the company to continue work which had become impossible in a dying organisation or under bureaucratic constraints. Whatever their origins, many new private companies have changed their sphere of activity, sometimes quite radically, in response to changing opportunities, until they have found their niche, though once they have invested in production facilities it becomes much more difficult to change direction. Many new private industrial enterprises were originally established as trading companies or provided business or information services, through which they identified worthwhile investment opportunities.

The owner-managers of new private enterprises often have a technical background, with a high level of education and work experience in research institutes or high-tech defence enterprises, but they rarely have any management background and they have developed their management practices and learned their management skills through a process of trial and error in the organisation and development of their business. Since such firms have often grown by exploiting promising market niches, rather than on the basis of the established skills of their organisers, the managers are rarely professional specialists in the sphere in which their enterprise works. In the period of initial growth of the business the acquisition of knowledge is slapdash, driven by enthusiasm and business activism, decision-making is based on intuition rather than rigorous analysis and there is a high potential for innovation. Success may be as much a

---

[1] According to research undertaken by the Association of Managers and the Institute of Sociology, 82 per cent of top managers in the private sector are also owners, as are 55 per cent of second-rank managers. A quarter of their sample of managers were majority shareholders in their company (Дынин А., Литовченко С., Черныш М., *Социальный профиль российского менеджера: результаты исследования*, Москва: Ассоциация менеджеров, Институт социологии РАН, 2004).

matter of luck as of skill or judgement.[1] However, once the business is established and the owner-managers seek to consolidate or expand its position, these skills turn out to be insufficient for carrying out more complex tasks related, in particular, to analysis of the market, ability to assess the current situation and develop long-term strategic perspectives. Many managers understand this very well:

> *'We are growing, and soon there will be problems with the managers, they will simply not be up to their jobs in terms of the level of their qualifications. We have sales. It is very difficult there. There nobody can say where we are going. We need a very strong economist there. We have an accountant, she does a lot, she does a colossal amount of work, but she is not an economist. And it is like that everywhere. It will be very difficult. Well, we all began together'* (MK2).

At the same time, management in private business is a pretty closed group. Despite the acute need for specialists, it is very rare to hire a person from outside except perhaps for a marketing specialist, to whom a particular mystique is attached. On the one hand, there is a considerable reluctance to sack existing managers, both because they are often long-standing personal friends and because they have information which could be valuable to competitors or dangerous if reported to the authorities. On the other hand, most new private enterprises do not have the kind of money needed to hire the necessary specialists on the market. Thus the management team of new private enterprises is made up not so much of specialists in particular areas, as of trusted people, reproducing the traditional soviet model of the 'ideal worker' in which loyalty is valued more highly than skill and professionalism. Rather than hiring specialists, the tendency is for senior managers in new private enterprises to follow part-time and correspondence courses in management and economics to improve their qualifications. Turnover amongst the management team is almost zero and, given their age (most are between 35 and 45), change in the composition of top management is only likely to come if the enterprise grows significantly (or if there is a falling out among the partners).

The management of new private enterprises tends to develop spontaneously, but lags behind the growth of the enterprise since the owners are reluctant to take on new managerial staff. This leads to the tendency for one person to take on a number of management functions and for there to be a minimum of hierarchical links in the management chain, with many managers being directly subordinate to the director. This makes it very difficult to identify a formal management structure, since responsibilities are not clearly allocated and demarcated, as tasks may be assigned spontaneously by the director.

The most important operational management function is that of getting orders, because the activity of the whole enterprise depends on this, and this function is often taken on personally by the director or his trusted first deputy. Sales

---

[1] The authors of the study of the 'social profile of Russian managers' characterise the kind of managers who emerged in the 1990s as 'crisis' managers (ibid.).

managers are the most highly valued employees, they are the most likely to be given training at the expense of the company, and they are likely to be paid generous commissions. Supply, which was the bugbear of the soviet enterprise, is much less of a problem and those responsible for organising supplies have lower pay and status in management.

New private enterprises typically try to minimise risk and take advantage of tax and other concessions for SMEs by registering themselves officially as a number of formally independent firms, which carry out different aspects of the business. The fixed assets of the business might be owned by one firm, which leases them to the others. Other firms will be formally responsible for production, for sales, for transport and distribution and so on. Usually these are all purely paper transactions, undertaken for accounting and reporting purposes, and have no substantive implications for the management of the company. The fragmentation of the business into a number of independent companies helps to protect the business from the authorities by making it opaque. This system also facilitates the removal of funds from the company accounts and their diversion into 'shadow' cash transactions, which avoids taxation and other payments, and the separation of the assets and liabilities of the undertaking into different companies to facilitate shedding liabilities through insolvency and liquidation.

There is considerable scope for conflict within the management team when the intuition of joint owners diverges, or the intuition of the owner does not coincide with the professional judgement of a hired manager. It is very common, therefore, for co-owners to fall out and go their separate ways, taking their managerial colleagues with them and often founding a competing business in the same sphere, or for professional managers to leave the business, often joining a competitor, in each case taking with them valuable business contacts.[1]

MK2 is a furniture manufacturer which was established in December 2000 when a previous furniture company, which had existed since 1995, split into two independent firms as a result of a disagreement between the two owners. The previous company had been built up from virtually nothing by a group of friends, two of whom were the founder-owners of the company, who had studied together at a aviation institute and had then worked for a time as specialists in various large enterprises. When the enterprise split, the owner of MK2 managed to take with him the sales director of the previous venture, and correspondingly the connections with their traditional customers, by giving him a 45 per cent share of the new company, and also managed to hold on to the other managers and to keep a significant part of the modern and expensive equipment, although he had to build new premises. MK2 is formally registered as three different firms for tax and reporting reasons. It has been profitable and has grown rapidly, now employing sixty people.

---

[1] In almost all of our case-study new private enterprises which involved more than one founder, the founders have fallen out and one or more of them left within the first five or six years of the business.

SO1 was also created by graduates of an aviation institute at the end of the 1980s, their firm being first established in 1991 to provide disinfection services. In 1994 the enterprise similarly split up after a disagreement between its founders and the two resulting enterprises became fierce competitors, at first locally but later on the national market. SO1 effectively withdrew from the local market, handing it over to small local companies, and set up a national network which now extends to eighty-nine Russian regions. In 2000 a further conflict erupted between the general director and the production director, and the latter left to set up a rival company, the former partners having now become uncompromising competitors. In 2001 the company was raided by the tax police and heavy fines imposed, which the owner is convinced was the result of a tip-off from his competitor. In order to avoid such complications and minimise the tax burden the company has formally moved its headquarters to a neighbouring region and created a network of independent businesses. The lesson drawn by the owner from his experience is that '*there must be one owner*'.

Tensions between owners of new private businesses and their hired managers are especially likely to arise because owners make heavy demands but are very reluctant to delegate authority to hired managers. '*Maybe it would be easier to hire managers and tan their hides. But there are also minuses in that. They have to be supervised. They have their own interests. They begin to work for their own pockets*' (director, **SO1**). Even when they create collegial bodies, the directors recognise that they are only decorative: '*We are still small, but we have to get used to some sort of order. The Board of Directors can have an influence on some trifling questions. If they are right and persuade me of this, why not? But they do not make any serious decisions; they do not own the money. We play at these games. I do not really consult with them on anything. Basically it is only an exchange of information*' (director, **MK2**). If the owners are to hold on to their managers in such circumstances, they have to make sure that they are well rewarded.

The management of most new private enterprises is very centralised and concentrated in the hands of the owner-director, who tends to intervene in all aspects of the management of the company. The owner-director usually controls all the financial flows and authorises all spending, but it is rare for there to be any systematic forms of accounting or monitoring of expenditure.

MZ7 is a small precision engineering company which makes an innovative new product. It was founded in 1991 by three friends, of whom one split off in 2001 and a second died in 2004. On the death of the latter the finance director, who had been his associate, also left and has not been replaced. There is no system of accounting for or controlling expenditure and frequent attempts on the part of the director and chief engineer to introduce formalised control in order to reduce expenditure arising from faults and breakdowns have not been successful, because nothing has been done to encourage staff to handle equipment more carefully and reduce the production of faulty products.

In larger companies, particularly if they operate on a number of different sites, it is necessary to have more elaborated management systems, including systems of budgeting.

MK3 is a furniture factory which had originally been established as an *artel'* (co-operative) in 1919. It fell into deep crisis in the 1990s and by the end of the decade was heavily in debt and working at 5 per cent capacity, with wages unpaid and more than half its 400 employees on administrative leave. The factory was bought by a new private furniture company which was expanding from its own production base and drafted in a completely new management team. Within two years the company was employing 600 people, although only about 150 of the original labour force remained: the best had left and the worst were sacked after the merger. The two factories are under common management, implemented through a system of budgeting, but the director of each enterprise has the freedom to reassign funds within the overall budget. Managers at lower levels do not have overall budgets, but limits are set on each category of spending.

TP1 was established in 1993 by three friends, who eventually decided to focus their business on supplying and installing high-quality household fittings. The company now employs almost 600 people in a network of regional branches. Originally the owners managed the company themselves, but one dropped out and in 2003 they hired a general director who only lasted five months (*'He was not right, well, we didn't know whom we needed. At first we made a mistake'*). His replacement had worked for ten years as deputy director of a western company and was keen to introduce western management methods. He introduced a system of rigorous budgeting, but was not satisfied with the financial plans proposed by the heads of branches and subdivisions and so introduced a new system under which the budgets were drawn up by the financial control department, whose staff had come from the western company and were familiar with the methods. The heads of branches and subdivisions were unhappy with budgets imposed from above, but were forced to accept them by threats of the sack.

MK1 is a furniture producer which followed the opposite course to TP1. The company was established in 1994 to produce high-quality office furniture from imported components, initially with a hired director. The management was chaotic and the director was sacked in 2003 because the owners were not satisfied with the financial results. One of the owners took up the post of director. The new owner-director undertook a systematic rebuilding of the management structure. *'Until then we did not have a clear division of responsibilities in the company . . . people interfered in the production process and took any old decisions'* (commercial director). The director's first step was to appoint a new team of senior managers, with a very clear vision of whom she wanted: *'I know for myself exactly. . . . I instructed the personnel agencies and myself searched only for men. I even know what he* *looks like, how he conducts himself and that it is a man of a certain age – not a young lad and not an old man. I know that a woman will not be successful. She will not pass an interview . . . well because I'm a woman myself'.* She appointed four young men in their twenties to the senior posts, although informants considered that she had thereby excluded better-qualified women. The chief accountant is a woman and, although formally a member of the senior management team, her influence is limited to her own department.

New private enterprises mostly supply local markets, mainly selling direct to consumers through their own retail outlets or selling direct to enterprises and organisations and only occasionally selling through dealers and wholesalers. This is partly because the wholesale trade is still underdeveloped in Russia and wholesalers' margins are high, but also because small businesses want to keep as much control as possible of their sources of cash income. Managers of new private enterprises generally report that they face a less harsh competitive environment and have more market opportunities than do traditional enterprises,[1] but high costs of transport and distribution mean that they find it difficult to expand beyond their native region. Only two of our case-study new private enterprises felt that they faced stiff competition in their local markets, both coincidentally furniture producers who were being squeezed between large Moscow and Saint Petersburg companies, on the one hand, and local cheap handicraft producers, on the other. A number of our case-study enterprises had tried to expand into the markets of neighbouring regions with limited success, while attempts of regional companies to break into the Moscow market had generally ended in costly failure. Because of financial constraints, new private industrial enterprises also find it difficult to make significant changes to their product range, let alone to change their sphere of production altogether, in response to market changes. This gives added importance to their capacity to market and sell their existing products.

New private enterprise directors report increasing quality, introducing new products, conducting market research and developing a marketing strategy as being among their main immediate priorities to make their business more effective,[2] although they are limited by their financial, organisational and professional capacities in what they can achieve in this direction. Small and medium enterprises do not have the capacity or resources to undertake market research, which in any case is not very reliable in the unstable Russian market conditions, but generally get feedback directly from their customers or their own retail outlets. Most companies try to promote their products through advertising and conduct a limited amount of *ad hoc* marketing and market research, checking the prices of competitors, looking for new sales outlets and business partners. One common method of promotion is to offer customers additional

---

[1] Фаминский В. И. (ред.), *Стратегии поведения частных предприятий на рынке в современных условиях*, Москва: НИСИПП, 2004, p. 89.

[2] Survey of directors of 100 SMEs conducted by the Samara branch of ISITO in 2002. Only the renewal of plant and equipment ranked higher, but this was generally seen as a longer-term objective.

services. For example, furniture companies sell a range of complementary products and offer their commercial customers a turnkey service under which they will fully furnish and equip an office. Suppliers of technical equipment may provide installation, training and maintenance (which is normal for western customers, but is not part of traditional soviet practice).

The vulnerability of new private enterprises means that it is even more important for them than it is for traditional enterprises to reduce their costs to protect their competitive position and to minimise their expenditure to protect their cash flow. This is their prime consideration in making fixed investments. One of the principal barriers to the development of new private enterprises is the difficulty and cost of securing finance. The vast majority of investment funds therefore come from the owners' own resources, occasionally supplemented by loans from friends (particularly when setting up the business) and business partners, particularly suppliers in the form of commercial credit. A survey in 2000–1 found that only 20 per cent of small and medium enterprises had taken even short-term bank credit in the previous five years. The same survey found that the investment priorities of small and medium enterprises were the purchase, repair and modernisation of equipment, buildings and transport facilities,[1] and these were also the priorities of our case-study enterprises. As in the case of larger enterprises, even small enterprises put a premium on self-sufficiency, to protect themselves from the unpredictability of the external environment and from extortion from monopoly suppliers and to reduce their outlay on renting premises and transport facilities, so they seek not only to modernise and expand their core production facilities, but also to extend the degree of their self-sufficiency.

In rare cases there will be sufficient funds to buy expensive imported equipment to develop the product range, improve quality or lower costs. Such acquisitions are facilitated by the better terms on which such equipment can be obtained, either through low-interest credit or leasing arrangements. Importing foreign packaging equipment is often seen as an important element of a marketing strategy. However, in most new private enterprises, limited access to investment funds restricts the ability of the company to compete on the basis of the reduced costs and increased quality achieved by installing modern equipment, so they have to continue to resort to *ad hoc* marketing efforts, opportunistic methods of cost reduction and recourse to self-sufficiency.

The limitations of management in the new private sector

The absence of a clearly formalised management hierarchy with a clear demarcation and allocation of responsibilities, which is partly a result of smallness but also a consequence of the reluctance of owner-directors to delegate, becomes increasingly problematic as the enterprise grows and management tasks become more complex, so that it becomes beyond the capacity of the director to maintain constant supervision of all aspects of the work of the enterprise. This is the point which many of our case-study new

---

[1] Stephen Batstone, *Russian SME Observatory Report 2001*.

private enterprises have reached, and it is the point at which the continued survival of the enterprise is most at risk.

T1 is a printing and publishing company created by two friends in the wake of the August 1998 crisis. The present co-owners were offered a printing machine to pay off a debt, so they founded the company and opened a printing works, beginning from nothing and learning the trade from books. Within a year they had three machines and expanded into publishing. Initially, there was no clear division of responsibility between the two owners and management was based on the principle *'The one who knows best about something does that. If it is necessary to go and get some paper, the one who is free goes'* (director). Later one of the owners left and the owner-director took on a deputy for production, to co-ordinate production with orders, a chief accountant and a head of the binding shop, who turned out to be incompetent and was replaced by a technology manager who co-ordinates printing and binding. The director is enthused by his mission 'to publish good books', but tries to realise this mission on the basis of enthusiasm and a presumed team spirit rather than through the systematic management of a complex business. He keeps all financial information to himself and there is no system for the accounting and control of spending. There is no middle management layer, with the director intervening and interfering in everything. The company has grown rapidly, but management is disorganised and planning haphazard, imposing significant costs through delays in the delivery of supplies, overtime payments and equipment breakdowns.

The fish-processing factory *RZ1* has a hyperactive owner-director who organises supplies, manages external contacts, works on the organisation of the enterprise, participates in developing the technology, works with personnel and so on. Naturally, virtually none of the other managers can keep pace with their chief. This leads to quite big conflicts and several senior staff admitted, *'We cannot keep pace with the director'*. In the six months prior to our research several managers and specialists, including the head of the personnel department and the head of the trade department, left the firm at the same time. Conflicts between senior and middle management arise regularly. The director accuses the middle managers of incompetence, a lack of responsibility and an inability to work for the future. The middle managers complain about instability, the lack of clear planning and even petty tyranny. The claims of both sides have some foundation. The fact is that the firm has outgrown the capacity of its management.

MetZ5 was founded in 1995 by a group of private metal traders to process waste metal. It is now owned by the director and his wife and employs 260 people to produce high-quality alloys and castings. The general director concentrates on external relations and strategic decision-making, while the executive director is responsible for operational management. They have found a market niche which was not interesting for the giant metallurgical enterprises that at that time were oriented to export markets. Most of the production workers and line managers came from the neighbouring giant metallurgical factory and the production shops still have elements of the traditional industrial culture of a large soviet industrial enterprise, but these values are being eroded without any effort to replace them with new values so that an increasingly instrumental orientation to work prevails among the workers. The office workers, on the other hand, share a quite different clannish culture, which emphasises self-reliance and individual achievement. The top managers are a group of long-standing friends of the general director, with no background in the industry, although they have subsequently followed management training courses. The general director regularly invites his friends to join the team, even if there are no posts for them, in which case there is a reallocation of responsibilities or a new niche is found. The key quality of a manager is not their professional skill but their loyalty and commitment to the owner-director. The management structure is accordingly very unclear, with a very imprecise allocation of responsibilities and the status and authority of the manager depending more on informal relations than on the formal position. Or, as one respondent explained it, *'There is a mismatch, but I would not say that it is formal/informal. Functionally in any case each person has their duties. The only thing is that they are not assigned to them on the basis of their post'.* Respondents insisted that this fluid management system works because it is a small enterprise, but it is not clear that it will continue to work if the enterprise continues to grow.

In all these cases, then, the director retained tight control and orchestrated a rather fluid management team, while the final case underlines the continuing reluctance of the director to relinquish this style despite enterprise growth.

There are considerable differences in the corporate management of our case-study enterprises, each of which has its own particular features which makes each one of interest in itself. However, we can identify some clear patterns from the analysis of the case studies as a whole, which can be summed up very briefly. On the one hand, there are substantial differences between the management values and management practices to be found between the three different types of enterprise that we have defined, traditional independent enterprises, traditional enterprises which have been integrated into holding structures, and new private enterprises. On the other hand, despite the adaptation of corporate management to the demands of a market economy in general, and to subordination to capitalist owners in particular, there has been very little change in the spheres of personnel and production management. What we find at the present stage of development of Russian capitalism is the attempt to subordinate the production of things to the production of profit largely by means of traditional soviet methods of personnel and production management. In the next three chapters we will look more closely at these aspects of management practice in order to identify, in particular, the stresses and tensions to which this combination might give rise in order ultimately to assess to what extent these traditional management practices are consistent with the new demands placed on them.

6 Labour relations and personnel management

The priority of traditional enterprises through the 1990s was to survive the crisis, and in terms of personnel management this meant trying to hold on to the core of their labour force through the period of decline, in the hope of a subsequent recovery. The solution to holding on to the core of the labour force was finding ways to enable key workers to continue to earn, even when there were few sales and orders. Many enterprises switched from piece-rate payment systems to paying time-wages so that main production workers would earn even when there was no work, and shops took on all kinds of additional work to provide income. However, the tendency was for the most skilled and enterprising employees to leave for better-paid jobs and better prospects elsewhere, leaving behind those who were less competitive on the labour market. At the same time there was very little new hiring, so by the end of the decade many traditional enterprises were left with an ageing, low-skilled, low-productivity labour force, often with low discipline and low morale.[1] With the improved macroeconomic conditions after 1998, enterprises were faced with major personnel management issues. However, as will be seen in this chapter, in most enterprises shop chiefs were left to address these issues on their own initiative. Only in a small minority of enterprises was there any development of systematic personnel management policies and practices.[2]

Personnel management systems in soviet enterprises reflected the character of the soviet social relations of production. Principles of personnel management were expressed in declarations, regulations and bureaucratic procedures, but in practice personnel management was largely subordinate to the day-to-day management of the production process. In the soviet enterprise

[1] Капелюшников Р. И. *Российский рынок труда. Адаптация без реструктуризации*, Москва: ГУ ВШЭ, 2001, p. 232.

[2] This chapter draws heavily on the chapters by Petr Bizyukov ('Службы персонала – управленческая периферия' [Personnel services as the periphery of management]) and Lyudmilla Cheglakova ('Изменения в практиках управления персоналом' [Changes in the practice of personnel management]) in Кабалина В. И. (ред.) *Практики управления персоналом на современных российских предприятиях*, Москва: ИСИТО, 2005.

the personnel department (*otdel kadrov*) was nominally responsible for personnel management, but personnel policy was rarely developed in the personnel department. Employment levels, wage scales, social welfare funds and training programmes were determined by the ministry and handed down to the enterprise. The real centres of personnel policy in the enterprise were the production services and the leading bodies of the 'social-political organisations' (Party, trade union and Komsomol) which were found in every enterprise. The personnel department performed predominantly registration functions, maintaining personnel records. The personnel department had a correspondingly low status, carrying out a multitude of repetitive routine operations which did not require special knowledge or highly qualified staff, so that it was on the periphery of the management apparatus.

With the collapse of the soviet system the enterprise was in a position to determine its own wage and employment levels, social spending and training needs. The Party and Komsomol were removed from the workplace, and the trade union, no longer under the leadership of the Communist Party, began to transform itself, so the system of personnel management also began to change. The personnel department was often renamed, becoming the 'personnel management service' (*sluzhba upravleniya personalom*), although it is an open question how much had changed apart from the name on the door. One task we set ourselves in our research was to discover just how much had changed in the management of the employment relationship in post-soviet enterprises.

Our study of personnel management in contemporary Russian enterprises led us to two fundamental conclusions. First, the majority of decisions relating to the functions of personnel management are still taken outside the personnel department, so the main actors in personnel management are not specialist personnel managers but other groups of managers, and most particularly middle (line) managers, and the function of personnel management is decentralised and fragmented. Second, the personnel department has a greater role to play the more complex the organisation of which it is a part since the more complex the organisation, the greater the amount of interaction between its parts. The more traditional the enterprise and the simpler its organisation, the less does the personnel department participate in personnel management.

The two central issues we want to address are what the functions of personnel management are and who carries out those functions. We start by looking at the characteristics of heads of personnel departments, in comparison with other management specialisms. The next major section of the chapter then considers the range of functions with which the personnel departments become involved. In particular it addresses the question of the typical division of power and responsibilities in performing these functions between the personnel department itself and other groups of managers. The final main section then discusses how this division of labour varies between different types of enterprise.

A portrait of the personnel manager

The heads of the personnel departments in our case-study enterprises were usually the most competent, best-qualified and often the most experienced members of staff in their departments and so were clear leaders in their field. However, personnel management is not a well-developed or highly regarded discipline in Russia and it is very difficult to find people with the knowledge and ability to innovate in this sphere. The general director of *NKhZ* complained of his inability to find an effective personnel director: *'So far I have not seen a candidate who would suit me. They, as a minimum, must know more about personnel management than I do. I am self-taught and I want someone to make professional proposals regarding the solution of my problems'.*

To assess the location of personnel managers within the structure of management of the enterprise it is necessary to compare them with other managers at the same level, whom we take to be the heads of the marketing and finance departments and chiefs of major production and auxiliary shops. The first and most obvious feature of personnel managers is that they are predominantly female – more than 70 per cent in our sample of enterprises – whereas finance directors may be male or female and heads of marketing and shop chiefs are predominantly male. There are no significant differences in age between the different posts, or in the length of service at the given enterprise or in their present post, except that heads of marketing tend to be younger and have shorter service, which is in keeping with the novelty of the profession. Finance directors are much more likely than other managers to have come directly into their post on joining the enterprise.

There are significant differences in the level of education of the different occupations. First, most finance and marketing directors have higher education, while as many personnel managers as shop chiefs do not. Second, most of the other managers have a specialist education corresponding to their occupation, technical for shop chiefs and economic for finance directors, but the personnel managers have a much more varied educational background. On the other hand, they are a little more likely than any of the other professions to have followed additional courses to develop their professional skills, allbeit only for an average of seven months. There are no significant differences in the way they came into their posts (most were by promotion) or in their ownership of shares, or in their subjective views about the aims of the enterprise.

So the typical personnel manager is a middle-aged woman of about 40 who has worked at the enterprise for a long time and has worked for the majority of that time in her present post. The length of her tenure suggests that she is somebody who is well integrated into the enterprise and knows her job and the enterprise very well. She does not earn nearly as much as the heads of the finance and marketing departments and her status is correspondingly significantly lower. She is not markedly traditional, humanitarian or liberal in her views, which combine liberal and traditional elements. One can presume that she shares the views of other senior managers and sees herself as a proponent of their values, policies and so on.

The functions of personnel management and the role of the personnel department

We start by asking the functions of the personnel department, a question that we put to the head of the personnel department in all of those enterprises which had such a department (in some cases it consisted of only one person). This identifies the range of personnel management functions in these enterprises, but it also indicates that the involvement of the personnel department itself in performing these functions is variable and often quite limited.

Registration and record-keeping

The first function, carried out by more than 90 per cent of personnel departments, is the traditionally dominant function of the soviet personnel department, registration. This involves maintaining the personnel records and labour books, recording statistical data on employment and labour turnover, keeping pension and military service records and so on. This is not so much fulfilling a personnel management function as recording the results of personnel management decisions that have already been taken: to hire somebody, to fire somebody, to promote somebody or to discipline somebody. It is obviously extremely important to keep records, and workers have a particular interest in those records being kept accurately because their future employment, pension, various benefits and compensation depend on their work record, but keeping records is not at all the same as making management decisions. On the other hand, the responsibility for recording decisions can involve the personnel department in altering decisions that have already been taken. Most managers are not very familiar with the details of labour legislation and in their relations with the personnel department adopt the approach that 'I need to do this and you work out how to formalise it!' For example, a manager might demand that the personnel department formalise the illegal sacking of somebody, or insist on hiring somebody on illegal terms. An authoritative personnel department will intervene and demand that the manager should either follow the proper procedure, for example correctly draw up the documents to provide a legal basis for dismissal, or abandon the idea. The personnel department often does not have sufficient authority to insist that the proper procedures are followed, as is shown by the fact that workers win the vast majority of cases in which they contest the legality of their punishment or dismissal through the courts, because the proper procedures have not been followed and documented.

Hiring and personnel selection

The second most frequently performed function is 'personnel selection', which is also reported by almost all personnel managers (though less frequently in new private enterprises, where this function is often handled personally by the director). However, on closer examination it turns out that in most enterprises the actual selection of personnel is undertaken not by the personnel department but by middle managers, the heads of shops and subdivisions, who control the selection of personnel for their own departments. The most common procedure is one in which the personnel department plays a role in finding candidates for positions, with the hiring decision being taken by the head of the relevant subdivision. In other cases, however, the whole process of recruitment and selection, often through personal connections of current employees, is undertaken by the subdivision and the personnel department merely completes the formalities of hiring and perhaps formally approves the decision made elsewhere. In the most common case, though, the subdivision reports a vacancy to the personnel department, which looks for candidates for the position by advertising directly and perhaps through labour market intermediaries (the Federal Employment Service, private employment agencies), although as a rule enterprises only turn to labour market intermediaries if they cannot find candidates for themselves. The personnel department then carries out a preliminary selection, filtering out those candidates who do not meet the minimum requirements for the post because they do not provide evidence of the necessary qualifications, they have a criminal record or have been dismissed from previous jobs for disciplinary violations (most commonly theft or drunkenness).

Many companies also have some strategic guidelines which have to be taken into account in hiring and these have the potential to give the personnel department a greater involvement in the process of personnel selection. For example, some companies have a rule of not hiring those who have previously left or been dismissed from the company, while others display a positive preference for those with previous experience of work there. Quite a few companies have a strategy of 'rejuvenating the labour collective', giving priority to young people in hiring, while others have a policy of encouraging 'labour dynasties' by hiring the children of those already working for the company. Some personnel departments keep lists of people who have previously worked at the enterprise or who have inquired about employment so that they can immediately contact them in the event of a vacancy arising.

In practice, of course, the terms and conditions of employment on offer affect the extent to which the personnel department can be selective in filtering applicants and sometimes the company has no choice but to consider those with inadequate qualifications or a poor disciplinary record. Many enterprises in the light, food-processing and engineering industries which have managed to recover since 1998 are still paying relatively low wages and so can make only limited demands on applicants for jobs. In such enterprises the main requirement of the candidate is that they have a Labour Book and *'the person should be conscientious, without bad habits'* (**KhBK1**), or more bluntly, *'they should not be drunk'* (**MZ8**) or *'whether the person is a drinker'* (**NKhZ2**). As in soviet times, they hire just about anybody who comes looking for a job. As the head of the personnel department of **SM1** acknowledged, *'sometimes you have to take the first person who turns up, just to get somebody to fill the job'.* At the bread and pasta combine **KhBK2** *'hiring a person works like this: he arrives, if there are not medical contra-indications he goes to the shop chief, but by now we foremen can tell whether the person will work or not'* (bread shop foreman), but another foreman in the same enterprise confessed that he is pressed for time and is ready to take anybody: '*in hiring a person the decisive word is that of the person himself*' (pasta shop foreman).

Only the more successful enterprises, which can pay relatively good wages and/or offer a good package of social benefits, can make more exacting demands for education, qualifications and experience. For those enterprises which are able to be selective, personal qualities are often at least as important as professional skills and experience, with loyalty being the value rated above all others. At the foreign-owned detergent factory *KhZ1*, the general director explained:

> '*The principle according to which staff are selected for the team . . . These are the two basic factors: professionalism and loyalty to the firm. These are the absolutely necessary two, and there should not be one without the other. . . . Here it is not registered, here it is not formalised*'.

Loyalty and professionalism are also the key hiring criteria in the foreign-owned *MetZ1*. The general director of the telecommunications company *TK1* similarly explained that the criteria for personnel selection were '*professionalism, loyalty and the cohesion of the team*', although here too the criteria were not written down anywhere. Thus, the values traditional to soviet enterprises of support for management and lack of conflict in management relations are reproduced even in foreign-owned firms. However, these demands are expressed in a new 'western' terminology.

Although the methods of hiring and selection of personnel remain within the framework of traditional soviet practices as far as most positions are concerned, there is some differentiation in the practice of recruitment applied to different categories of staff, with young specialists increasingly being hired on a competitive basis when the main criteria are qualifications and personal characteristics. The personnel department is also typically assigned the responsibility of finding candidates for the more problematic positions in the social structure of the enterprise, particularly for auxiliary personnel and other groups with high potential and real turnover, or for highly skilled positions in which there is a severe shortage of qualified applicants.

The practice of hiring through friends and relatives of current employees was common in soviet enterprises and such forms of closed hiring remain common today, particularly where there are shortages of the appropriate categories of labour. The advantages of such a form of hiring are that it provides a means of identifying reliable candidates for jobs, for whom the intermediary would provide some kind of surety, and it is likely to facilitate the adaptation of new employees, reduce labour turnover and strengthen the degree of social integration of the organisation.[1] It is also economical, requiring only minimal investment of the resources of management and the personnel service, and can provide a means of filling positions rapidly. There is a widespread use of hiring

---

[1]   Simon Clarke, *The Formation of a Labour Market in Russia*, Cheltenham: Edward Elgar, 1999, Chapter Five.

of the main categories of staff through friends and relatives, while top managers and specialists are commonly found through professional connections and recommendations, or are assigned by the holding company from its own staff. Enterprises generally turn to the external labour market and open personnel selection in only two situations: to find candidates for the most unskilled and low-paid positions which are marginal to the enterprise and for which candidates are unlikely to be found through recommendation, or, conversely, if there is a shortage of high-skilled employees with the professional and skill characteristics required by the enterprise.

The deficiency of hiring through friends and relatives is that it might exclude consideration of much better-qualified candidates because professionalism and skills corresponding to the requirements of the job are secondary in relation to the fact that the employee is 'one of ours'. This may be overcome by combining formal and informal criteria in the selection process.

> At the telecommunications company *TK1*, the fact of acquaintance with someone employed by the company is not a ground for appointment. The general director recognises the existence of informal channels but does not see them as the most preferable. *'Of course people come by recommendation, but everybody comes on an equal footing. I cannot say that in this respect there is any kind of preference'*, and the company has a strict rule of not hiring relatives of current employees, in the belief that this *'sooner or later tells on'* their work. In such a case social connections serve as a channel of information, rather than as a channel of appointment. Nevertheless, many people come to the company through social connections, telling their acquaintances about vacancies: *'I came to TK1 through an acquaintance, 70 per cent of the people came here through acquaintances'* (engineer).

Once the personnel department has drawn up a list of candidates, responsibility for the actual selection is nearly always passed to the head of the relevant subdivision. Candidates will be interviewed by the head of the subdivision, who will decide which candidate is most suitable for the position. Sometimes the decision has to go to the general director for approval, particularly in small enterprises and/or for more skilled or senior positions. The personnel department then completes the formalities. The major limitation of this procedure is that the head of the subdivision does not usually interview all the suitable candidates for the position and select the best one, but more commonly simply takes on the first person who seems satisfactory, without a thorough assessment of their qualifications or comparison with those of other candidates. The head of the subdivision has a heavy workload and urgently needs to fill a vacancy, so does not have the time or inclination to undertake a rigorous selection procedure. However, middle managers jealously guard their prerogative of selecting the personnel with whom they will have to work, which gives them a certain amount of patronage, and they strongly resist attempts to centralise personnel selection.

As noted earlier, in some companies the personnel department plays a more active role in recruitment, particularly when the enterprise faces a shortage of skilled labour. Many enterprises lost a large part of their most highly skilled workers during the 1990s and confronted shortages of skilled labour once recovery got under way after 1998. This is a particularly acute problem in mono-industrial towns, in which there is a relatively small pool of potential employees on which to draw. Technical colleges reoriented their training programmes during the 1990s, since there were few openings for those with industrial qualifications at that time, so there was no longer a supply of qualified young workers and specialists. Many companies have reconstituted traditional relationships with neighbouring educational institutions which had broken down with the collapse of the soviet system, and provide placements for students completing their diploma work, which provides the company with a flow of young people with professional training and an opportunity to identify promising candidates. When workers require quite extensive training, there is also the problem of retaining them until they have reached their full earning capacity. All of these activities give the personnel department a greater role in the process of personnel selection.

MZ2 is a fairly advanced engineering enterprise which went through a deep crisis in the 1990s, but has reoriented production in order to secure a healthy recovery. It has an ageing labour force and suffers from a serious shortage of skilled labour. However, the reserve of skilled workers in the city has disappeared: *'There is a shortage of people with the necessary skills. There was a large outflow of people over the eight years in which there was stagnation. Specialists left and we took on new people – cleaners, those who had been driven out of other factories. Today we have eaten up all the able-bodied population of the city with the necessary skills'* (deputy general director for personnel). The enterprise sought to lure former employees back by offering them special bonus payments and the personnel department organises recruiting missions to bankrupt enterprises in other cities and selects the best of their redundant employees. Recently connections have been established with educational institutions, with the aim of restoring the practice of agreeing orders for the training of specialists and workers, but the deputy general director for personnel recognises that the old ways of assigning students to their jobs will no longer work: *'We understand that this work is not very effective, today there is no longer a system of distribution of specialists who have graduated from the technical schools. We understand that this is a reserve, if these people come to us for their practical work, they will see that one can work here normally, there is a large programme of social protection of workers. This makes the enterprise attractive'.*

The enterprise has also had to hire young specialists and workers, despite their lack of the necessary experience and skills. Young workers undergo training, often long, up to a year, on the job, in the course of which the administration tries to keep them at the enterprise and encourages the intensification of their labour with additional payments. *'We set the pay of the new arrivals, young workers – basically young workers come and for a time they undergo training or retraining . . . so during this period we establish additional payments for them, depending on their output. Well to give them an interest in such work'* (head of the department of labour and wages). They also hire supernumerary young specialists to work alongside experienced incumbents, usually working pensioners, until such time as the existing specialist retires, encouraged by an attractive early retirement package, and is replaced by the newcomer.

Although the revision of labour legislation has expanded the opportunities for Russian enterprises to hire employees on less secure and more flexible contractual terms, our case-study enterprises do this only to a very limited extent, and the most common form of hiring is still the traditional indefinite labour contract, with about a third of enterprises using fixed-term and temporary contracts or subcontracting.[1] There has also been only a limited tendency to the individualisation of labour contracts, with only half the case-study enterprises providing individual conditions even in the contracts of senior managers, and only 10 per cent providing such conditions for all their workers. The drawing up of labour contracts is therefore also largely a routine task, since most employees sign a standard contract.

Disciplinary function

The third most common function of the personnel department is involvement in the disciplinary system, although this too is less commonly a function of the personnel department in new private enterprises. Again, closer inspection shows that the administration of the disciplinary system is primarily the responsibility of line managers and the role of the personnel department is usually limited to registering disciplinary violations and punishments that have been reported to them. Like personnel selection, discipline is a function which line managers jealously guard for themselves because it is an indispensable lever in their management of their subordinates which they wish to use with discretion. At the same time, senior management may want to tighten discipline and to this end the personnel department (or the security service) may be instructed to organise a clamp-down, which might involve tighter checks on punctuality and sobriety at the entrance or searches and checks on early departure when people leave work, or might even involve raids on workplaces to make sure that disciplinary rules are being maintained. However, many line managers object strongly to being compelled to *'wash our dirty linen in public'* (**SM1**) and such interventions provoke antagonism on the part of line managers. From their point of view, all disciplinary problems should be resolved within the shop or department *'by our own methods'* and only irresoluble problems referred upwards.

---

[1] In fact fixed-term contracts are no less secure than the traditional permanent contracts (Simon Clarke and Inna Donova, 'Internal mobility and labour market flexibility in Russia', *Europe-Asia Studies* 51(2), 1999: 213–43).

Conflict resolution

In their fourth function of 'receiving complaints and resolving conflicts' the personnel department is also responsible more for registration than for decision-making. Staff of the personnel department often participate in commissions, such as the labour dispute commission or the commission negotiating the collective agreement, but their participation in these bodies is either purely nominal or at best to take the minutes and record the decisions. Again it is the heads of the subdivisions that play the main role here, and they certainly would not tolerate the active intervention of personnel managers in dealing with these issues, despite the fact that they are a central feature of the management of personnel.

Where there is a trade union organisation in the enterprise, its role in dispute resolution varies, depending on its degree of activism, but the trade union is almost universally integrated into the management structure, so that even in the best of cases it serves as mediator rather than pressing the interests of its members. In these cases the role of the trade union as a branch of enterprise management further undermines the status and role of the personnel department.

Training

The next most important functions are training and the appraisal of workers and specialists, features which again underline the varied but limited role of personnel departments in such activities. Training encompasses a wide range of activities and throws the role of the personnel department into clear relief. It is important to note that the scale of training has declined considerably since soviet times, when every enterprise was given a plan for training which it had to achieve, even if much of that training was a formality. Nevertheless, following the collapse of the soviet system of training there has been some recovery as enterprises have developed training systems that are appropriate to their present and anticipated future needs. In most enterprises training provision is *ad hoc*, to meet the immediate training needs of particular individuals, primarily those newly hired or promoted, but some larger enterprises, particularly those integrated into holding companies, have more systematic training programmes.

At the minimum an enterprise will have a system of on-the-job training, perhaps associated with a system of apprenticeship, for newly hired workers. This kind of minimal organisation of training, found predominantly at small enterprises and those with simple technology, does not involve the personnel department at all. The main task is to provide the workers with the necessary skill and socialise them into the workplace: *'young people need two or three weeks to get into the job, more experienced workers help the young ones'*. The resources for the reproduction of apprenticeship are the social and ideological resources of mutual assistance and mutual benefit handed down from soviet times. Responsibility for this is usually laid on the lowest level of line management (foremen), who either provide the training themselves or find a tutor from among the experienced workers.

In most cases apprenticeship is pretty formal and the tutor is not paid, or is paid only a very small bonus, providing very little instruction. In practice it seems that the new worker is usually left to work things out for him or herself and the main function of the tutor is precautionary, to make sure that the apprentice does not make mistakes which could lead to serious wastage, breakages, accidents or injuries. *'The specialisms are such that no particular training is necessary. You simply need to explain once or twice on a concrete example, and the person can already work independently'* (foreman, *MZ5*).

Specialists might be inducted into their jobs in a similar way, or might be expected to find any necessary training courses for themselves.

Even where there is a more extensive training programme, it is sometimes still under the control of line management and the production services. The technical services develop training programmes, determine the categories to be trained and the duration and forms of monitoring. The personnel managers carry out the organisational work, gathering the trainees, preparing the training premises and materials, organising lecturers and so on. For example, at *KhZ3* there is an intensive training programme controlled by the heads of subdivisions and the general director, while training at *MZ4* is controlled by the chief engineer. In these cases the personnel department at best administers and then records the outcomes: who has undertaken what training, where and with what results (diploma, certificate and so on). Sometimes this provides the basis for somebody's promotion or for assigning them to the 'personnel reserve' as a candidate for promotion when a vacancy arises.

More generally, however, where there is a more intensive training programme there is a specialist, or even a whole section, in the personnel department with responsibility for training. At most of our larger case-study enterprises there is a comprehensive training programme which includes initial training courses (in health and safety, technical skills and so on), sometimes combined with on-the-job training or apprenticeship, and further training courses for workers and specialists.

Training for specialists takes a wide range of forms. In some enterprises specialists are expected to find and take training courses under their own initiative, sometimes at least partially paid for by the enterprise. In other enterprises there is a strictly regulated training programme which defines who will be trained, in what, where and by whom. This training is also generally controlled by technical and line managers. Staff of the personnel department, particularly where there are specialists with responsibility for training, may participate in deciding which training institutions to use, but usually their role is still primarily that of registration (drawing up lists of those to undertake training, recording the outcomes) and organisation (finding trainers, organising their hiring, organising premises, examinations and so on, or booking places and making arrangements for travel and accommodation where training is provided elsewhere).

Training sometimes also plays a motivating role, for example at the telecommunications company *TK1*: *'some employees have been sent on* *expensive training – this is at the same time an incentive. They give us good travel expenses: a hotel up to 1,500 roubles and $20 a day for subsistence'* (engineer). Particularly successful employees are selected, with the agreement of their immediate managers: *'This concerns specialists and engineers. When they achieve a certain degree of success in their work, the employee can be sent to another city, to another division of another enterprise for training'* (director).

In larger enterprises, particularly those which are part of holding structures, the personnel department may be more centrally involved in the organisation and provision of training, although even here training may be under the control of production departments, which identify training needs and the means of satisfying them. At *MZ2*, for example, there is a systematic training programme and the personnel department does not simply record and service the programme; it has a special section with five staff which is also responsible for drawing up the lists of people to be trained and laying down the schedule of the training programme. The same is true of another large enterprise which is part of a holding structure, *MetZ3*. At *TF1*, in sharp contrast with our earlier cases, the head of the personnel department has even managed to wrest control of the form of training of new employees from a powerful shop chief.

The knitting factory *TF1* is very atypical of light industry enterprises in that it has a deliberate and precisely formulated personnel strategy and the head of the personnel department is one of the most influential members of the senior management team, a member of the Board of Directors who is involved in all strategic decision-making. She has worked at the enterprise for twenty years, initially in preparatory production, and has been head of the personnel department since 1989. Her main priority is to reduce labour turnover in order to overcome an acute shortage of seamstresses. This led her to insist on organising brigades of novices, despite the opposition of the chief of the sewing shop who wanted to retain the traditional form under which the novices were attached to brigades of experienced workers. In the opinion of the shop chief, work in a skilled brigade allows young people to get involved in production faster, but the basic argument of the chief of the personnel service was that young people first need to adapt and get used to the work before joining already established collectives. *'During the adaptation period we try to hold them together. We organise excursions around the factory, meetings with representatives of the trade union, with the economist, with the chief of the labour department. This is to give answers to questions which arise for workers in the first two to three months of work. I have noticed that when people undergo group training, it helps more'* (chief of the personnel service). The chief of sewing production still does not share this point of view, but the head of the personnel service prevailed.

In some holding companies there has been a resurrection of the soviet practice under which training is undertaken in accordance with the plans drawn up centrally by the personnel department of the holding company, which decides which categories of people will take which courses. In this case the technical and line management of the subsidiary may be almost completely divorced from this process, whose implementation is the responsibility of the personnel department of the subsidiary which is responsible for selecting people for training and implementing the decisions made above. The line managers can make special requests for particular training courses to be provided, but it is still the personnel department of the holding company which makes the final decision as to whether or not to meet those requests, no doubt after consulting technical specialists in the headquarters.

At *KhZ1*, which is part of a foreign-owned holding company, the Russian headquarters draws up a personnel development plan each year, specifying how many people will undertake what training, with an associated budget. Requests for training are submitted to the personnel department by the heads of shops or subdivisions on the basis of recommendations from foremen. The personnel department determines where the training will be undertaken and payment is from the enterprise budget. The shop chief has his own budget, which includes an item for training. If it is necessary to increase the sum allocated to training, a request has to be submitted to senior management, explaining the need for additional training.

Appraisal

Appraisal of workers and specialists is ranked alongside training among the functions of the personnel department. Appraisal consists of both evaluation and attestation. The former involves evaluation of the current activity of employees over a particular period in order to obtain information about the use of human resources in the enterprise or organisation. Attestation is a qualifying procedure, the aim of which is to award or confirm the skill grade of the employee.

Formalised procedures of evaluation, in the sense described above, are hardly ever found in Russian enterprises. This does not mean that there is no evaluation of the work of the organisation at all, but it is undertaken mainly on the basis of data about discipline (offences, reprimands, rewards and so on) and task fulfilment, which is reflected in pay, and also on the basis of informal relations (relations with colleagues, management and so on). This system is hardly adequate to provide an objective evaluation of the activity of staff, let alone to get an overall evaluation of the use of human resources as a whole in the organisation. Disciplinary records are particularly misleading because disciplinary control is usually based on informal agreements between line managers and staff about the limits of acceptable behaviour, not on centralised rules and standards of discipline. Pay similarly does not always provide a reliable basis for evaluation because it does not so much reflect real effort as attachment to a particular post or professional category and at the same time the degree of loyalty to the line manager. In these circumstances the evaluation of the staff member is essentially informal and its main vehicle is the immediate manager of the staff member. This means that there is simply no general and comparable information about the current activity of the staff of various subdivisions, that is, about the use of human resources in the organisation. It is dispersed among the low-level managers.

The inadequacy of the methods of evaluation of the use of human resources in the enterprise is in marked contrast to the rigorous methods, inherited from the soviet period, for accounting for the use of material resources. Every enterprise maintains a balance sheet which provides a regular, centralised evaluation of the use of material assets and is comparable with that of other enterprises. It is impossible to imagine a system of accounting for material assets (materials, equipment, wages, monetary resources and so on) in which the head of each subdivision maintains accounts in whatever way suits him or her so that it is impossible to have any generalised evaluation of the use of resources at the level of the enterprise. Although it is a commonplace to declare that people are the most valuable resource of the organisation, and every enterprise has a fully developed system of accounting for things, there is no centralised, formalised procedure for accounting for the current use of human resources. The implication is obvious: just as under the soviet system, under capitalism in Russia it is more important to account for the use of material assets than to account for the expenditure of labour – things are more important than people. Without a proper system of accounting for material assets, the company will suffer serious losses from the misuse of equipment and from theft and embezzlement. The Tax Inspectorate imposes immediate heavy penalties for the absence of a balance sheet. By contrast, the penalties imposed by the State Labour Inspectorate for violations of the Labour Code are insignificant. People can usually be replaced, so there is much less need for rationality and economy in relation to employees. This is why one finds the wasteful expenditure of labour and use of human resources everywhere. But while the wasteful use of raw materials is an immediate loss, the wasteful use of human resources incurs almost no immediately obvious costs. Employers can fine workers for production losses; they can pay at a lower rate for overtime, or even not pay at all; they can pay unskilled wages to highly skilled workers. It is only when the enterprise finds itself facing acute shortages of skilled and reliable employees that it even begins to turn its attention to the more rational use of human resources.

Attestation is a very common procedure and is part of the system of training and promotion, although sometimes it is undertaken systematically, without any reference to training. In soviet times attestation was carried out on a large scale, but it was either a purely formal procedure or a means of getting rid of undesirable employees, and the situation has not changed much since then.[1] Thus, at *TK1* attestation is seen by management as a means not only of

---

[1] S. Shekshnia has expressed similar concerns about the procedures of assessment and appraisal in his book *Kak Eto Skazat' Po-Russki: (современные методы управления персоналом в современной России)*, Москва: ООО «Журнал «Управление персоналом», ЗАО «Бизнес-школа «Интел-Синтез», 2003.

increasing competition between staff but also of getting rid of 'unsuitable' people, while at *ET1* attestation is used to identify people for redundancy.

The attestation of managers and specialists is still conducted in the traditional way – a commission is established, procedures drawn up (plans for interviews, questionnaires, examinations, tests and so on) and employees are put through them in turn. Often the results of the attestation are reviewed only as a formality, but just as often they may be used to carry out so-called 'unpopular measures'. For example, it might be a means of introducing a general reduction of grades and corresponding reduction of pay (*ET2*) or for dismissing particular employees (ET1). Only in rare cases does the system of attestation have a more positive role to play. At *MZ2*, for example, where management systems have been modified according to western models, there is a system of attestation for both workers and specialists which is closely related to the training procedures, with the personnel department drawing up the procedure and actively participating in it. But in the majority of cases the attestation commission consists of functional and line managers who make the major decisions and define the parameters of attestation.

Manpower planning

The personnel managers of about half our case-study enterprises reported that they participate in labour force planning, but this seems to be a substantial exaggeration of their role. Our case studies showed that personnel strategy and labour force planning are closely related. The minimal form of personnel planning is adaptive reaction to the changing situation. Most commonly this is a response to requests from heads of subdivisions complaining of a shortage of staff, which happens more often in small enterprises. Sometimes reactions to immediate needs are accompanied by requests to plan ahead, for example to replace anticipated retirees. Only one-third of personnel directors reported that their enterprise had a personnel strategy, which would imply that they undertake some labour force planning, while two-thirds reported that the strategy at their enterprise was determined by the director, which would suggest that these enterprises have a strategy which exists only in the head of the enterprise director. So it would seem that in the majority of cases the personnel department does not participate in labour force planning.

The most commonly used means of planning and regulating the size of the labour force is the staff list, which enumerates the authorised posts in each subdivision. The staff list may be altered from time to time as a result of changing technological or production needs, economic pressure to get rid of surplus staff or instructions from the personnel department of the holding company. But whatever the reasons for the change, the enterprise personnel department plays a subordinate role, even if their opinion has some influence on decision-making.

However, our case studies also include some enterprises in which the personnel department does play a significant role in the personnel planning process, being involved not only in labour force planning but even in developing the personnel strategy of the enterprise. For example, in *TF1* the head of the personnel service has considerable authority and conducts a centralised personnel policy. Large enterprises are more likely to have an overall personnel strategy as part of a centralised system of management and in this case the personnel department is likely to play a significant role in developing and implementing this strategy. Labour force planning is most likely to be found as an accompaniment to a strategy of 'rejuvenation' of the labour collective, to bring in more young employees, which we will discuss below.

Wage policy

Traditionally the personnel department in soviet enterprises was not involved in wage-setting. This was the responsibility of the department of labour and wages (OTiZ), which was part of the economic service. In many of our case-study enterprises this situation persists today, but in some cases the department of labour and wages, or the relevant specialists, have been transferred to the personnel department. This does not necessarily imply any recognition on the part of senior management of the importance of personnel management and correspondingly an increased significance for the personnel department. In the best of cases it is the result of a rationalisation of the management structure, but a common feature of this change is that the status of the staff of the department of labour and wages has fallen as a result of their transfer to the personnel department. For example, at *SM1* the department of labour and wages was dismantled and its chief transferred to the personnel department into the post of engineer. On the one hand, her administrative duties were expanded as she took on the work formerly done by three people who had previously been in her department but, on the other hand, the shop normsetters were removed from her responsibility and made responsible to the shop chiefs.

Overall, then, this analysis of the functions of the personnel department leads to the conclusion that in the bulk of enterprises the personnel department is still primarily engaged in registration, recording the decisions taken by other services and other levels of management. The personnel management functions are basically decentralised and divided between various groups of managers. Decisions relating to personnel are usually taken by line managers. Sometimes, particularly in new private enterprises, these functions are carried out by senior management. The personnel department makes decisions about a very narrow range of issues and its decisions are usually only preliminary or recommendatory. This situation is the result of a number of factors, but the most important are the low priority accorded to personnel matters and the leverage of the shop chiefs.

First, personnel management is not regarded as a priority direction of management activity. Labour costs constitute only a small proportion of total production costs, so there are few savings to be made from the more efficient use of labour power and the priority for cost reduction is to reduce energy costs and wastage. The principal barriers to the growth of the enterprise are considered to be presented by the technical capacity and the degree of depreciation of the plant and equipment, on the one hand, and the market, on the other, so the priority for the allocation of funds is maintenance and repair of equipment and investing in sales and marketing. Responsibility for the effective use of labour power can be left in the hands of the shop chiefs, who know the capacity and requirements of their own production units.

Second, shop chiefs are very jealous of their powers in their own domain and resist attempts to interfere in the management of their shops. Thus, for example, they insist on their right to decide whom to hire for positions in their shops and to maintain discipline and to handle conflicts on their own initiative, without outside interference. Even if the senior management or the holding company decides to impose uniform personnel policies and practices throughout the enterprise, the personnel department rarely has the authority to override the opposition of shop chiefs, so these policies have to be imposed by more authoritative departments or directly by the general director.

Typology of personnel management systems

Having identified the personnel managers and outlined their functions, we can stand back and take a more systematic view of personnel management systems. We can draw up a typology of personnel management systems in contemporary Russian enterprises on the basis of two factors. The first criterion is the existence of personnel management as a specialised management function, which is taken to be indicative of the significance attached to personnel management in the enterprise. The second criterion is the degree of centralisation of the personnel management function. Centralisation does not necessarily imply a rigidly hierarchical management system, because it is quite compatible with the delegation of authority. There is a degree of interdependence between these two factors because as the management function becomes more specialised there is a tendency for it also to become more centralised.

Non-specialised personnel management

The first type that one can distinguish is the non-specialised system of personnel management. This type is common at small enterprises and its main feature is the almost complete absence of a separate personnel department and concentration of personnel management functions in the hands of a particular group of managers, usually middle management. One-third of our case-study enterprises did not have a personnel department at all, and one-sixth were only in the process of establishing one. Even fewer new private enterprises, which tend to be smaller, had a personnel department. The personnel service then consists of one person who combines these duties with others.

At the new private fish-processing factory *RZ1*, the personnel manager is also the lawyer who draws up contracts, represents the company in legal proceedings and so on. At *KhDK1* there is no personnel department, but there is a senior personnel specialist who is subordinate to the general director and who is responsible not only for personnel work but also for other aspects of record-keeping, drawing up enterprise orders and even basic accounting tasks. At the construction company *ST2* there is no personnel department as such. One person fulfils the functions of the personnel department and the department of labour and wages. In the senior management circle they say openly that she was hired as 'the general director's person'. She was originally hired as the health and safety engineer and was transferred to the position of head of the personnel department four years ago when the former head left. After a year she was also given responsibility for labour and wages, which merely involves monitoring the calculation of wages by the site foremen. At the moment she is completing technical university, reading for a degree in management. At *KhBK1* the personnel department comprises one person who was appointed a year ago and who previously worked as the director's secretary. The new personnel director has no written job description, but is directly subordinate to the general director and her responsibilities were agreed verbally. She is currently following a course in personnel management. But here, in personnel management as in other management areas, *'everything comes from the director'*.

In these cases the personnel manager has a limited set of functions to fulfil; as a rule these are dealing with hiring, firing and simple forms of training. There is no planning, appraisal or any more complex responsibilities. The heads of subdivisions do not need anybody else interfering. As they see it, they know everything about how their people work, who needs training, who should be dismissed and who should be paid how much. The heads of subdivisions may simultaneously carry out the registration functions, keeping records and guiding the personal affairs of their staff.

This is the form of universal, comprehensive, unspecialised management which is found in small enterprises, where the manager can keep track of all their staff. The lack of specialisation in this case is found not only in relation to personnel management. Economics, marketing, technology and supply are all handled by one or a few people who are responsible for everything and manage everything. While the enterprise is small and the director can keep everything under their personal control such a system does not give rise to any particular problems. But as the enterprise grows it is necessary to move beyond this universalism and towards specialisation. Otherwise 'unmanaged zones' appear at the enterprise, which simply escape the attention and effort of managers who are responsible for everything. Problems associated with the transition from unspecialised to specialised management arise because this requires a redistribution of authority. This means that 'universal' managers have to give up some familiar functions and construct relations of subordination. This gives rise to opposition and often the transition from universalism to specialisation is long drawn out and the number of 'unmanaged zones' increases. This is especially difficult in the case of new private enterprises, where the owner-director has to reconcile him or herself to delegating authority to hired managers.

Decentralised personnel management

The majority of medium and large enterprises use a decentralised system of personnel management. The essence of this system is that here, despite the existence of a personnel department (whatever it may be called), almost all decisions relating to personnel management are taken outside the department. The personnel department primarily carries out registration functions; sometimes personnel managers have the right to an advisory voice but no more than that. The personnel management functions are dispersed between several centres. Hiring, firing and some training are carried out by the chiefs of shops and structural subdivisions. Planning of the staff, the parameters, content and schedule of appraisal, the scale of redundancies, changes in wages, hiring and training of senior specialists and managers are the prerogatives of the senior management of the enterprise. The financial and economic services might also be centres of decision-making; they determine the need for and scale of hiring and also of redundancies. The economic service pays a great deal of attention to the question of the scale of payments and also the development of the system of wages and bonuses. The personnel department is only involved in recording, formalising and implementing decisions made elsewhere. The decentralised model differs from the unspecialised model in that here there is already a specialised management, but the main defect of such management is the absence of a unified approach to the management of human resources.

Centralised personnel management

The third model is centralised and implies the existence of a single centre for personnel management and the transfer of most of the personnel management functions to this specialised service. Above all this model is found at large enterprises with modern technology and enterprises which are part of vertically integrated holding companies. In the latter case centralisation is often a feature of the policy of the holding company. Personnel management is taken more seriously in large holding companies not because their labour power is more expensive, but because it is a feature of the centralisation and co-ordination of all aspects of management decision-making. In these cases, many personnel functions are centralised, but in the personnel department of the holding company rather than in that of the enterprise. Thus the personnel policy in two-thirds of our enterprises which are part of holding companies is determined by the holding company and almost one-third of enterprises which are part of holding companies do not even have their own personnel department. These centralised services take many significant decisions: they determine the number and skill composition of the labour force, the size of the wage fund, the directions and scale of training, redundancies and many other functions. Neither the personnel department of the enterprise nor line management nor even senior management of the enterprise has any significant influence on the decisions taken. The systems of personnel management in holding companies therefore tend to reproduce or reintroduce typical soviet systems and practices, with the holding company taking the place of the ministry.

The personnel department at *KhZ1*, which is part of a foreign-owned holding company, has been combined with the department of labour and wages, which has four staff: a senior specialist and an economist for wages and payments, an inspector for personnel (senior inspector of the personnel department) and an engineer for staff training. The department has responsibility for all the 'traditional' personnel work, but it is immediately subordinate to the personnel manager of the holding company, so the enterprise does not take any decisions about personnel management independently, but is completely subordinate to the holding company in its personnel policy.

The outcome also tends to reproduce the deficiencies of the soviet system, as the centralisation of personnel management in the holding company fails to take into account the particular features of individual enterprises, which are therefore likely merely to follow the soviet tradition of paying lip service to the instructions coming from above. For example, in one enterprise the personnel department responded to the strict formal demands of the holding company by drawing up documents reporting on the implementation of the toughest and most laborious tasks, for example carrying out a quick comprehensive appraisal of specialists, managers and workers, while either failing to carry out the tasks at all, or reducing them to the minimum.

A few large enterprises (*MetZ2* and *MZ2*) which are not part of holding companies conduct a personnel management policy which is co-ordinated with technical and economic policies and is given equal weight to them. In these enterprises the personnel department conducts sophisticated analytical work not only relating to current tasks but also to future prospects. Even at these exceptional enterprises not all personnel management functions are concentrated in the personnel department, but such key functions as hiring, training and motivation are centralised in these cases. One other enterprise (*TF1*) follows a similar centralised policy and the personnel department is actively involved in social policy, even though it is not a large or modern enterprise. In this case the reason for adopting such a system can be attributed to the personality and career history of the head of the personnel department, as discussed above (p. 137), a reminder that such features can contribute to variations around the primary patterns we have identified.

Personnel management in new private enterprises

The characteristics of the labour force of new private enterprises are rather different from those of traditional enterprises. The new private enterprises that grew up in the 1990s hired the more enterprising staff who had left former state enterprises, as well as young people who were already ideologically adapted to work in a market environment in sharp contrast to the paternalistic employment relationship of traditional enterprises. The employment relationship in new private enterprises is one in which the employee is expected to work hard and conscientiously in exchange for a wage, on pain of summary dismissal. For this reason new private enterprises are much less likely to develop the elaborate systems of punishments and rewards characteristic of soviet and post-soviet enterprises.

However, this does not mean that new private enterprises have made any radical innovations in personnel management. Rather, they continue in a simplified and harsher form the practices characteristic of traditional employers. They do not have any elaborated personnel management strategy, merely a few general ideas about their desire to improve the production process and, as in the past, the personnel management functions are dispersed throughout the enterprise between line managers and functional services. Personnel management tends to be the last aspect of management to which the directors of new private enterprises turn their attention, and a personnel manager is the last specialist manager to be hired. Surveys consistently show that the predominant concerns of new private enterprise directors are sales and marketing, on the one hand, and technical equipment, on the other. In most new private enterprises the role of personnel management is restricted to the traditional clerical functions of recording staff details and is combined with another management function or is the responsibility, for example, of the director's secretary. Meanwhile, the management of labour relations is left largely to the discretion of line managers.

Another feature of the management of labour relations in new private enterprises, in comparison with traditional enterprises, is the minimal elaboration of internal formal rules and so the unequivocally informal regulation of labour relations, with a very high degree of managerial discretion. Where rules are developed, it seems that these are primarily for the sake of external appearances and not for the purposes of internal management. For example, many new private enterprises have formalised quality control procedures, even obtaining ISO certification because it is increasingly required to obtain contracts, but this does not imply that these procedures are implemented in practice.

Employees in new private enterprises are much less likely than those in other enterprises to have a formalised job description, almost half of our new private sector employee respondents either having no job description or having been given one only verbally. This implies that these employees can be moved freely between tasks and locations and will be required to do whatever management instructs them to do, providing managers with the flexible labour force they need to cope with the uneven demands of production. The director of a printing and publishing enterprise (*T1*) was quite frank about his reasons for not providing a written job description:

> *'People often ask me to write them down, but I say to them "This is a little list to cover your back. I will never write such a list for you". What does writing a job description mean? In a large enterprise they are necessary. In our small enterprise, if we write them either a person will do everything which, in principle, is not possible, or he will say: "But that is not in my job description"'.*

The majority of workers we spoke to also felt that it was to their advantage not to have a formal job description, primarily on the grounds that everything was settled informally in any case, and that while they would be tied by the terms of a contract, there would be no way in which they could enforce the employer's compliance.

In our case-study enterprises there was no significant difference in the form of contract provided by new private as opposed to traditional enterprises. Despite the increased possibilities of hiring on temporary and fixed-term contracts provided by amendments to the labour legislation, more than four-fifths of all employees are still hired on the traditional basis of permanent, indefinite hire. Three of the case-study new private enterprises also used temporary hire, with contracts of less than a year, but these affected only a small number of employees and their use was seen more as a symbol of a progressive market-oriented business. As one director put it, *'we simply used the experience of other serious businesses'* (**MK2**).

The fixed-term contracts are usually on the same terms as regular contracts and are normally transformed into a permanent contract when they expire, so employees regard them as regular contracts and often don't even know that they have a temporary contract. Indeed, most employees do not know what are the terms of their contract and do not regard them as significant, the traditional entry in their labour book being much more important. As in the case of job descriptions, employees did not think that a written contract gave them any advantages since their terms and conditions of employment were in reality determined within the framework of informal relations with the employer. A written contract could only be to the advantage of the employer:

> *'An agreement, in the end, is written mainly in the interests of the boss'. 'He is the boss, if it is not profitable for him, he will not observe the conditions. In which case he will say: "if you don't like it – go, leave". Where can you turn? Nobody can control him'* (workers, **MZ7**).

Whatever the terms of the contract and the guarantees of the law, particularly in a small enterprise with no trade union, the employer can get rid of an employee without any difficulty whenever he wants to. In some cases (for example, **MZ4**), employees are required to sign an undated letter of resignation at the same time as they hired, so that they can be dismissed without compensation at any time.

From passive to active personnel policy

During the 1990s enterprises were preoccupied with survival and in those conditions managers 'do not see personnel management as a problematic area demanding special effort on the part of management'.[1] It is only when circumstances change and recovery begins to get under way that managers start

---

[1] Дудченко О. Н. и Мытиль А. В., 'Зависимость формирования новых правил трудовых отношений от позиции руководства и избранной им стратегии', *Становление трудовых отношений в постсоветской России*, (Под ред. В. Ядов), Москва: Академический проект, 2004, p. 113.

thinking about personnel policy as an important aspect of the adaptation of the enterprise to the changing environment so that the enterprise can best take advantage of the opportunities presented to it. However, the degree to which personnel policy becomes a focus of attention depends on a wide range of factors.

One extremely important factor is the comparative advantage that the enterprise enjoys in stabilising and improving its economic situation in a market environment. From the traditional soviet production-oriented perspective, the priority is the maintenance and renewal of the production technology, and those enterprises with the most up-to-date or best-preserved facilities (not such a high degree of depreciation of the machines, because *'we looked after them'* (*KhDK1*)) were in the best situation to benefit when demand began to recover. Because of high fixed costs and a substantial amount of idle plant, the key to survival and eventual success was to restore the level of capacity working rather than to reduce current costs.

Those facing a stagnant market may see the secret of future success as lying in engineering a change in the product range and developing a new sales programme. The competitive success of the firm in these cases depends mostly on technological decisions.

The bakery *KhBK1* was faced with the stagnation of its core market for bread products and limited profitability resulting from the regulation of bread prices by the local administration. It therefore developed new types of fancy breads and pastries which sold to the growing middle-class market and were not subject to price control.

MZ1 produces electrical equipment and experienced a severe decline during the 1990s. Following its acquisition by a holding company it used its own resources of highly skilled design and production staff to develop new products, using the existing antiquated machinery, which enabled it to conquer new and more profitable markets.

If the enterprise is not so well endowed technologically it may seek the way forward in marketing as a way of side-stepping problems in the technology and organisation of production.

The cement factory *SM1* was a relatively low-volume producer with outdated equipment which was acquired out of bankruptcy by outside owners in 2002. The new owners concentrated on expanding the market by developing new products, such as specialised breeze-blocks, and new kinds of packaging, such as 25-kilogram sacks and 'Big Bags' of one tonne capacity for retail and wholesale customers respectively, to supplement the traditional 50-kilo packs. The Big Bags are very attractive for wholesale customers and will sharply reduce loading times while significantly reducing the labour cost of packing.

In all of these situations the enterprise's development strategy does not involve any consideration of questions of personnel management, until the stage at which it becomes necessary to find additional workers. Personnel management can be left to shop chiefs, as an aspect of their management of the production process, as has traditionally been the case, and no special personnel management policies are necessary. As the director of the bread and pasta combine **KhBK2** noted: *'There is work with personnel but it is implicit. The enterprise works better and people's pride in the enterprise grows'.*

Across our case-study enterprises, a number of factors can be identified as providing significant stimuli to the adoption of new personnel management practices. The first is the pressure of competition, which forces the management to review its practices more carefully. *'When imports appeared, and our competitors, well here they began to stir. In this respect we also began to stir'* (**ETZ1**). Many enterprises have had to consider their personnel management practices as a result of a decision to seek ISO 9000 quality certification, which is required by many major Russian contractors and facilitates access to export markets. *'Really, the active "team" work of those managers responsible for personnel work and for quality is related not so much to the organisational structure as to the priority tasks of the enterprise – ISO certification and the reform of the payment system'* (**KhBK1**). In **ET1** *'the work of the personnel management service is drawn up in the framework of the general quality strategy and policy'.* ISO certification requires the institutionalisation of a comprehensive set of personnel management policies, although of course whether or not these policies are actually put into practice is another question.

Significant technological developments also call forth new initiatives in the sphere of personnel management. The acquisition of new equipment and increasing production entails the selection and training of staff to operate the equipment. At **ET1** they face a problem of a shortage of skilled personnel which has arisen as a result of the growth in the volume of production and technical re-equipment: *'If we do not keep pace and . . . it is necessary to introduce new equipment, or there are some urgent orders, then the number increases . . . production at the present moment demands that people should have the appropriate training and not just middle education'* (ET1). If the equipment is imported, it may be necessary to send operators and technicians abroad for the appropriate training. Of course, many enterprises are still working with equipment that was installed long ago, whose operation requires experience more than high levels of technical knowledge and so does not impose any particular demands on personnel management.

Integration into a holding company does not necessarily lead to significant changes in personnel management practice. In itself, integration into a holding company and subordination to the personnel policies handed down by the holding company is a return to the traditional centralised system of management. Only if the holding company has a positive policy of transforming personnel management practices, and appoints a new personnel manager to implement such a policy, do we see significant change.

The aims of personnel policy

For the majority of enterprises not only the methods but also the aims of personnel policy remain very traditional: to recruit and retain the labour force required (*'the retention of experienced, skilled and loyal staff'* (**KhZ1**)) and to ensure the effective use of that labour force by maintaining high levels of motivation. These aims are generally achieved not through a coherent personnel policy formulated and implemented by an authoritative personnel department, but by a combination of employment, wage, social and disciplinary policies formulated and propagated by the senior management or the holding company and a fragmented and decentralised system of personnel management, with the personnel department, economic services, line managers and the trade union all playing a role. Much of the policy and practice of personnel management in the vast majority of enterprises is left to the discretion of line management, who make the decisions about hiring and firing, about disciplinary sanctions, about the disposition of the labour force, about work schedules and working hours, and who often play a role in determining the size of wages and in the allocation of non-wage social and welfare benefits. These aspects of personnel management are all regarded as an integral part of the line manager's responsibility for ensuring the smooth achievement of its tasks by the relevant subdivision.

The elements of personnel policy which tend to be articulated by senior management primarily concern the employment policy of the enterprise, determining the number to be employed, the desirable characteristics of employees and cultivating appropriate labour motivation. The priorities in these respects depend to a considerable extent on the inter-related factors of the character of the labour force inherited from the past, the production technology, the economic prospects and the form of ownership of the enterprise.

Many traditional enterprises lost a significant proportion of their labour force in the crisis years of the 1990s. Those hardest hit were left at the end of the decade only with those who could not get work anywhere else, by reason of age, infirmity, demoralisation or a poor disciplinary record. The priority of these enterprises was to raise morale, improve labour discipline and motivation and to recruit experienced and reliable former workers and promising younger employees to bring the labour force up to strength.

NKhZ2 was established in 2001 by outside investors buying part of what had been an integrated chemical complex which had declined sharply during the 1990s and had been at a standstill for two years, with only a skeleton staff retained to maintain the equipment and the remainder being sent on administrative leave. The neighbouring plant produced industrial alcohol and drunkenness was a real scourge. *'Turnover was very high. People who stayed here either did not want to look for another job or could not find one because of their weak competitiveness'* (general director). Since getting back on its feet wages have been increased substantially and the labour force has doubled, but turnover is still high, primarily as a result of drinking and other disciplinary violations, and the enterprise still suffers from labour shortages.

Many traditional enterprises were able to recover after 1998, despite their antiquated equipment and lack of investment funds, because they still had a reserve of loyal and reliable workers who had not left by reason of their age and their loyalty and attachment to the enterprise and who would continue to work hard to overcome all the obstacles for very low wages. This is particularly characteristic of enterprises with a predominantly female labour force in light industry and food processing, many of which have retained their independence because they are not attractive to outside investors or holding companies. The management of these enterprises sees its aim as being above all to secure the reproduction of the enterprise as a productive social organisation. This aim is translated into the priorities of personnel policy: *'to preserve the labour collective'*, *'to preserve the skeleton'*, *'to maintain a fully staffed technological chain'*. As the personnel director of *SM1* put it: *'My strategy is to bring the staff up to strength so that there are not any gaps'*. The general director of *SM4* spelled out his priorities and expressed his pride in his stable collective:

> *'I have one aim – to keep people and for them to get reasonable pay. Although they say that Russians work badly, I know one thing, they pay badly . . . The nucleus is stable: the management staff from the foremen to chief engineer are people who have worked here from seven to twenty years. People do not leave, people work'.*

The heavy reliance of these enterprises on the loyalty and commitment of an experienced labour force means that they attach a high priority to maintaining the stability of the labour collective. This implies a commitment to keeping people employed and enabling them to earn their wages, whatever might be the fluctuations of the production cycle.

The bakery *KhBK1* tries to ensure that all vacancies are filled in the first instance by internal transfer or promotion. *'We try to use internal reserves. If we have an appropriate colleague, why not take him? As far as the workers of the bread shop are concerned, a large part of the labour force there is an internal reserve. We try to change people, rearrange things a bit. If it is necessary. If one person leaves the job completely, we put another one there. If one person is temporarily absent, we put another one there on a temporary basis'*. To replace main workers during the summer they take on students from the neighbouring technical school as temporary workers.

The work of the frozen foods combine *KhDK1*, is very seasonal, with demand for ice-cream in particular being much higher in the summer. The collective is very stable, with 79 per cent of the 500 employees being over 40 and many being of pre-pension and pension age. Shop chiefs use any and every method to try to make sure that there is work for people. This is achieved by the flexible management of labour. *'In winter we have nowhere to put our people. But we also try, we also contrive things. We try things where there is a lot of work but a small output. So here is a 30 gram pack, six people make 500 kilos. And this is good, people work . . . In April we made 100 tonnes of half kilo packets. We also thought where to put people, they had to do something. I said, make some mixtures, they keep for six months even if they lie in the freezer. Then in summer we will not work so intensively because we have the mixtures. We did it. We put a ventilator in the room and made a homemade room and it was minus 44 there, that is, we achieved the same result as in the shop. That is through rationalisation, but nobody thanked us for this, nobody anything. Not a kopek, nothing. And in that way my people worked on mixtures, they earned. All initiative'* (head of the ice-cream shop). Nevertheless, because of the seasonal character of the work they have to lay off some workers temporarily during the winter and they hire a small number of temporary workers in the summer. The latter used to be pensioners, who would return regularly year after year, but now they rely mostly on local technical college students.

In enterprises which are controlled by outsiders or integrated into holding companies, the owners or holding company dictate the personnel policy and they are much more single-minded than inside owners in pursuing narrowly economic objectives. While independent enterprises emphasise the stability of the labour collective and the need to maintain its productive potential, enterprises which have been acquired by outside owners, and particularly by foreign owners, are required to 'optimise the number of staff', which is a euphemism for making staffing cuts in order to reduce costs and increase profitability.

MetZ1 is an advanced tool-making company which was acquired by a foreign owner in 1996. The enterprise employed 1,500 people in 1988 and now employs only 260, with the number being reduced gradually by redundancy so that workers would not enjoy the protection they would qualify for in the event of a 'mass redundancy'. While traditional enterprises still protect the more vulnerable employees (pensioners, single mothers, the disabled) in the event of compulsory redundancy, MetZ1 has consistently sought to keep the most highly skilled and industrious workers, or at least those showing most loyalty to the firm, and targeted the less productive, including pensioners, disabled and pregnant women and single mothers.

Redundancies imposed from above are often a very blunt instrument, since the holding company or the outside owners have little idea of how many people are really required for particular operations.

At *MetZ3* the holding company imposed a strict economy regime focused on a sharp reduction of the labour force, with a freeze on hiring which, in association with high labour turnover, gave rise to serious anomalies. In one shop they urgently needed to check the output after repairs, but there was nobody in the laboratory to do this because the whole shift of three people had left and not been replaced. One of the principles according to which redundancies were to be made was a maximum number of engineering-technical staff to be employed in relation to the number of workers in each subdivision, even though different subdivisions need a different number of engineers, depending on the characteristics of the technological process. As a result of this instruction, specialised technical services like the laboratories, which initially had a higher proportion of specialists, had to cut the number of their specialists by a third to a half, which was not appreciated by the managers: *'the brain of the factory, they have taken the backbone and destroyed it'*. The redundancy policy led to substantially increased workloads for many of those who remained, and the pay rises that had been expected in compensation never materialised, so many of the most skilled workers and specialists left voluntarily, and eventually had to be replaced by new young people. *'There was a big reduction in shop number one. Now they are hiring new people there. But experienced specialists left, and they're turning somersaults with the young people and faults are increasing'*.

Redundancy is one area in which the trade union sometimes tries to intervene on behalf of its members, at least to ensure that legally prescribed procedures are followed. Often, as at *MZ2* and *ET1*, the trade union tries to ensure that those made redundant are found jobs elsewhere in the enterprise.

At the foreign-owned *MetZ1* the trade union president complained that he was not able to defend those selected for redundancy because the management discreetly paid people off to persuade them to go voluntarily. The foreign-owned *KhZ1* has also achieved substantial voluntary redundancies by offering employees more favourable compensation than that prescribed by the law, while foreign-owned *LPZ2* has tried to save on redundancy compensation by reducing staff through a freeze on appointments and liquidation of vacant posts. At the bread and pasta combine *KhBK2*, the director explained his thinking behind a reform of the payment system, which was supposed to link pay to individual productivity: *'I think that those who work badly will leave of their own accord and those who do a lot of work will be interested in staying because they will receive good wages. I hope to reduce the number employed naturally'*. In fact the reform failed to achieve its purpose because it led to insignificant differences in pay, which did not seem to the workers to bear any relation to their individual effort or productivity.

Successful new private enterprises have the problem not of reducing a labour force inherited from soviet times, but of building up a labour force suitable to meet the opportunities confronting them. New private enterprises, like traditional enterprises, are worried about the quality of their human resources, but the rhetoric of their personnel priorities sounds closer to western values.

Their managers do not speak of their workers so much as a 'labour collective', but are more likely to regard them as valuable human capital.

> *'If a person leaves, that is an unambiguous loss of money for the shareholders. An engineer or billing clerk who works at our billing base is not a hot-dog seller on the street with a sanitary book whom you can train in a day. Any member of staff who leaves us is a loss of money, a loss of the intellectual potential of the enterprise. Thus it is important for us to capitalise our human potential'* (finance director **TK1**).

The cultivation of human potential involves the selection and retention of high-skilled competent specialists who have the capacity for training and intensive work, constantly increasing the level of competence of the staff and forming a cohesive collective, able to work *'as a unified mechanism'*. These are the personnel priorities of advanced new private enterprises.[1] In such new private enterprises, employees expect that the management will live up to the market values which they espouse by demonstrating their respect through the pay packet, and paying relatively good wages is a central part of the personnel policy of successful enterprises in the new private sector.

Despite their different objectives, all enterprises face some common problems. Three issues in particular have been the foci of innovation in personnel policy and so merit closer attention. These are the attempt to increase the flexibility of the use of labour, an orientation to the rejuvenation of the labour force and activities to strengthen the motivation and commitment of employees.

Labour flexibility

The soviet employment system was based on a very rigid division of labour, corresponding to the equally rigid soviet production system, in which production tasks were, at least in principle, predictable, repetitive and scientifically organised. Each worker was assigned to a particular task, covered by a precise job description, which he or she was qualified and certified to perform. In practice things never worked like this. The unpredictability of supplies of parts and raw materials, the unreliability of machines and equipment and constant labour shortages meant that the rhythm of production was very uneven and the core workers, on whom the line management relied, always had to double up and fill in for one another. During the 1990s production became even more unstable as enterprises adapted their production plans to fluctuating sales, cash shortages restricted their ability to secure supplies, and the deterioration of plant and equipment was exacerbated by the lack of maintenance and unavailability of spare parts. In order to earn, enterprises and

---

[1] Of course, there are many new private enterprises in trade, catering and domestic manufacture which take advantage of the vulnerability of those without marketable skills to employ them for long hours, on low wages in bad working conditions, but such enterprises fall outside the present study.

their separate shops tried to develop new products which could be made by their skilled workers with their existing materials and equipment, which gave workers an incentive to expand their skills. Many skilled workers retired, died or left to find better jobs elsewhere and their work had to be taken on by colleagues.

With most enterprises working far below capacity, many people could only work a full working day by working in two or more professions, and acquiring an additional trade became the principal means for workers to protect themselves against redundancy and strengthen their position in the labour market. As Veronika Kabalina noted at that time: 'Facing a shortage of labour, they encourage workers to learn related occupations. Thereby they obtain a full interchangeability of workers and that provides greater flexibility in the management of production'.[1] Thus, the spontaneous responses to the crisis of the 1990s led to a great increase of flexibility in the deployment of labour and in the use of working time and to a great increase in the multi-skilling of the labour force as a basis of multi-tasking, which has become the norm in many enterprises. In many cases this is still based on informal agreements between line managers and workers, but in many of our case-study enterprises it has become a specific objective of management policy. This means that such multi-skilling and flexibility are officially registered and attract the payment of a bonus, which increases the incentive for workers to acquire a range of skills.

Three-quarters of personnel managers, particularly in new private enterprises and holding companies, reported that increasing labour flexibility through multi-skilling was an object of their personnel policy.

At the advanced engineering factory, *MZ8*, where the number employed fell from 25,000 in 1988 to a low of 8,000 in 1998, the combination of professions is becoming a more widespread compulsory practice as a result of the shortage of staff. This is possible thanks to the high skill level of the employees. When production worked at full capacity, workers had narrow specialisms, everybody made a particular concrete part or assembled a concrete item. Now many workers combine functions. Skilled workers also quite often have to clean up around the machines in the section. For workers the combination of functions is recorded and recognised officially, but for technicians the combination of functions is usually more informal. Many of these jobs are held by women and do not constitute a full workload on their own. For example, a tooling engineer also works as a loader and as a storekeeper, explaining it thus: *'There are not the people, there is a lot of work, the pay is low. Or here they will ask for a secretary, there for a toolmaker's assistant'.* For being a storekeeper she is paid an additional 40 per cent for the widened zone of responsibility. Another example is when a senior foreman replaces a packer or simply helps her with the packing. Transfers of workers between shops are rare because they are limited by the strong specialisation of shops and production sections, but they may happen in the event of an urgent order or, conversely, a stoppage. Then, in order to

---

[1] Кабалина В. И.. 'Изменение функций и статуса линейных руководителей', *Социологические исследования*, 1998, № 5, p. 40.

maintain the earnings of workers, the shop management tries temporarily to transfer the workers to another section or to put them to work cleaning the territory of the factory and the work areas. Transfers, unlike the combination of professions, are not part of the personnel policy here.

At the electrical equipment factory *ET1*, employees are increasingly required to work beyond their job descriptions or in related professions. This is usually implemented through verbal agreement between the foreman and workers and is not registered in any documents, so does not directly attract any additional pay. If it is officially recorded by the shop chief it is paid an additional 30 per cent of the basic rate for the job, but this is often too little to provide an incentive, in which case the assignment is compulsory. Workers are also sometimes required to carry out subsidiary work: *'Many have to do unnecessary work, which has absolutely nothing to do with their job description, people have to go and mow the lawn, which is not their responsibility'* (foreman).

At the reinforced concrete factory *SM4*, the concrete mixing shop relies very heavily on multi-skilling and the mutual replacement of workers: *'Every one of our workers can carry out another job, at least two or three. Because my workers are permanent and have already mastered many professions'* (shop chief). However, workers are not very keen to take on the additional work because there is little material incentive to do so. According to one of the foremen, *'They do not want to do it, but sometimes there is combination of professions. It is necessary because of the shortage of people. This is, of course, taken into account, but I must say that the incentive is pretty small. The only thing is the KTU* [Coefficient of Labour Participation]*'.* Nevertheless, when it is necessary people help out. *'Everybody behaves with understanding. Everybody knows that if we do not meet the schedule there will not be any wages'* (shop chief). According to the foreman, transfer to another workplace is the main cause of conflict in the shop: *'The shop chief gives instructions, and they take an additional person from another section. People, of course, are unhappy about this, they do not want to do it, "we are comfortable in this work, why are you moving us?" But you say that we are one shop, we all eat from the same pot. . . . There are no special supplements, so there is no enthusiasm. Sometimes we have to turn to the shop chief, we call the worker over and discuss it together. If he still refuses, that is a delicate question, we do not have the right to punish him. We try to reach agreement'* (foreman).

At the foreign-owned detergent factory *KhZ1*, the personnel policy is to encourage the combination of professions. This combination is formalised in writing and a bonus of 30 per cent is paid for the duration of the replacement of an absent worker. To serve as such a replacement, the worker has to have the qualifications and experience to work in that profession. This gives the workers an incentive to acquire an additional profession.

These patterns of multi-tasking or multi-skilling were also combined with the pursuit of other sources of flexibility. New private enterprises (probably less respectful of labour legislation) were much more likely to be seeking to increase the flexibility of working time, while independent traditional enterprises were more likely to be planning to increase the use of temporary workers and those in holding companies to employ people on short-term contracts to fill gaps. More than a third of new private enterprises and holding companies, but no independent traditional enterprises, had a policy of increasing the use of part-time work and/or of sub-contracting.

Rejuvenating the labour force

The collapse of the soviet system of training and the virtual closure of recruitment in the crisis years of the 1990s means that a whole generation of workers is missing from these enterprises, with a substantial proportion of the skilled workers, managers and specialists approaching or beyond pension age. This makes the retention of existing employees and the recruitment and training of a new generation of workers an important priority for many of these enterprises, although one which many of them have not even begun to address. Some enterprises have made a point of their priority of '*rejuvenating the labour collective*' (**KhZ3, MZ2, MZ3, MZ5, MZ8, SM4, MetZ3, TF1, ET2**) and we have already seen a number of examples, such as that of MZ2, which has managed to reduce the average age of the labour force from 46.2 years in 1997 to 42.6 years in 2003 by the methods described above (p. 133). However, it is not always easy to reconcile the retention of experienced personnel with the attraction of young people to the enterprise.

At *MZ5*, for example, the trade union and the personnel department have been pushing for the payment of a bonus for length of service, to facilitate retention, but other senior managers have resisted the proposal because they want to ensure that they can pay good wages to young people. Here the experienced workers are resentful that there appears to be an attempt to push them out and to bring in young people in their place. The same situation has arisen at *TF1*, where they are making a concerted effort to recruit and retain young women.

The motivation and commitment of the labour force

A central thrust of personnel policy in all enterprises is the attempt to strengthen the motivation and commitment of employees. Management tries to ensure '*that people understand that here they are not just little screws – we respect them, we value their work, we value them as specialists, as masters of their trades*' (*MZ2*). Of course, people appreciate it if such respect is demonstrated by a financial commitment in the form of high wages, but most traditional enterprises in the less prosperous engineering, light and food-processing industries producing for the competitive domestic market are not able to pay high wages, so they rely on the reproduction of the traditional soviet work ethic to reinforce the loyalty, motivation and commitment of the labour force. Because of the low pay and severely limited resources, there is very little scope for introducing any innovations in personnel policy in these enterprises, nor is there any possibility of strengthening labour discipline or following a selective hiring policy. These enterprises seek to maintain labour motivation by appealing to traditional soviet labour values, which are reinforced by the reproduction of traditional soviet practices through which the management displays its respect for the workers and fulfils its paternalistic caring role. Obviously, the retention of these traditional practices is most complete in enterprises with a large number of long-serving employees, where the management has remained in place since soviet timesand people simply reproduce the environment which is familiar to them.

> The bakery *KhBK1* had a very low reputation as a place to work in the soviet period, with low wages and predominantly unskilled labour, poor labour discipline, with hard drinking and theft, and heavy reliance on prison labour. Because bread was one of the few products to remain in demand through the 1990s, though consumption still fell by half, the enterprise managed to survive the crisis and continued to pay wages, making it much more attractive to work there. The expansion of the product range, establishment of a marketing department, a chain of retail outlets and a transport section have led to a doubling of the number employed, to 500. The senior managers, who now own a controlling interest in the enterprise, have all worked there for decades – people literally work here until they drop down dead. The personnel policy of the management is to preserve the labour potential of the enterprise by holding on to the core workers who have worked there for a long time, know the specific features of production and are loyal to the management. These 'old' workers preserve the 'traditions' and labour values of the enterprise (traditions which in reality were only forged in the struggle to survive through the 1990s), and transmit them to the newcomers. In order to promote these traditions the management has maintained egalitarian principles of reward and has sought to preserve the social policy of the enterprise unchanged from soviet times, so that one often hears people in the factory proudly proclaim, *'here it is like in socialist times'*. The trade union president commented on the traditional attitude to social protection: *'The enterprise must pay its employees well, but they look after their social protection themselves – that is a purely western structure. We have not moved towards that at the moment'*.

The reproduction (or, in this case, regeneration) of this traditional environment is welcome to the existing labour force, but it does serve as an additional barrier to the recruitment and integration of younger workers, which in the long run is essential to reproduce the labour collective. For young workers the provision of funeral benefits, bonuses for war veterans and sinecures for the elderly and disabled is no substitute for earning a living wage, so in the longer run this strategy to preserve the labour collective may be self-defeating unless it is complemented by the payment of higher wages.

Those enterprises which are integrated into a holding company are more likely to have the resources to pay higher wages and correspondingly to recruit and retain more highly skilled and conscientious workers. This is not so much because they can call on the resources of the holding company as because they tend to be in the more prosperous branches of production, based on the extraction or processing of Russian natural resources (gas, oil, coal, metals, timber) and/or on an advanced technological legacy. These enterprises also tend to rely more heavily on a highly skilled core of the labour force than do independent enterprises in engineering, light industry and food processing, which they can only retain if they do pay a satisfactory wage.

Most successful enterprises do pay wages significantly higher than those prevailing in the local labour market and most holding companies have begun to undertake propaganda activities in the attempt to cultivate a 'modern' type of corporate culture appropriate to the new capitalist system, based on the contractual relationship according to which the employer undertakes an obligation to reward the employee commensurately with the services rendered by him or her. For these enterprises, the principal means of stimulating labour motivation is an incentive payment system, but this has to be reinforced by the cultivation of appropriate labour values.

Traditional soviet labour values and personnel practices which seek to reinforce them are not, however, confined to the less prosperous independent enterprises. We also find cases in which they are retained or are being reintroduced in enterprises which are part of holding companies and even in those which are foreign owned. This is particularly the case in mono-industrial towns, where the enterprise has a smaller pool of labour on which to draw, but is not under such pressure to increase wages because it does not face competition from other employers.

At the open-cast coal mine *U1*, owned by an aggressively capitalist Russian corporation, the owners have deliberately sought to restore the traditional soviet system of production relations. On the one hand, they have re-established an extremely strict centralised administrative system of management, and on the other hand, they have revived and developed the traditional social and welfare system at all the enterprises in the holding company. This was not the spontaneous initiative of the holding company, but was forced upon it. In 2001 the new owner of the holding company sent in a new team of managers who pursued a strict economising strategy centred on reduction in pay levels, reduction of the number employed and liquidation of all 'unproductive expenditure'. This strategy ran into internal management opposition: the head of the wages department at U1 was sacked for resisting the policy of reducing pay but was immediately elected president of the trade union branch, from which post he continued his resistance to the policy of the new management and thereby secured the support of the workers and the regional administration. The display by the workers of their attachment to the traditional social and welfare programmes (and pressure from the regional administration) persuaded the new management that these were a very cost-effective mechanism for securing social integration so that they became enthusiastic proponents of the 'new social and welfare system', which includes subsidised holidays for workers and their families, free workplace health centres and hot meals, sporting, artistic and cultural events and community activities, including the traditional street-cleaning. For some workers the new programme was a sign of a return to the 'good old times' and for others it was an indicator of the economic success of an enterprise which was ready to spend money not only on production but also on social programmes.

A number of researchers have commented on the preservation of the traditional soviet models and forms, with some modernisation through the addition of alternative elements,[1] or at least a change of names. Vladimir Yadov concludes from his research that in practice enterprises continue to use 'old forms in new roles'.[2] The revival of traditional practices is common to many of our case-study enterprises and extends far beyond the resurrection of elements of the traditional paternalistic social and welfare policies. Many enterprises have revived the practices of socialist competition (under new names), of encouraging rationalisation and innovation, of awarding honours, of holding corporate festivals and cultural and sporting events. U1 has revised socialist competition in the form of a competition between its various subsidiary enterprises.

At the giant engineering enterprise *MZ2*, which has seen a western-directed modernisation of its management structures and practices, *'we are reviving many of those traditions which we had in the past, at a qualitatively new level – holding the five-minute meeting [before work begins], assemblies, informing the staff, they have revived the factory newspaper, measures to encourage people, entries in the Honour Book, awards'*. In preparation for the annual professional holiday in 2003 the general director instructed that the names of twenty workers and specialists be entered into the honour book.

At the crane-making enterprise *MZ5* the young general director has reintroduced the factory honour boards and is working out a new regulation on competition with the trade union: *'He says, what did you have before, let's take a look at it. Well, he looked at the regulation on competition, he says, come on let's do it, we decided that we should take it up . . . well at the moment we are thinking about how to stir people up, to support activity. Well, in the past there was socialist competition, people made their commitments. This is all being revived, but it is not finished yet'* (trade union president).

---

[1] Кирдина С. Г., 'Трудовые отношения в редистрибутивных экономиках: случай России', *Политика социального партнерства (российский и зарубежный опыт)* (Отв. ред. М. В. Каргалова, К. Д. Крылов), Москва: ТК «Велби», Изд-во «Проспект», 2003, pp. 37–55.

[2] Ядов В. (ред.) *Становление трудовых отношений в постсоветской России* Москва: Академический проект, 2004, p. 3.

The new foreign owners of *LPZ2* introduced a comprehensive programme to propagate a new corporate culture and strengthen the commitment of employees in an attempt to facilitate the planned intensification of labour. At first this was met with derision by the local managers because, according to the head of the department of corporate relations, it was associated with slogans from the soviet time persuading people of the need to build communism. *'Basically, we already knew all of that. All the soviet principles had simply been given different names: Socialist competition – Labour contest, and rationalisation proposals'* (trade union leader). However, the new culture was quite rapidly embraced by the local senior managers, who saw opportunities to advance their careers. They are able to participate in corporate evenings, participate in seminars locally and abroad, and claim credit for the achievements of the enterprise. As the president of the trade union observed with unconcealed envy: *'they are self-confident and converse with representatives of the holding company in a common language'*. But the new corporate culture has, if anything, widened the gap between management and workers. The workers live in a different world, their corporate events still the traditional ones organised by the trade union. Just as in soviet times, when foreign delegations appear, the foremen teach the workers 'what to say' and to change their overalls.

Across the case-study enterprises, we can conclude that personnel management methods have changed little since soviet times. Most enterprises have no personnel management strategy, and the personnel management function is dispersed, with most significant personnel decisions being made by line managers. Attempts to centralise personnel management decision-making, particularly in the spheres of discipline and hiring, tend to founder on the resistance of line managers, who do their best to subvert or ignore attempts to reduce their authority. The centralisation of personnel management in holding companies tends to suffer from the deficiencies that such centralisation faced in soviet times, of being inflexible and inadequate to the circumstances of the specific enterprise, provoking the same response, of at best a ritualistic performance of the prescribed functions. The most significant change in the employment relation, which is the increased flexibility in the use of labour associated with multi-skilling and multi-tasking, has developed spontaneously, in response to the pressures on production management, rather than as a deliberate personnel management strategy, although in some enterprises it is reflected in the payment system.

The principal innovations in personnel management as far as the personnel department is concerned have been, first, the recognition in a small number of enterprises of an increasingly urgent need to recruit and retain more young people and, second, concerted attempts to improve labour motivation by reinstating some of the traditional elements of the soviet work culture, expressed in various kinds of collective celebrations and events and embodied in various social and welfare benefits.

7   Changes in payment systems

The principles of scientific management that underpinned the soviet system focused on the payment system as the means of encouraging labour motivation and channelling it in desirable directions. A properly designed payment system would provide workers, specialists and managers with the incentives to increase the quantity and quality of their labour. The proper design of the payment system was the preoccupation of labour economists, and proposals to reform the payment system were constantly proclaimed as the means of overcoming the deficiencies of the soviet economic system. The weaknesses of the traditional soviet payment system were considered to lie in its 'levelling' tendencies, which led to an egalitarian wage distribution, and the associated failure effectively to link individual payment to individual effort. However, periodic attempts to reform the payment system to overcome these tendencies were crowned with failure as they disrupted the organisation of production and provoked conflict in the workplace by violating the widely held collectivist values and expectations.[1]

The traditional soviet payment system was based on individual piece-rates for main production workers and time-wages and salaries for auxiliary workers, managers and specialists, with additional bonuses for overfulfilling norms and plan targets. During the late soviet period, with the introduction of the brigade organisation of labour, collective piece-rate systems became more common. The introduction of the brigade system was also associated with the application of the coefficient of labour participation (KTU), through which the pay of the brigade was supposed to be distributed differentially between the brigade members according to their labour contribution. In practice brigades sought to deal with differential contributions not through differential payment, but by replacing less effective members in order to strengthen the brigade so that all could earn more. To the extent that the KTU was effective, it was used as a discretionary instrument of line management to assign punishments and rewards for specific failures or particular effort.

---

[1]   Bob Arnot, *Controlling Soviet Labour*, Basingstoke: Macmillan, 1988.

Approaches to the reform of the payment system

Generally enterprises are quite conservative with regard to the reform of the payment system.[1] Wage reforms in the soviet period proved very disruptive, provoking widespread conflict, and to make radical changes in the payment system is still to risk serious trouble, if workers' expectations are violated or if line managers find that their levers of management are undermined by a badly designed payment system. We find that, even fifteen years after the collapse of the soviet system, more than a quarter of our case-study enterprises still use state tariff scales (the traditional state 'Unified Skill–Tariff Handbook', branch or other tariff systems) as the basis of their payment system for production workers, and in total more than two-thirds of enterprises use them at least as the point of reference.[2] Enterprises which are part of holding companies and even new private enterprises are no less likely than independent enterprises to hold on to the traditional tariff scales. Nevertheless, the majority of enterprises, particularly those which are part of holding companies had made some changes to their payment system in the previous two years.

In most enterprises changes to the payment system have been quite limited, partial and *ad hoc* and only a handful of enterprises, mostly foreign owned, have made radical changes to the payment system. In holding companies, innovations in the payment system are generally dictated by the head company. At independent enterprises the initiators of innovations are usually the heads of the planning-economic services of the enterprise, less often other functional departments, sometimes even shop chiefs. These changes were developed by the relevant department together with top management, usually without reference to the Board of Directors and only very rarely with the participation of the trade union and employee representatives. Although there is a wide range of consulting firms offering their expertise in this field, not one of our case-study enterprises used a consulting firm or other external source of information in making changes to its payment system.

This conservatism in making changes to payment policy is reflected in the socio-demographic characteristics of those responsible for the payment system at the enterprises. Over three-quarters of those responsible for wages whom we questioned were women, with an average age of 45 and an average fifteen years' service at the enterprise, the majority having started working there in soviet times, and one in ten having occupied their present post since soviet times. The majority had taken their posts through internal promotion or transfer, only one having been appointed on a competitive basis. Eighty per cent of them

---

[1] This chapter draws heavily on Inna Donova's paper 'Изменения в системах оплаты труда' [Changes in payment systems] in Кабалина В. И. (ред.) *Практики управления персоналом на современных российских предприятиях*, Москва: ИСИТО, 2005.

[2] The Russian Labour Flexibility Survey (RLFS) of 524 enterprises in 2001 found a very similar incidence of the use of state tariff scales, 27 per cent using them and a further 34 per cent using them as a point of reference (my calculation from RLFS11 Data).

were graduates, three-quarters of whom had degrees in economics, the remaining quarter in technical subjects, but only a minority of them had undertaken any additional training since 1990, most of which was in short courses, despite the fact of working in an area which has seen the most dramatic changes since that date. The majority of these labour economists see themselves as low paid (in comparison with marketing and production managers). Thus, the majority of those responsible for the payment system can be expected to be oriented primarily to reproducing the existing system and would not be expected to initiate dramatic changes.

The role of the department of labour and wages, like that of the personnel department, is primarily the execution of routine administrative tasks. Some, mostly smaller, and particularly new private enterprises, do not have a department of labour and wages, or even any specialists in the field.

The new private fish-processing factory *RZ1* does not have a department of labour and wages or a planning-economic department. These functions, in reduced form, are distributed between the accounts department, the general director and his deputies. Thus, one of the staff of the accounts department is responsible for checking the output records of piece-workers and the chief accountant then calculates everybody's pay. The chief accountant also, on the instructions of the director, draws up plans for the reform of the payment system.

In other cases the department is a section of the planning-economic department or, very rarely, of the personnel department, often in smaller enterprises consisting of only one or two people. Where there is a department, its most common functions were the calculation of wages and setting output norms, which were carried out by almost all of those questioned. Two-thirds of the departments were responsible for monitoring spending on wages and social payments, and just over half were responsible for identifying effective criteria for incentive payments and for planning the payment system, which implies that in about half the enterprises with a department of labour and wages it is not responsible for the design of the payment system. These are predominantly cases in which the payment system has not been changed for a long time, or in which changes to the payment system are dictated by the general director or the head office of a holding company.

The head of the department of labour and wages generally does not participate directly in strategic decision-making, even in areas which are directly related to their responsibilities. Thus, only a quarter of the department heads questioned participated directly in decision-making about employment and work organisation, another 40 per cent were consulted before or after decisions were taken and a quarter were not involved at all, with those in enterprises which are part of holding companies being significantly more disengaged from employment decision-making. In almost half the latter enterprises the department of labour and wages was not involved at all in decision-making about wages and in all enterprises the department was generally not involved immediately in discussion of social policy. It goes without saying that the department of labour and wages was largely excluded from other areas of decision-making, such as production, price-setting, planning and investment.

There is a marked difference in the character of changes in payment systems between those initiated by the enterprise itself and those which are initiated by a holding company. Those initiated by holding companies are generally part of a process of establishing a uniform payment system throughout the enterprises of the group and are primarily aimed at bringing expenditure on wages under stricter control. There is a more confused set of motives for changes initiated by the enterprise itself: reduction of costs; strengthening of control over workers; the intensification of labour; attempting to transfer risks of the enterprise onto workers by linking wages more closely with the results of the work of the enterprise as a whole; but they are generally motivated by a desire to overcome particular management problems by modifying the payment system. In this respect, changes in the payment system often represent an attempt to use an incentive system to compensate for weaknesses of production management. In the vast majority of independent and new private enterprises the choice of payment system is oriented to increasing productivity, while in the majority of enterprises which are part of holding companies the primary purpose is simply to control and reduce expenditure.

In those enterprises in which there have not been any changes in the payment system, or in which changes are only local and not fundamental, incentive payment systems are simply accepted as traditional social norms, an element of the organisational culture. This is reflected in the explanations of the payment system provided by managers: *'it has been like that here for a long time'*, *'that is how it is here'*, *'it has always been like that'*. Retention of the traditional system is not necessarily the result of a conservative resistance to change. In some cases it is based on a conviction that the traditional system is tried and tested and does not need to change.

In the view of the head of the department of labour and wages at *MZ8*, a very traditional engineering factory where the payment system has been unchanged for many years, no changes are needed in the organisation of pay, the existing system is harmonious and systematic and should not react to changes in production: *'the system of pay disciplines the chaos in the organisation of production. It is not right when they try to plug holes in production with pay'*.

Planning and controlling spending on wages

During the crisis years of the 1990s every enterprise was living from hand to mouth and no enterprise was able to engage in any kind of planning. The labour force rose and fell spontaneously, depending primarily on the level of wages and whether or not wages were paid at all. Wages were determined by a crude balance between the constraints of the labour market and the financial resources at the disposal of the enterprise. The total spending on wages in the course of a year or a month was unpredictable and, with predominantly piece-rate payment systems, uncontrollable. Many independent enterprises still do not have any system of planning employment or spending on wages. Some small and medium new private enterprises similarly do not have any planning systems, because their management systems are informal and decision-making is *ad hoc*, by the owner-director.

With the stabilisation of the economic situation, and particularly with the subordination of enterprises to outside owners and their integration into holding companies, the owners make every effort to bring spending under control in order progressively to reduce it. This applies to all categories of expenditure, including spending on wages, which amounts, for our case-study enterprises, to an average 22 per cent of the cost of production.[1] This underlies the tendency to the centralisation of control of wage spending and the drawing up of strict budgets against which spending on pay can be controlled. The traditional soviet system of budgeting for wage payments was through the wage fund, which defined the amount that could be spent on wages at the level of the enterprise and its subdivisions. The wage fund was controlled through the strict regulation of the staff list, which defined the number of authorised posts, and centrally dictated rates of pay and allowances, which together determined the size of the wage fund against which the monthly spending on wages was monitored.

In many enterprises the wage fund is still based on the authorised staff list, as it was in soviet times, but this means that where the shop has control of its own wage fund, as is the case in about half of our case-study enterprises, line managers can keep some posts vacant and thereby generate additional resources that they can use to pay for overtime, various supplementary payments to favoured workers and so on. While this considerably eases the task of the line management, and provides a strong incentive for workers to cover for vacancies or for absent colleagues, it considerably weakens the centralised control of wage spending. For this reason there is a tendency, particularly in holding companies, to move towards planning the wage fund on the basis of the actual labour input, not the staff list.

At *NKhZ2* the finance director has repeatedly stressed his intention of moving from planning the wage fund from the staff list to planning it from the labour input, so as to make it possible to exert more strict control on spending for the payment of overtime, combination of professions and weekend working, which has become widespread as a result of the constant shortage of staff.

---

[1] According to the official statistical data, wages and social insurance payments accounted for 17.9 per cent of the costs of industrial enterprises in 2003, but according to an official survey of 28,000 enterprises and organizations wages accounted for 21 per cent of costs in 2002 (Rosstat, Moscow *Statistical Bulletin* № 6 (99), 2003). Wages accounted on average for 24 per cent of production costs of the enterprises surveyed by RLFS in 2001.

At *MetZ1* the shops have no wage fund of their own and everything is decided centrally. Here, according to enterprise specialists, *'if there was a proper system of planning it would exclude the possibility of foremen influencing the salary of workers by increasing the amount of overtime'*.

At the other extreme, there are enterprises which use a 'reactive' method of determining the wage fund, barely covered with the fig leaves of norms and job rates.

At *KhDK1*, the orders are closed in accordance with the enterprise's job rates for each kind of work. The job rates are set by the planning department, supposedly on the basis of 'scientific' norms, but there is no serious economic analysis and in reality the job rates are calculated on the basis of a general impression of an acceptable level of pay. *'We considered that should be about normal. Well that is how it is, approximately'* (ice cream shop chief about the calculations of the planning department).

At the confectionery factory *KF1* the head of the department of labour and wages emphasised that the process of forming the wage fund in the enterprise was centralised and the fund was strictly under her control. *'The wage fund is structured by subdivisions. The shop chiefs do not take part in this in any way. It is strictly centralised. The wage fund sits in one pair of hands. The general director keeps watch over it and I must manage this fund. The shop chiefs can influence the amount paid to workers, but the fund for paying for this . . . he does not influence the size of the fund. This is my fund, it is planned by me'*. But in reality the wage fund was determined as the amount due to be paid in wages and bonuses on the basis of the figures returned by the production shops and the sales department, which was then distributed among the employees according to the same figures, so the wage fund simply corresponds to the amount paid out as wages and does not set any constraint on the payment of wages at all. In effect, the problem of production is considered to be the task of the foremen and depends on the conscientiousness and experience of the workers, who are paid according to how long they work, how much they produce (and how much the sales department manages to sell). With this system there is no pressure on the line managers or production workers to increase productivity.

In general, even in those enterprises which do have some system in place to plan spending on labour power, it is quite primitive, only taking into account the direct costs of labour expressed in the wage fund, without considering the costs of hiring and training employees, spending on work clothes and health and safety measures, non-wage benefits and social and welfare facilities or bonus payments made out of profits or cost savings. There is no systematic attempt to implement a system of labour force planning which would take into account the direct and indirect spending on labour and the returns on that spending. This is another manifestation of the weak conception of personnel management that remains as a legacy of the soviet past.

The fact that the employers have an immediate economic interest in controlling and reducing spending on wages, and managers and specialists in interviews repeatedly declared this to be a central feature of the management of pay, does not necessarily mean that Russian enterprises are seeking to reduce wages to the minimum. While they would like to pay as little as they can, many recognise that paying low wages is not consistent with securing the skilled, stable and motivated labour force which they need to achieve high levels of productivity and product quality, particularly when they are expecting workers to work with old and unreliable equipment, often using inferior raw materials. Low pay for workers also makes the job of the line managers much more difficult because they have fewer incentives at their disposal to encourage conscientious workers and they have to spend a lot of their time finding and training replacements for those who leave as a result of low pay. Thus, although pay at our case-study enterprises is generally low, at least by West European standards, there is a very big difference in pay between the lowest- and the highest-paying enterprises. The median monthly salary of the 703 workers in our case-study enterprises who reported their wages for the previous year was 4,500 roubles ($150). The lowest wages were at the knitting factory, *TF2*, where the median monthly wage was 1,950 roubles ($65), the highest at *SM3*, where the median wage was 22,500 roubles ($750).

While low wages may lock an enterprise into a vicious circle in which low productivity continues to justify low wages, managers are understandably wary about simply increasing wages as a means of solving this problem. As the general director of the petrochemicals enterprise *NKhZ2* commented:

> 'Well, representatives of shop seven recently wrote me a petition about the level of pay they wanted. They said, we want so much. I do not accept such an approach. I realise perfectly well that it is difficult to live on the 6,000 roubles ($200) which they receive at the moment. But if they were not getting that from us, at our neighbours over the fence they would get $150. If we were to pay the salary today, on the basis of our present capabilities, if a person oversleeps and we lose one million roubles of production (such things happen), what increase is there to talk about? That is what we have to struggle with. . . . Yes, all of us work to make money. But that raises the question of how that is done today: "First you pay us, and then we shall think about whether or not we will work for you" is unacceptable. . . . Often people give just one answer – give us money, and everything will be good, we will become clever, amenable, hard-working'.

To upgrade the labour force requires spending on a comprehensive programme, including training, personnel selection, improving the working environment and the technology, in addition to paying better wages.

Innovation and the dual role of the payment system

The payment system in a capitalist enterprise has to perform two functions. On the one hand, it must provide sufficient pay and prospects for the enterprise to be able to recruit and retain employees with the skills and personal qualities required. On the other hand, it must provide an instrument for the motivation of employees, to reward those, individually and collectively, who make the greatest contribution to the success of the enterprise. The payment system has to perform these functions while confining wage payments within the limits of profitability.

In the soviet system there was not officially a labour market and there were not substantial differences in pay, but priority enterprises were able to recruit and retain the best workers by offering an attractive 'social package', including housing, health care, child care, cultural, sporting, leisure and recreation facilities and so on. The low-priority industries, light industry and food processing for women, construction and engineering for men, paid lower wages and had far inferior social and welfare facilities, but they also had more relaxed discipline, a slower pace of work and more flexible working hours. In the soviet system payment was conceived much more as an instrument of labour motivation than as a labour market instrument, with workers being penalised and rewarded through the differential distribution of the wage fund. The payment system was always regarded as problematic in the Soviet Union and there was endless discussion around proposals for wage reform, but reforms were few and far between and when they were introduced generally provoked enormous disruption and high levels of conflict without achieving their intended aims.

This view of the payment system as being essentially an instrument of labour motivation persists to a very considerable extent in post-soviet Russian enterprises but, as we shall see, both traditional and innovative attempts to use the payment system to this end have tended to come up against the constraints of the labour market and the demands for the centralisation of management control or have weakened the control of labour by undermining the powers of line managers. In the rest of this section we will look at problems which have arisen in relation to the use of the payment system as an instrument of motivation in our case-study enterprises.

The erosion of the piece-rate payment system

The traditional soviet payment system involved the payment of main production workers on piece-rates and the remainder of the personnel on time-wages. Piece-rate payment systems were widely adopted in the first decades of the twentieth century in the leading capitalist countries, from which they were borrowed by the Soviet Union, as an aspect of the Taylorist 'scientific management of labour'. In the capitalist world the weaknesses of piece-rate payment for most categories of labour soon became apparent. On the one hand, piece-rate payment systems had to be complemented by costly monitoring and quality management systems if quantity was not to be achieved at the expense of quality. On the other hand, piece-rate payment systems effectively ceded control of the pace and intensity of labour to the worker. Piece-rate payment was no substitute for the effective management of production. However, the Soviet Union retained its ideological commitment to the 'scientific management of labour' to the last.

One of the main changes observed at our case-study enterprises is the increasing use of time-wages in place of piece-work in the payment of workers. Fewer than a third of our enterprises still pay all of their workers on piece-rates, about a quarter use time-wages and the remainder a mixture of both systems.[1] However, the reasons for the shift to time-wages are not the use of increasingly complex technologies and the changing role of living labour in modern automated production that make piece-rate systems redundant, since there has been little change of production systems. Piece-rate payment has been abandoned because it leads to unjustified and unjustifiable differences in earnings between different groups of workers and employees.

The reinforced concrete factory *SM4* used to set the pay of managers and specialists in relation to the piece-rate earnings of workers but in 2004 they changed to the payment of a fixed salary for these categories because the uneven workloads led to large wage differentials for managers and specialists working in different shops. This led to considerable dissatisfaction among the line managers, who complained that they were suffering not for any fault of their own but because of the inability of senior management to provide them with work. The workers, of course, were in the same situation but were not in a position to make their feelings known so strongly. For the first three months under the new payment system, the managers and specialists earned about 50 per cent more than the workers, but as production increased so did the workers' piece-rate earnings and the differential fell to about 15 per cent.

MZ5, which makes cranes, is revising its payment system with the aim of increasing incentives and improving the motivation of labour. A new system of pay is being introduced for production workers, on the basis of a proposal from the head of the preparatory shop. This involves a transfer from a piece-rate plus bonus system to a time-wage plus bonus system. *'Piece-rate payment stimulates labour, but it requires a lot of expenditure on monitoring. The new system is being introduced with the aim of freeing the norm setters of the department of labour and wages, the foremen and the shop chiefs from the task of evaluating the work and checking the data on the orders'* (general director). The other reason for the change was that the job-rates had become very outdated and payment according to those rates led to a lot of conflict with workers, because nobody wanted to work on the low-paid jobs, so the shop chiefs had to manipulate the rates.

---

[1] The RLFS 2001 survey found that 46 per cent of their respondent enterprises paid workers on piece-rates, 15 per cent on time-wages and 38 per cent used a mixed system. In the 1996 survey 61 per cent of enterprises had paid workers on piece-rates (my calculation from RLFS data).

Under the new system every worker has an individual salary, which is determined by the line managers: *'we approached it individually, on the basis of the capacity of the worker, so that there would not be levelling'*, and in addition there is a bonus of 100 per cent of the basic salary if the section fulfils its monthly plan and a further 100 per cent depending on the foreman's assessment of the worker's conduct and discipline, confirmed by the shop chief. This represents a considerable increase in the power of line managers. The workers were very critical of the proposals but, although they were consulted, their criticisms were ignored. *'Tariff payment plus 100 per cent for fulfilling the plan suited us. But if there are conflicts, the foremen or the chief at any time can begin to play their trump card. At any time they can take away any percentage of the bonus . . . for example, you start to smoke but the director is there. And that's it. The rules here are like in a Pioneer camp – fifty minutes you work, ten minutes you smoke. They immediately point to a regulation – violation. It's the same with lunch: a minute late and that's it. Everything is at the discretion of the shop chief. Well that does not suit us . . . in the other shops they have tariff and bonus. If they do not fulfil the plan, they do not receive the bonus, but that's not too bad. But with us here it's the lion's share of pay'* (workers). The abolition of piece-rates also means that workers can no longer boost their earnings by working overtime or at weekends, nor can they control their own pace of work by building up a reserve or covering for one another. The shop chief conducted a meeting of the collective at which the proposal was discussed: *'Everybody, of course, was against it. But the majority agreed. There was a vote. We're like guinea pigs, they are conducting an experiment . . . nobody listens. The foreman has no competence in these matters, everything is decided by the shop chief. That is, they decide it up there. All the shop chiefs are against, apart from ours'* (workers). The reform also reduces the freedom of manoeuvre of the shop chiefs. Under the old system *'some unscrupulous chiefs can cheat with the orders. The top level of management cannot track whether or not they have really done this work, or the work is difficult or less skilled. But nobody here thinks about anything. They send the plan to the shop, the shop fulfils the plan, they get their money and they go away'* (general director).

The clothing factory *ShF1* moved in 1996 from a piece-rate payment system to a complex system which was essentially time based. This was intended to give management more control and simplify the calculation of wages, laying off the staff who had been responsible for this work. The change meant that workers no longer had any ability to affect their own wages and led to a huge conflict. It was introduced *'with shouting, swearing, tears and conflicts. Well, what were the seamstresses used to? They made five seams – they calculated how much that cost, they made another operation and again they calculated. They knew every job-rate by heart. That is how they worked before, when we sewed simple items in large runs it was possible. But now, when the range has been extended, it has got more difficult, the runs have become small, another approach to pay was needed'* (deputy director for production). Managers sought to persuade workers to accept the change at meetings and pressure was put on those who tried to resist (for example, by closely monitoring the quality of their work).

Only a minority of enterprises have given up the piece-rate payment system altogether, but those who retain it have to have ways of ensuring that workers can continue to earn even if there is not enough work for them to do by giving them additional payments under some pretext to take them up to their usual average monthly earnings.

At **ET2**, despite the declared principle 'pay is normative with output' social pressure compels the management of the enterprise in some cases to 'advance money' to shops and sections which have problems with the volume of work or for objective reasons have overspent their wage fund.

At the new private precision-engineering enterprise **MZ3**, which has a piece-rate payment system, there is some kind of tacit agreement among all the managers that the workers should not receive less than 4,000 roubles a month. *'For example, a worker comes up to us. Here the salary is 4,000. They say to him: 4,000 pay, 50 per cent bonus'* (chief accountant).

At the new private furniture factory **MK2**, during the seasonal fluctuations of demand newly hired workers are paid additionally approximately at the average level of wages: *'In the first six months we pay workers additionally, workers are not guilty if there is a seasonal fall in demand for furniture. But everything is done by the seat of the pants. You see what a person receives in wages. He will not work for such pay, he will leave. And you value your staff, you take your money and pay them additionally'* (general director).

At the frozen food company **KhDK1**, the workload of the loaders, who are paid on piece-rates, fluctuates substantially, so they have a minimum hourly rate below which their wages cannot fall.

At the bakery **KhBK1**, payment is formally a piece-rate determined by both the results of the production process as a whole and the individual contribution, but in reality when wages are calculated there is an equalising mechanism. The piece-rate payment in production subdivisions is calculated by the brigade according to the amount produced (delivered) and should reflect the contribution to the general result of the work of the shop and the enterprise. However, in practice the size of the wage does not depend on the efforts of the brigade since the volume of work is determined from outside according to the flow of orders. The piece-work component of the wage is distributed equally between the workers of the brigade by the foreman or brigadier, taking account only of the number of shifts worked.

One exception to the tendency to replace piece-rate with time systems of payment is with regard to sales and marketing personnel, who are very often paid on a commission basis. This is probably because the senior management has some doubts about the usefulness of their work and has little idea of what it involves, and so has no way of monitoring and evaluating their work.

A very small number of our enterprises, which are undoubtedly technologically advanced and using highly skilled labour, have successfully used time payment systems for a long time. Rather than trying to use the payment system to compensate for management failures, these enterprises pay relatively high wages, have careful personnel selection and regular appraisal and employ capable managers so that work is well organised and people are willing to help out where necessary without demanding immediate additional payment.

The telecommunications company *TK1* has paid a salary to all its employees, with virtually no bonuses, since it was first established. The personnel director claims credit for this innovation, which is now in line with the pay policy of the holding company as a whole. The enterprise has a salary scale with quite high differentials, so that managers earn about three times as much as ordinary employees. Each post is assigned to a position on the salary scale, and each position has quite a substantial salary range, with the highest pay for the post being about double the lowest pay. A new appointee will normally be hired at the bottom of the range and their salary reviewed twice a year.

Problems of norming

The effectiveness of a piece-rate payment system depends on the effectiveness with which output norms are set for each operation. The ideology of the 'scientific organisation of labour' prescribes that equal pay should be the result of equal skill and effort in different operations, and that work at the prescribed intensity should generate a normal wage. The idea that the organisation of norming at the enterprise is the basis of the rational organisation of work and planning of the labour input of the production programme is still canonical in enterprises which retain piece-rate payment systems. The 'scientific' character of the organisation of labour rests on the presumption that the output norms, so-called 'rational norms', have been determined scientifically by engineers and work-study specialists. In the Soviet Union, this was done in a large number of scientific research institutes attached to the various ministries, with the norms being published in fat reference books which were used by the normsetters in the enterprises. Where rational norms had not been developed, or special circumstances applied, so-called 'statistical-experimental' norms, derived from the achieved output of the workers rather than from 'scientific' study of the operations, were used. Moreover, the familiar problem of the negative influence of periodic increases of output norms on labour productivity frequently arises. The workers are not motivated to increase production because they know that if they do so, the output norm will simply be revised so that they have to do more work for the same pay. The management therefore tries to force the pace by ratcheting up norms, which leads to conflict in which the line managers, who have the task of enforcing the new norms, often take the workers' side.

At *KhZ4* the workers took advantage of the recovery of the enterprise to achieve a larger volume of work in order to earn correspondingly more pay. However, the management of the factory, observing the significant increase in productivity, responded by tightening the norms, which led the workers to hold back for fear of provoking further tightening.

At the engineering factory *MZ2*, each part is evaluated by the norm-setters (through experience – 'approximately') in terms of the amount of time needed to carry out all the operations, and so the corresponding cost of the part. From time to time the normsetters are instructed to increase productivity and they cut the time allowed for each operation so that the sections have to carry out a larger number of operations to fulfil their task and receive a bonus. However, the shop chiefs (and the workers) see this process the other way around. From their point of view it is not that increased productivity has led to a reduction of time and labour input, and so a reduction of the price of the job, but the reverse – the normsetters have cut a certain natural inherent cost of the operation to make the workers work faster. This impression is reinforced by the fact that the increase of the production norms is anticipated by the reduction in the price, which must stimulate an intensification of labour which could then, again as an accomplished fact, be consolidated in a new production norm. The workers know this and do not force a speed up of the operations, but the shop chief has to speak about the *'labour cost in monetary terms'*. The job prices periodically give rise to discontent which, however, does not develop into conflict since the power of the foremen in the distribution of work (and, correspondingly, bonuses) among the workers is very considerable. In some cases, if the workers and the line managers can prove that the norm has been set incorrectly according to the prescribed procedures, they can successfully appeal for it to be revised. The bonus fund for the shop, out of which the bonuses of workers and managers are paid, is composed largely of savings out of wages, so the line managers have a strong material interest in the intensification of the labour of the workers under their control.

The ineffectiveness of piece-rate payment systems as a means of increasing labour productivity has been well known in the capitalist world for a very long time, but it is hardly a new discovery for Russian managers, since it was a very well-known feature of the soviet system which no amount of rhetoric about 'scientific' rational norms could conceal. Thus enterprises tend to use direct administrative methods of controlling labour costs rather than organisational-economic ones, adjusting the norms to ensure that workers receive adequate pay.

The frozen food company **KhDK1** uses output norms drawn up by the Scientific Research Institute of the former ministry, which have hardly changed for years. New kinds of work are normed by specialists from the planning department. However, workers and line managers do not understand how pay is calculated and do not know on what basis it is reviewed (for example, various additional payments are increased or reduced). The payment orders which the heads of subdivisions submit are not necessarily implemented because the accounts department has the right to correct the calculation of pay. This constantly gives rise to friction between the accounting group and the shop chiefs, who press the interests of their subordinates. The head of the ice-cream shop constantly initiates increases in the job rates for particular kinds of work. She invites specialists from the planning department to evaluate the labour costs: *'I constantly say, let us increase it. Here is the frosting. There they earn very little. So I say, watch it, stand and look at it, they really do produce little and earn little. So they increase them a bit'.*

The small specialised construction company **ST2** used to calculate wages on the basis of the norms prescribed by the state for the construction industry, but the management considers that these norms are much too stringent and do not take into account the increased quality demands which mean that many jobs take twice as long to complete as they did in the past. Therefore these norms only provide the reference point for calculating wages *'because if you pay according to the normative documents for construction, then people would never earn anything'* (general director). However, the state norms are still the basis on which labour costs are calculated for state contracts and they are the starting point for contract negotiations with private customers. This is one reason why state contracts are unprofitable, and the company has to negotiate higher prices for private contracts to cover the full wage costs. In principle wages are calculated by the foreman on the basis of the official norms, but in practice there is no system of control of the output of the workers and the wages are calculated by the site foreman fairly roughly, on the basis of a subjective assessment of the contribution of each person, so that everybody earns a reasonable daily wage.

In some cases there has been a change in the level at which incentive payments are calculated, for example from individual to collective piece-rates or bonuses, or vice versa, or additional parameters have been introduced to link individual earnings to the results of the work of the brigade or division. Although such changes can make the payment system more opaque and can introduce more scope for subjective assessment by the line managers, if pay increases at the same time the system is regarded by workers as fair and effective.

The expansion of the bonus system

During the crisis years of the 1990s, when production and earnings of the enterprises were unstable and unpredictable, there was a tendency for enterprise management to try to shift some of the risk onto the workers by increasing the proportion of the wage which was accounted for by the bonus. This was often done initially by paying compensation for inflation in the form of bonus payments, which in principle could be annulled if the enterprise could not afford to pay, rather than by indexing the basic wage. Enterprises also shifted the risk onto the employees by linking bonus payments not to the fulfilment of the production plan, but to the economic results, in the form either of sales revenue or the financial outcome. Increasing the proportion of wages that was paid in the form of a bonus in principle gave management much more discretion in determining the wages of employees, but in practice this was the case only to a limited extent because the expectation was that everybody would receive the bonus in full. Thus the bonus system effectively only gave management a negative sanction, using deprivation of bonus as a penalty for disciplinary offences. On average across our case-study enterprises the fixed component accounts for a bit over half the total wage, ranging from zero in three enterprises to 90–100 per cent in three others. Nearly all traditional enterprises, though only two-thirds of new private enterprises, paid bonuses to production workers. Around three-quarters paid bonuses for skill and qualifications, for harmful working conditions and for combining professions, about half for the quality of work and a quarter for length of service.[1]

Managers and specialists tend to think that the greater the proportion of the wage that is not guaranteed the better, because this provides greater incentives for the workers. On the other hand, Russian labour economists suggest that a high level of bonus payments is an indicator of poor management. The less well organised is production, the lower the quality of the norming of labour and the more indeterminate the range of duties of the worker, the lower is the share of tariff payment and the higher the share of incentive, and vice versa.[2] The problem with the use of bonus systems as a motivational device is that the indicators on which the calculation of the bonus is based have very little relation to the effort and initiative of individual workers or even of their particular subdivisions. When asked on whom their earnings mostly depended, more than half of the workers questioned said 'on the enterprise administration', just under a quarter 'on the head of my subdivision', 5 per cent 'on the foreman' and only 15 per cent 'on me'. So rather than being an incentive payment system, the bonus is widely seen as merely a means of shifting the burden of failure from the enterprise onto its employees.

---

[1]   In the 2001 RLFS three-quarters of enterprises reported paying bonuses, the bonus on average amounting to 40 per cent of the wage. Unskilled workers were slightly less likely than skilled workers to be paid a bonus and their bonus was a little smaller as a proportion of the wage. Just under half the enterprises paid bonuses for skill and qualifications, combining professions and work in harmful conditions, fewer than one-fifth paid bonuses for seniority and for the quality of work. The 2002 Rosstat wage survey reported that the tariff part of the wage made up 41.8 per cent of the wage in industry.

[2]   Мазманова Б. Г. *Управление заработной платой*, Москва: Финансы и Статистика, 2003.

MZ6 once supplied the military-industrial complex. It went through a severe crisis in the 1990s, but recovered by redirecting its activity to the production of industrial equipment for leading industrial branches: power engineering, the railways and oil and gas. It was acquired by a regional investment group which oriented it to supplying the latter branches and put in a new young management team with instructions to increase the profitability and market capitalisation of the company. In February 2003 a new payment system was introduced, initially for engineering-technical staff, the essence of which was to reduce the fixed part of the salary and to increase the share of the bonus, which was to be calculated on the basis of the achievement of the current sales plan by the factory as a whole. The idea was that this would encourage an intensification of labour and strengthen subordination by increasing the identification of the employees with the success of the company. However, the new system was introduced without any consultation with the employees, who responded very negatively to the proposal because they could not see any connection between the sale of the product and their own efforts in production. *'Excuse me, but I would rather have guaranteed earnings, something definite, say something like two-thirds, and one-third depends on me . . . but when you have, excuse me, one-third guaranteed pay and you don't know about two-thirds, somebody over there missed out on the sales and you will earn nothing because of it'* (foreman of experimental section). Workers were not convinced by rhetoric about the need to work in a single team for a single aim. Some people left as a direct result of the change and even senior managers did not like the new system, seeing it as a return to the old soviet form of propaganda: *'for a single aim, just like before – for the victory of communism!'* (head of planning-economic department).

The fertiliser factory ***KhZ2***, which is part of a large vertically integrated holding company, uses a time-plus-bonus system of payment. The general orientation of pay policy is to increase the proportion of non-guaranteed payment and relate it to the results of the activity of the enterprise as a whole and the labour of the individual employee. The enterprise has worked out four regulations on bonuses to provide incentives for employees, but these provide only the most general guidelines, without any clear criteria on the basis of which bonuses can be applied. This gives line managers a great deal of discretion in awarding the bonuses.

For the majority of new private enterprises and those within holding companies the basic criterion for payment of main production workers is the results of the enterprise for the majority of independent enterprises it is the results of the work of the individual or the brigade. However, there is a tendency for the more sophisticated enterprises, particularly those which are part of large holding companies, to move from basing bonuses on a uniform indicator of the production or sales of the enterprise as a whole to indicators for the separate divisions, with the intention of linking bonuses more closely to performance.

At the cement factory *SM2*, which is now part of a horizontally integrated holding company, the department of labour and wages is responsible for confining spending on wages strictly within the limits of the wage fund approved by the holding company. Under the previous owner the wage fund was based on the state tariff scale plus a bonus based on plan fulfilment by the enterprise as a whole. The new owner is moving to stricter control of wage payment, with a bonus based on the results of the division. The implementation of the new system is being discussed with the shop chiefs and shop economists.

At the metallurgical factory *MetZ2* the wage fund for each shop is calculated on the basis of the planned volume of production and the bonus is based on the plan fulfilment of each shop. At present the payment system does not play a significant motivating role, but the new foreign owners have demanded that the factory management create a pay system which would play such a role, and the department of labour and wages has been instructed to create such a system: '*they are trying to get us to interest the employees, that was not the case in the past*' (leading engineer for the organisation of labour).

Some enterprises have developed their own methods to try to overcome the limitations of the existing bonus systems, although the outcome generally serves to reinforce the conclusion that centrally managed bonus systems provoke conflict and disorganisation rather than motivating workers.

NKhZ2 used a simple bonus system according to which a percentage bonus, usually up to 35 per cent, was paid to all employees on the basis of the financial results of the month. In the spring of 2003 the general director introduced a new system, based on scores determined by a monthly appraisal of the performance of each subdivision and each individual employee, both on a ten-point scale according to prescribed criteria. The general director had read about the use of such systems for rewarding managers in a management textbook and decided to apply it more generally in order to tie pay more directly to performance. Not surprisingly, the system has led to considerable conflict as shop chiefs contest a low evaluation of their shops or their subordinates. '*Not long ago there was a case when the chief power engineer considered that our work to commission a compressor was unsatisfactory. I wrote a memorandum to the director of the factory with a request to review the conflict over the change of ratings. The question was resolved in the presence of the director. We partially defended our score, you also have to fight for your people*' (shop chief). Workers also question any reduction in their scores. '*When they receive the wages list, our phone begins to ring: why not so much, but why so much? We pick up the rating sheet and explain that there it says 9.8 points, he asks again, why? I cannot answer that. That is worked out by the immediate manager. How the manager assesses his participation, quality. . . . And although the amount of work is calculated there, in the rating sheets we do not see this. The assessment has simply been reduced because he has quarrelled with his boss, we do not know this'* (head of the department of labour and wages). Many managers and specialists (including the head of the department of labour and wages and the finance director) see the new bonus system as *'not sufficiently worked out'*. Line managers find it less effective than the coefficient of labour participation (KTU) because of the lack of clarity and degree of subjective judgement in the criteria. It also does not provide an incentive because it is basically a system of punishment. Line managers complain that, unlike the KTU, the money saved by depriving the guilty of their bonuses is not available for redistribution to others: *'KTU, I think, was more suitable, because there you could cut from one person and give more to another at his expense. And there I operated with money, people understood that better'* (head of the repair shop).

It is difficult to overestimate the role of bonuses at the enterprises. Bonus payments are the main factor in the differentiation of pay at new private enterprises and those which are part of holding companies, although they are less significant in independent enterprises where working hours are the main factor in pay differentiation. Amounting on average to almost half the earnings of the worker, they have become a universal management tool. Bonus regulations provide for the award of bonuses for individual skill and the absence of faults, length of service and improvement of professional skill, training of beginners and replacement of absentees. By means of the bonus, the general tasks of personnel management are also supposed to be accomplished: retention of core personnel, maintenance of discipline, encouragement to improve skills.

However, although initially created as an incentive system, bonuses for the fulfilment of production and sales plans were immediately incorporated into the workers' expectations of a normal wage and, as in the case of piece-rate payments, workers were very aggrieved if they lost their bonus through no fault of their own, so the bonus lost any kind of incentive function that it might have had and its payment became the norm. Many of the workers interviewed did not know how much of their wage was fixed and how much was accounted for by the bonus. The result has been that bonuses at the case-study enterprises have been used more and more widely, not as a positive incentive, but as an instrument of punishment, with the partial or full deprivation of bonus becoming the standard punishment for all kinds of disciplinary violations. Deprivation of bonus is used to punish shirkers and latecomers, the unconscientious and disloyal, bunglers and the alcohol-dependent. For example, many bonus regulations are associated with the system of quality control, but in practice punishment for spoilage, rather than encouragement for high-quality work, prevails. Moreover, some bonuses are even conceived at their introduction as a means of imposing penalties.

Labour market pressures and pay increases

Enterprises have to be competitive in the local labour market if they want to avoid the heavy costs imposed by shortages of labour and high labour turnover. This severely limits their ability to use wages as a motivational or a disciplinary factor. In general, the main determinant of pay levels for all but senior managers and specialists is the local labour market. *'We pay what labour costs on the labour market'* (head of the planning-economic department, *MZ6*). Any successful enterprise tries to keep its wages above the average in the local labour market in order to recruit and retain the employees it needs. Thus, only a handful of our case-study enterprises were paying wages below the local average. Many employers complain that the level of taxation on the wage fund, including compulsory social insurance payments, prevents them from increasing wages as much as they would like (the total weight of taxation, according to Rosstat's survey data, is on average only 12.9 per cent), and half the specialists we interviewed in our case-study enterprises felt that this was the case in their own enterprise. However, many employers, particularly in the new private sector and those in senior positions in all sectors, avoid such an inconvenience by reporting extremely low official pay, which is subject to taxation, and paying the bulk of the salary unofficially in cash.

It is not easy to determine exactly where the enterprise stands in the local labour market, because there is a wide range of factors to take into account in comparing one place of work with another, so the process of adjusting wages is not a simple one. In general, with double-digit inflation, most of the case-study enterprises increase pay regularly, on average once or twice a year (although five enterprises reported that they had not increased pay over the previous two years). However, only a fifth of enterprises cited increases in their product price as the source of pay increases, the vast majority citing increased labour productivity and/or economies on energy and raw materials as the source of the increase.[1]

Pay increases are usually on the initiative of management. In enterprises which are owned by holding companies the final decision about changes in the level of pay is taken in the head office of the holding company, it is not taken in the enterprise. In some cases this will be on the recommendation of the general director and his senior management team, but in other cases the holding company may be single-minded about the need to cut costs, so will not sanction a pay increase that is not paid for out of increased productivity, or it may have its own pay policy, which it applies across all the enterprises under its control.

The detergent manufacturer *KhZ1* was owned by a Russian holding company until 2001, when it was acquired by a foreign owner. Under the new owner the personnel department has been integrated into the department of labour

---

[1] Respondents to the RLFS in 2001 were asked about the sources of pay increases and 43 per cent said that the source was productivity increases, 31 per cent profits, 4 per cent economising on energy and raw materials (16 per cent had not had a pay increase).

and wages and is completely subordinate to the personnel department of the head company. The new owner has a unified pay system at all its Russian enterprises: this is a system of time payment with the point on the salary scale being determined by qualifications and experience, and a regional coefficient and additional bonuses being paid for combining professions, working unsocial hours or working in harmful conditions. There is a further small bonus paid if the factory exceeds its sales target. The sales staff has a different bonus system, with a substantial proportion of their salary depending on achieving sales targets. Since the new owners took over there has been a series of large pay increases, part of which has been targeted at reducing the substantial differentials that had developed under the previous ownership between the pay of managers and that of the rest of the employees. Thus senior managers and specialists were excluded from a substantial pay rise for other categories of staff in July 2002.

In small and medium enterprises, particularly in the new private sector, where the director concentrates all the decision-making powers, the decision to increase wages might be taken by him unilaterally with an eye on the local labour market. *'You look at other enterprises and approximately you conceive the wage level'* (director, **MK2**). However, no employer likes to increase wages voluntarily and so senior management often introduces pay increases only as a result of some internal or external pressure.

In some regions there is external pressure on enterprises to increase pay. According to the revised Labour Code that came into effect in 2002, the federal government is obliged to adjust the legal minimum wage upwards in stages until it reaches the level of the official subsistence minimum. However, in some Russian regions the local administration has taken it upon itself to accelerate the process and has pressed local employers to raise their minimum wage to the level of the regional subsistence minimum. Such an obligation is also sometimes contained in regional tripartite agreements, though more often as wishful thinking than an effective obligation. Enterprising employers have found various ways around such demands:[1]

At **MZ4** the demand of the oblast administration to raise pay to the subsistence minimum put the factory in a difficult position because it would have required them to increase pay by about 10 per cent. Rather than pay such an increase, it was decided to transfer low-paid workers onto a shortened working day.

Pressure from within the enterprise for an increase in pay levels can come from a number of different directions. If the enterprise is experiencing high labour turnover and is finding it difficult to recruit new staff, the head of the personnel department might make representations to the director about the need to increase wages, but such representations are likely to carry little weight on their own

---

[1] Капелюшников Р. 'Механизмы формирования заработной платы в российской промышленности', *Вопросы экономики* № 4, 2004: 66–90.

because of the low status and authority of the personnel department. If representations come from the personnel department alone, the inability to recruit suitable employees is more likely to be attributed to the incompetence of the personnel department than to the inadequacy of the wages.

The trade union, where it exists, plays an equally limited role in pressing for pay increases, although the trade union president is often very ready to take the credit once an increase has been awarded.

> At the engineering factory *MZ2*, which has an influential foreign minority owner, there have been frequent pay increases, but the administration increases pay on its own initiative without any pressure from the trade union. The trade union president insists that these increases are also an achievement of the trade union committee. *'But here one always has to understand that when there is a pike in the lake the carp cannot doze, right? There is a trade union and they will always know that this question will be put and they will always come to them with it. So, even when things are forging ahead there is a role in this for the trade union'.*

> At the foreign-owned *KhZ1* the payment system is fully specified in the collective agreement and the trade union is centrally involved in the discussion of pay. Informants gave credit to the trade union for the much improved pay and social benefits, even though the improvement was merely the result of the application of the uniform policy of the holding company to the enterprise. *'All of these social benefits were only adopted under pressure from the trade union . . . and if there had not been a trade union we would not have got any of this'* (head of the electrical shop). The workers did not share the confidence of the shop chief in the power of the trade union, only two of the sixteen questioned seeing the trade union as the defender of their interests in questions of pay.

In some cases the periodicity of pay increases is incorporated in enterprise collective agreements and branch tariff agreements, but in one in four enterprises in which there is a trade union organisation, the trade union plays no part at all in decisions regarding pay and in only a minority of cases does the trade union participate immediately in pay discussions; in other cases it is consulted or its participation is a mere formality. Not one of the trade union leaders questioned believed that the trade union played a decisive role in resolving questions of pay. In two cases they believed that the activism and determination of the workers themselves was crucial, in one case that the shop chiefs played the decisive role, but all the rest admitted that it was the enterprise administration that decided questions of pay. Workers had no more faith in the trade union than did their leaders. When asked who would best protect their interests in questions of pay, 40 per cent said the head of their subdivision, 20 per cent the director of the enterprise, 20 per cent said 'nobody', 16 per cent said 'myself' but only 27 out of 770 workers identified the trade union as the best defender of their interests.

At *MZ1*, a highly skilled electrical engineering factory, wages were below the local average and there had not been any increase in the pay of piece-rate workers for some years, although their earnings had risen somewhat because of the link between their job rates and the prices of the products. Moreover, the failure to increase wages was in violation of the management's obligation to index wages, which was included in the collective agreement. Ordinary workers held meetings in the shops on their own initiative and drew up a handwritten petition to the director requesting an increase in pay, with signatures being collected in the shops. The trade union president, while declaring his resoluteness – *'we may take it to court and resolve this question in that way'* – in fact did not even make any attempt to lead the initiative coming from below. Line managers tried to distance themselves from this action, but they did not hand over the 'ringleaders', saying smoothly *'Some of our people proposed . . . ', 'in this shop they decided to write . . . '*. It is particularly noteworthy that the appeal was more of a request and not a legal demand. It did not even mention the failure of management to fulfil the terms of the collective agreement. The trade union president did not react in any way to what was going on and did not participate in the meetings. *'I am waiting until a few more of these appeals have been gathered – they do not relate to the trade union committee, but to the director – and then we will decide this question in some way'* (trade union president).

In many large former state enterprises the trade union is still a part of the management structure and participates in discussions, signs a collective agreement and gives its approval to bonus regulations and extra payments for particular categories of workers, as well as dismissals, redundancies and so on. But the collective agreement unequivocally plays a significant role in the determination of wages in only one of our case-study enterprises.

KhZ3 is a very traditional independent scientific research and design institute which designs production facilities for the chemical industry and is still majority-owned by its employees, although it is dominated by its two biggest customers which are minority shareholders. It is the only one of our case-study enterprises in which the collective agreement plays a significant role in the determination of wages, since it prescribes the methods for the calculation of wages and for regular pay increases. Moreover, a major component of wages consists of a bonus made up of savings on the wage fund. Each department has the right to distribute these savings between its members as they see fit, and usually this is through a joint decision of all the members of the department.

Although the trade union is not a significant force in achieving wage increases, it would be a mistake to imagine that the workers themselves do not have an influence on changes in the level and systems of payment. The workers' representations are not channelled through the trade union, but either directly or, more often, through their line managers. The latter have their own interest in ensuring that the workers under their command are well paid and that they have the resources that they need to persuade workers to overcome all the obstacles to achieving the production plans. Their high status and authority in most enterprises also mean that they are the best placed to pressure the senior management to agree to increase wages.

At **ST2**, a construction organisation that specialises in prestige construction projects and so requires a highly skilled and reliable labour force, the site foremen usually take the side of the workers when there is a dispute over wages. The issue of wage increases is raised from time to time by the workers themselves, not through protest actions but in an individual form or through delegates. Typically they send one of the longest serving and most respected workers to make representations to the chief engineer, executive director or general director. The attitude to such demands on the part of the administration is calm and tolerant. *'The workers ask, and of course there is also dissatisfaction, but the situation in the city is that our people understand very well that we try to do everything for them, we try to find work. We have paid wages to the day every month for the last three years. People can see all this. So, basically, we have already worked together for many years. Everybody understands that it is difficult. But there have been not been any incidents, excesses as such'* (chief engineer). Although such acts by the workers are rare and the managers do not see them as pressure (*'they come to cry on our shoulders'*), they certainly play a role in activating the process of increasing pay.

At the cement factory **SM1** a new management team, representing new owners, came in following the bankruptcy of the enterprise in 2001. In October 2002 the main production workers presented an ultimatum to the administration, threatening to leave if pay was not increased. The demands were presented to the general director and his deputy at a general meeting, but they were not prepared to enter into dialogue, and asked the workers for one month to think about their decision. The shop chief of the workers involved took the side of the workers because the low wages deprived him of the possibility of management and control. During this time there were rumours that the administration had negotiated an arrangement with the management of a similar factory in a distant city to hire a complete replacement team of operators although, according to the head of main production, this would be impossible because of the unique characteristics of the production process at SM1. After a month both the workers and the administration were still in an aggressive mood, neither side wanting to compromise. The administration refused to meet the workers' demands and five of the seven core operators gave in their notice so that the basic production facility was threatened with closure. At this stage of the conflict the shop chief took on the role of mediator since the loss of the workers threatened the loss of his job, and he managed *'to persuade both sides'*: the administration agreed not to hire any new workers and the workers agreed to stay at work. His basic argument was that both sides would lose more than they gained. The enterprise would have lost core workers and even if it could find new specialists, production would fall. For the workers, resignation was a guarantee of unemployment, since their skills were of no use to other enterprises. The smothering of the conflict was helped by the production situation because the following month the shop worked at full capacity so that the workers met all their supply targets and their pay doubled.

Following this conflict, the administration introduced a new incentive payment system which, on the one hand, made it possible to increase wages but, on the other hand, made them entirely dependent on the production of cement. The situation after the introduction of the new payment system deteriorated rather than improving. The differentiation of wages which was a result of the new system meant that the shop chief had to spend most of his time going off in search of workers who would agree to do the necessary work in the shop. Moreover, the workers' wages were very low in the event of a stoppage or reduced capacity working, which were common occurrences as a result of the seasonal fluctuations in demand and the repair programme introduced by the new management which required production to stop. The repairs inflamed the situation even more, because they were undertaken by contract workers paid two or three times the wage of the regular workers who were temporarily laid off. The conflict left all sides discontented. The shop chief and workers were dissatisfied with the outcome, but continued to work sullenly as the shop chief played on the loyalty of the workers to keep the lid on the situation. The directorate was dissatisfied that an uncontrollable situation had arisen and that they had not succeeded in using strong methods to suppress the conflict.

Payment systems in new private enterprises

The employees of new private enterprises are generally those who have adjusted most fully to living in market conditions and have already made the decision to take a job or to change jobs in order to earn as good a wage as they can. Such people are much more likely to leave their jobs for better opportunities elsewhere than are those who have remained working in traditional enterprises. For this reason, new private enterprises are much more constrained in their wage-setting by the prevailing wage levels in the local labour market than are traditional enterprises. New private employers have much less scope to plead their inability to pay competitive wages than do the directors of traditional enterprises. At the same time, new private employers are constrained in the wages that they can afford to pay by the outcome of their economic activities, often living from hand to mouth, so they frequently base their payment systems on a relatively small basic wage or salary, with a bonus depending on the results of the work of the enterprise as a whole, usually in the form of monthly sales figures, which (unlike profit figures) are relatively transparent. In some cases the payment system is completely *ad hoc*.

Workers at the successful new private printing and publishing firm *T1* have no contracts or job descriptions and the management of labour relations is completely informal. All decisions about pay are taken by the director individually for each employee and rates of pay are secret. There is no department of labour and wages and no wage fund, nor is there any systematic accounting of time worked or labour productivity or even spending on wages. The management conceded that the reporting of wages for tax purposes was entirely fictitious. The owner-director described the payment mechanism as follows: at the end of the month he calculates the difference between income and expenditure, then deducts the rent and communal service payments. Out of this net income about 30 per cent goes to pay. Then he looks at the results of the work of each employee, judging subjectively *'how much he has done for the enterprise'* and calculates the pay: *'It is immediately evident to me, you come, you look and it is clear how each person works. I do not discuss it with anyone, I see a group of people who work well and I see the others. . . . I cannot pay the same wages to an idler, who sits reading a book and a person who works conscientiously'*. Pay is fairly stable from month to month, but the workers had no idea how their pay was calculated.

Many new private enterprises use traditional individual piece-rate systems of payment when they are first established, but subsequently they tend to adopt collective bonus systems in which the wage is related to the results of the work of the enterprise as a whole. Line managers see this as a positive development:

> *'In the past there was a problem of getting them to do anything apart from their own operation. They did their own work, and the grass did not grow, they had to go home. To load furniture, each one had to be asked, but now they do their own work and help others without being reminded'* (head of production, furniture factory *MK2*). Some companies have more sophisticated collective bonus systems. At the fish-processing factory *RZ1*, for example, each category of employee has a different indicator on which its wages depend. For production workers this is the output achieved by their section, for managers it is the profit of the enterprise as a whole.

Many directors of new private enterprises fancy themselves as amateur psychologists, specialists in motivation, and pick up ideas from books or the newspapers. This is one reason why they are particularly inclined to experiment with payment systems, especially in setting the salaries of those working in sales and marketing on whom a great deal of responsibility for the success of the enterprise is laid and who can command high salaries in the labour market. Amongst our case-study enterprises the payment systems for sales staff range from payment purely on commission, with no fixed salary, to a high fixed salary with only an insignificant variable bonus or commission. The latter is more common in traditional enterprises, but is also found among our case-study new private enterprises (*San1*) when they want to make sure that they hold on to experienced sales personnel who know the products and the clients well and may have been trained at some expense to the company.

In general, payment systems at new private enterprises are more flexible, simpler and more secretive than at traditional enterprises. It is very common for new private enterprises to pay a low official salary which is declared for the purposes of taxation and social insurance contributions, with an additional payment made in cash and off the books. This saves the employer money, but creates a whole series of problems for the employees. One immediate problem is that it is very difficult to get consumer credit if they have a very low official salary. In the longer term they will face problems because of their lack of pension contributions. This is, of course, less of an immediate worry for the younger workers who predominate in the new private sector, but it is recognised as a problem even by many employers: *'When people reach pension age, the problems will begin. We all need a pension. But we do not show all of our pay. Really here it is higher than at many other enterprises, but officially it is 1,500 roubles'* (**MK2**), but many companies depend for their survival on such 'double bookkeeping' so that they cannot give it up: *'if we did that, we would just shut down straight away'* (**MZ4**).

Conclusion

Until the collapse of the soviet system in 1991 wage rates were strictly controlled by regulations, norms and scales issued from Moscow, and wage spending was equally strictly monitored to keep it within the authorised limits. Suddenly, towards the end of 1991, enterprises were given the freedom to adopt their own payment systems and set their own wage rates. In the past fifteen years there have been very considerable changes in payment systems, but the problems that bedevilled attempts at wage reform in the past have persisted. The main reason for this is that management has tried to make the payment system carry a weight that it cannot bear.

The reform has continued to be dominated by the traditional soviet belief that the payment system can be used as a means of providing incentives for employees to overcome the limitations of technology and the disorganisation of production management. This belief is based on the fallacy that objective constraints can be overcome by the force of willpower. In reality workers do not have the ability or the capacity to overcome the obstacles set in front of them, and even if they were able to do so, in a market economy such efforts are only recognised and validated if the products that the workers heroically produce find a buyer. In practice, the limitations of technology, management and the market mean that workers have very little influence over their own output or that of their subdivision and their wages depend very little on their own efforts.

At the same time, if the management is not to lose skilled and experienced workers, it has to ensure that they regularly earn a wage that is sufficient for them to stay. This means that payment systems have to be constantly manipulated, subverted and amended to make sure that workers do not lose out if there is a shortfall of production or sales. The most honest and rational response is to abandon the pretence that an incentive payment system can overcome all the shortcomings of production management and to pay workers a regular time-wage, and this is the approach adopted in the more far-sighted, and especially in foreign-owned, companies.

The adoption of a time-payment system leaves open the question of the 'manageability' of production workers, if the payment system does not provide the workers with monetary incentives. This is resolved in the majority of enterprises by holding down the tariff wage and cranking up the amount that is paid in bonuses, whose withdrawal can be used as a punitive sanction. This transfers all the responsibility for the effective management of production onto the line management, to which we will turn in the next chapter.

8 Line management: between capital and labour

In soviet enterprises line managers had a high degree of autonomy in the methods by which they achieved plan targets. This autonomy was strengthened with the disintegration of the soviet system as enterprises struggled to survive by all the means at their disposal. With economic stabilisation since 1998 there has been an increasing tendency to the centralisation of management, as the enterprise is subordinated to the capitalist priority of achieving the profitable production of a marketable product. This tendency has been expressed in attempts to integrate line managers into the management hierarchy and to encourage them to adopt the ideology of capitalist management, with its priority of financial results over technical achievements, in order to ensure that they more effectively meet the demands of top management in the workplace. However, the attempt to achieve such an integration is strikingly contradictory. Line managers face apparently insuperable difficulties in their attempt to carry out the tasks assigned to them as a result of their contradictory position. Underlying these difficulties is the fact that line managers are at the intersection of the aspirations of top management and the reality of the workplace, squeezed between pressure from top management and from the workers they manage. On the one hand, they are responsible for the achievement of the plan targets, on the other hand, they depend on the discipline, loyalty and will of the workers to achieve these targets. In some cases this leads to resistance on the part of the line managers to the demands imposed on them from above, in some cases they ignore or passively subvert those demands, and in some cases they do their best to achieve the demands imposed on them, using their traditional methods.

These processes take different forms in different types of enterprise. There are considerable differences between traditional enterprises (where traditional practices are embedded in the organisation and in the values and expectations of the employees) and new private enterprises. There are differences between enterprises which are under outside ownership or are part of holding companies unequivocally subordinated to the production of profit, and independent enterprises where the production orientation and at least the rhetoric of collectivism often still prevails. There are differences depending on the characteristics of the labour force: the number employed, the degree of skill and experience required and the situation in the local labour market. In a brief discussion we cannot take all of these and other sources of variation fully into account, but we will draw attention to them where they arise. In particular, we will concentrate on the reproduction or transformation of management structures and practices in traditional enterprises.[1]

The expanding functions of line management

We have seen in our discussion of corporate management that the status of the production divisions within the management structure varies from one enterprise to another, depending on the character of the product, the extent to which the enterprise has adapted its management structure to the demands of the market and whether or not it has been integrated into a holding structure as a production platform. Whatever the status of the production divisions within the enterprise, their function is to deliver the range and quantity of products of the prescribed quality, according to a defined schedule and with the resources allocated for that purpose. It is this function that determines the status and place of line management in the enterprise. Line managers include both shop chiefs and foremen, whose status and role depends to some extent on the size of the production shops: a shop chief may manage anything from a handful to 1,000 or more workers. In the latter case, of course, his role is closer to that of a middle manager, while the line management role falls to the foremen.

We asked shop chiefs and foremen in some detail about their spheres of responsibility and their participation in decision-making. The reduction in the status of these middle managers is graphically illustrated by the extent to which they are excluded from strategic decision-making. In independent enterprises a bare majority of shop chiefs participated in decision-making regarding employment, production and work organisation, but in enterprises incorporated into holding companies fewer than a quarter of shop chiefs participated in decision-making even in these spheres which related directly to their functional responsibilities, and the majority were only consulted, or only involved once the decisions had been taken. When it came to questions of finance, wages, and even planning and social policy, the majority of shop chiefs were not even consulted before decisions were made and in questions of investment and price-setting the majority were not even involved in discussion after the decisions had been taken.

Shop chiefs, in general, only had the authority to make decisions within the confines of their shops and their sphere of competence is generally limited to the regulation of daily production activity, although even here there were tendencies to the erosion of this authority. In the majority of cases shop chiefs

---

[1] This chapter draws heavily on Natasha Goncharova's paper, 'Проблемы интеграции линейного менеджмента в управленческую иерархию' [Problems of integration of line management in the management hierarchy], in Кабалина В. И. (ред.) *Практики управления персоналом на современных российских предприятиях*, Москва: ИСИТО, 2005.

had the authority to hire workers and foremen for their shops, but in almost no case did they have any say in determining the terms of their contracts. In half the independent enterprises, though rarely in those incorporated into holding companies, shop chiefs could determine the pay of individual workers, but they could never determine the size of the wage fund available to the shop and only rarely had the authority to assign pay increases or to determine the social benefits provided. In most independent enterprises, but only a quarter of those incorporated into holding companies, shop chiefs had control of the work schedule. They were nearly always responsible for identifying candidates for redundancy, but hardly ever decided how many should be made redundant. As the shop chief of *SM4* said about his functional duties, *'I am only the executor'*.

> The bread and pasta combine *KhBK2* is a fairly typical subsidiary of a holding company. Despite the quite democratic rituals in the dialogue between top and middle managers, the latter do not have any real participation in decision-making and behave appropriately at meetings – they report, but do not propose anything. As a shop chief said about 'management': *'If there are any questions, they call me, that is, I tell them what is going on'*. The shop chiefs do not feel included in strategic management and they themselves see their task as being exclusively to fulfil the plan and maintain the quality of production. Senior management does not think highly of them. According to the chief of the personnel service, *'we have weak middle managers – almost all shop chiefs and foremen are production workers, they are not able to work with the collective, they do not understand the sense of the reforms'*. Moreover, shop chiefs, despite their formally high status, receive much lower wages than top managers. Thus, middle managers do not have any interest in promoting the realisation of the strategic plans of the enterprise and transmitting the ideas of management to their subordinates.

At practically every enterprise that we studied we found that the everyday management of work processes at the level of the shops was very traditional and had shown very little change. For the vast majority of shop chiefs, the main task of the shop is the traditional one of fulfilling the plan, although six of twenty-five shop chiefs in holding structures said their main task was to improve quality. Despite all the rhetoric about customer orientation, only one shop chief reported that the main task of his shop was to meet the customer's needs and not one said that their main task was to reduce production costs. The primary functions of the shop chiefs are to organise the production process, the distribution of work and the scheduling and control of the performance of tasks to deliver the output with the resources put at their disposal. As noted above, shop chiefs do not usually participate in the development of plan targets, or even in their revision.

In some cases, where there has been a decentralisation of the management structure, the responsibility of line managers has been substantially increased:

At the foreign-owned *LPZ2* there has been a decentralisation of management so that the fulfilment of the plan within the shop is completely the responsibility of the foremen. *'When there was a chief engineer, he was responsible also for production questions and technical safety. Now this post has been removed and his functions have been transferred to us'* (head of the chemicals shop). Whereas in the past the foremen worked alongside the workers, and their role in the process was like that of a brigadier, now they no longer participate in the work itself, but control its fulfilment. The increased status of the foremen is shown by the fact that they now have individual contracts (like all the managers of the enterprise) and have received a significant increase in their pay. The foremen here identify themselves with management, although they wear workers' overalls, unlike the shop chiefs, who wear suits and have their own private offices.

The achievement of plan tasks was almost universally recognised to be the sphere of competence of line managers, in which top management does not generally interfere. Thus, although shop chiefs have largely been excluded from strategic decision-making, the majority of them reported that the degree of their independence had increased. If top management is dissatisfied with the methods or the performance of line managers, the remedy is entirely traditional, to replace the line manager with somebody else and let the new person get on with the job.

The shop chief may have been displaced from the status hierarchy of management, but in their own domain they are the unquestioned ruler. Frequently shop chiefs are the only source of information for foremen and workers about what is going on in the enterprise. It is to the shop chiefs that workers take their grievances and it is the shop chiefs who resolve disputes. Seventy per cent of shop chiefs and 60 per cent of foremen considered participation in the resolution of labour disputes to be one of their functions

The basic functions of shop chiefs, foremen and brigadiers are in many respects identical and differ only in the scale of the workplace under their control and their level of responsibility. For example, 94 per cent of shop chiefs and 90 per cent of foremen named the control of the fulfilment of the plan as one of their functions and the vast majority named this as their most important function.

As a shop chief at the road-building firm *ST1* said: *'The functions of the section chiefs and foremen and so on are just the same as under communism, they are determined by the quarterly, annual and monthly plans. They are provided with everything they need and they organise production on the spot'*. In traditional enterprises the functions of line managers have not changed, although their degree of responsibility has increased. At the bakery *KhBK1* neither the shop chiefs nor the foremen were able to identify any significant changes in their work but *'the responsibilities have increased, certainly: the equipment is more complex, the volume has increased, but not the functions'.*

Shop chiefs try as far as possible to leave the responsibility for the direct management of the workers in the shop to the foremen. In a few cases the workers are left to get on with the work themselves.

> The open-cast coal mine *U1* has a highly centralised management, but it practises 'self-organisation of work' where often managers at all levels are in a supernumerary situation, they trust the workers and only monitor the results of their work. The workers in the elite excavator sections are very skilled and experienced, with pretty high levels of education, some to degree level. They have worked here for a long time and know the mining-geological conditions and how to use the technology well. Moreover, selection over recent years has meant that those who remain are the best of the best. The result is that many of the workers have at least as much technical competence as the foremen and even the shop chiefs. A group of such workers can take fundamental decisions about the organisation of work on the face. For example, the excavator operators can order a bulldozer driver to clear away a place for loading the dumpers, although this is formally the responsibility of the foreman and shop chief. This decision will then be reported to the shop chief and, if necessary, entered into the technical documentation.

Such self-organisation on the part of the workers does not always proceed so smoothly, in which case the line managers have to intervene.

> At the specialist construction company *ST2* the job rates are such that some jobs pay much better than others, leading to conflicts over the allocation of tasks. *'I give a job to the shop, I cannot give each individual his task. . . . We have got one old-timer, he takes the task from you, and gives one job to one person, another to another. . . . They had a conflict, but I told them, sort it out among yourselves, nobody but you can decide it. Well, it is all the same to me. Basically you must determine everybody's workload yourselves'* (director of the production base). However, the increasing quality demands mean that the foreman has to make sure that jobs are only given to those sufficiently competent to do them. *'Now the situation has changed a bit. We have divided the work into well-paid and not so well-paid. Now much of the material is expensive and we entrust it only to experienced people, painters. . . . We do not give high quality [work] to the plasterer because he is learning and has worked his whole life as a plasterer. Of course, he would like to work on high quality, but you need experience, you need the skill'* (site foreman).

Twenty-eight out of forty-six production directors questioned noted that the degree of responsibility and independence of line managers had increased. The vast majority of shop chiefs said that their functions, as well as their independence, had increased, and foremen too thought that their functions had expanded, not one reporting that they had contracted. In some cases there has been an increased workload due to the abolition of posts. For example, at *TF1* there were separate posts of controller and tally keeper in a brigade, but these functions are now carried out by the foreman. At *MetZ1* the foreign owner de-layered management and abolished the post of foreman so that the workers are now managed directly by the section head. In other cases the workload may have increased due to the acquisition of more complicated equipment, an increase in the total amount of production, more rigorous quality standards or an expansion of the product range. Frequently, the responsibility and independence of the line managers has increased because they have to cope with antiquated and unreliable equipment. But the biggest increase in the burden placed on line managers is that they have to achieve increasingly demanding tasks with considerably diminished resources. *'As they say, they praise me, but they also abuse me if something does not work out. All the same I am always the one responsible'* (Shop Chief, *LPZ1*).

In carrying out their tasks, shop chiefs continue to face many of the problems that plagued them in soviet times of uneven delivery of essential supplies, of poor-quality components and raw materials, of unreliable machinery and equipment and shortages of essential tools and spare parts, although now these problems are often the result of the incompetence or penny-pinching of senior management rather than necessarily of the system as a whole.

> At *MZ1*, which makes electrical equipment, responsibility for providing materials formally lies with the senior managers. However, they try to shift responsibility on to the shoulders of the shop chiefs. *'The deputy director for production does not want to decide anything. He keeps quiet at the operational meetings. I am constantly having to speak out myself in order to press for some decision. I get absolutely no help from him, all responsibility falls only on the shop chiefs. And if there are no materials, where can I get them from myself? They also contrived to give the post of "head of production" specially to a young man. Responsibilities are not understood, what he does is not clear, there is also no help from him, he only supervises'* (head of shop two). The director prefers not to delve into such situations: *'He is not a producer, it is very complicated with him, he does not understand us and we him. He does not want to delve into production, you start to explain something and he just says "that is your problem"'* (head of shop two). On one occasion the head of shop two was removed from his post for failure to fulfil his production tasks, although the real reason for the failure was the absence of materials which could not be blamed on him alone.

While the dramatic macroeconomic decline and the transition to a market economy may have made shortages a thing of the past for those with the money to buy, the lack of funds for investment, or even for the basic maintenance and repair of equipment, has made the problem for line managers of managing production with inappropriate, unreliable and decrepit machinery progressively more difficult than it was even in soviet times. This has made them even more dependent on the skills and commitment of their core workers than they were in the past.

Line managers no longer merely have to beat out the regular monthly plan, they have to achieve unstable and unpredictable production targets, which may change day by day in response to fluctuating sales. This may not lead to disquiet if the tendency is for the plan to be increased, because that means more work and so more wages for the workers in the shop, although it can lead to a big headache for the line managers if they are short of workers. At the same time, they have to do this while meeting ever stricter quality demands and with tighter restrictions on the expenditure of money and resources.

The pressure to cut spending is partly expressed in the pressure to keep the number employed to a minimum, often referred to euphemistically as the 'optimisation of numbers'. In the traditional soviet system, with its supposedly scientifically planned Taylorist production, workers were assigned to precisely demarcated jobs according to their specific qualifications and in principle were only expected to do their own job. The Labour Code imposed severe limitations on the ability of line managers to move workers between jobs or transfer them between shops, such transitions normally having to be fully documented and requiring the workers' written agreement. Of course, in practice line managers had to use all manner of means to persuade workers to take on work that was not formally theirs, or to work beyond their normal working hours, and relied very heavily on their core workers to achieve the plan. The Labour Code still imposes some restrictions on the freedom of line managers to move workers around, but in order to achieve their fluctuating production plans with unreliable equipment and a reduced labour force, line managers rely even more than they did in the past on being able to transfer workers from one job to another, which also puts a premium on multi-skilling for the workers themselves. This puts an additional burden on the line managers as they have to persuade workers to switch from one job to another or to stay late or work at the weekend to complete an urgent order or achieve the monthly plan.

In the majority of our case-study enterprises senior management had taken steps to strengthen discipline, adding to the pressure on line managers.

At *MetZ2* the general director signed an order imposing strict punishments for turning up at work drunk. Initially some employees did not take the order seriously, but the management claim that the problem of drunkenness at the enterprise has been virtually eliminated, although *'even now they go to work with a jar of gin. Through the entrance they hide it in their jacket and go quietly through'* (auxiliary shop foreman). The key figure in maintaining discipline is the foreman, who not only has to monitor his colleagues at work, but also has to keep a check on their behaviour out of work. If a worker turns up for work drunk, the foreman is considered responsible 'by default': *'It means he did not do his job. . . . We had a grinder. A young lad . . . he carried out all the work. But he overindulged in spirits. Once he disappeared and could not be found. He should have informed the foreman, but he did not inform him. That was it, I went to look for him. I found him. He was there in some village. He said – I am off sick'* (auxiliary shop foreman). They do not actually punish the foreman if the worker is caught at the entrance to the factory, but if it happens at the exit then the foreman takes practically full responsibility. The young foremen consider that this aspect of their work is too big an extra-production load. They think that it is impossible and unnecessary completely to control the behaviour of the workers even inside the factory, so long as they do their job. Moreover, it increases the degree of detachment of the foreman from his collective and provokes an atmosphere of distrust. *'He* [the worker] *can even get pissed after work here, somewhere in the showers. I will not see him. If he has worked the shift normally, then drinks in the showers, they will catch him at the exit. I cannot go and sniff at everyone, I am not a dog. . . . And he may be a silent alcoholic. He drank, but it was not obvious that he was drunk. He drank by himself, but he stood at the machine and worked'* (shop foreman).

At *MetZ3* the new management has tried to tighten workplace discipline. Although discipline is the responsibility of the foremen, the general director makes a point on his daily rounds of the production shops of pinpointing disciplinary violations. If the general director identifies a violation he immediately phones the quality director on his mobile telephone and reports who should be fined how much, where and for what. These regular phone calls annoy the quality director, who considers that his task is to remove the reasons for quality failures and that punishments are not his responsibility.

In order to ensure that people return promptly from their lunch breaks, the administration introduced a new system to control passage through the entrance and automatically report lateness, which proved chaotic as many personnel had to pass to and fro regularly as part of their jobs. This led to dissatisfaction, protest and sabotage among employees and the trade union had to call in the Labour Inspectorate. As a result, the management had to make concessions.

The new general director issued a notice requiring that the safety rule that everybody should wear a helmet on site should be strictly enforced. When the general director saw people in the factory without helmets, he began to scream and take away bonuses, although there were not enough helmets to go round. People then hid behind the equipment so that managers would not see that they were not wearing a helmet. This went on for several months.

The shrinking resources of line management

The expansion of the functions and responsibility of shop chiefs and foremen has not been associated with an increase in the managerial resources at their disposal. Far from it, the attempt to strengthen senior management control in order to subordinate the enterprise to the constraints of the market or the dictates of the owners has markedly reduced the resources available to line managers and the degree of discretion that they can exercise in disposing of these resources. In the opinion of many of the line managers interviewed, they have to deliver the plan in the absence of real material and administrative levers of influence on workers.

> The shop chiefs at *MZ1* have to operate in the rigid framework of the monthly plan, about which they are not consulted, producing electrical equipment with antiquated machinery and inadequate supply of materials, while not having any real levers of influence over the workers. Line managers, talking about their work, frequently said that they had to '*twist and turn*' to get it done.

The resources available to shop chiefs, foremen and brigadiers have been significantly reduced. In the late soviet period line managers could in principle regulate workers' wages through the coefficient of labour participation (KTU), which would be used to raise or lower the wages of individual workers according to their contribution to production, disciplinary record and so on. The main limitation of this system was that it was only possible to reward one worker by penalising another, since the average coefficient was unity, which risked provoking conflict, so the line manager was always under pressure to award a uniform KTU to equalise wages. It is also difficult to use KTU where production is organised collectively or on an assembly line, where there are no objective indicators of the work of each individual, because in this case the assignment of the KTU is on the purely subjective judgement of the line manager. Where there was a brigade organisation, the KTU was usually set by the brigade itself, which had the same equalising effect. The system of KTU was abandoned by many enterprises in the crisis years of the 1990s, when the priority was survival rather than plan fulfilment, but with recovery this meant that line managers had lost their preferred lever of influence over the workers.

> At the petrochemicals plant *NKhZ1*, the KTU was abolished as a part of the centralisation of control of spending when it was integrated into a large holding company. The shop chiefs are proposing a return to the KTU system: '*They sometimes come from the shops and ask, the question has already been hanging over us for a long time, to reintroduce – we had it in the past – the coefficient of labour participation. . . . The shop chiefs want these coefficients of labour participation again. Because they cannot always punish the worker. There is an order or something else like that, but they would prefer to work with the coefficient of labour participation. . . . But now we only punish according to the list* ' (head of department of labour and wages).

In most soviet enterprises the line managers also had their own funds which they could use to make additional incentive payments to workers to persuade them to work beyond the normal expectations. The payments were small, but they were symbolically significant and provided a very useful lever for the line managers. Nowadays people want real money and the symbolic value of additional payments has been considerably eroded, but such funds can give line managers a powerful management lever.

A clear example of the effectiveness of this system is the fertiliser factory **KhZ2**. For carrying out particularly difficult work, workers receive some payment, as a rule, from the shop chief's fund. The bonus system at the enterprise also leaves the shop chiefs quite a lot of freedom in decision-making. In fact, they themselves decide how much bonus to pay each worker. There are two additional bonus funds at the disposal of the shop chiefs, for introducing technical innovations and for carrying out especially important work, the latter having been introduced at the suggestion of the shop chiefs. Money from these funds is used basically to encourage workers to master adjacent specialities, raise their skill level, or carry out functions which have not been stipulated by their job descriptions. However, shop chiefs also use it as a way of supporting the pay of particular groups of workers whom they feel are underpaid. *'They use this fund as a way of paying a hidden increase in wages. Well, say, the chief considers that this person is undervalued in this system. There are such cases'* (head of planning-economic department).

The shop chief's fund is used for the same purposes at the cement factory **SM1**. Distribution of the bonus fund is also completely handed over to line managers at the electrical equipment factory, **ET1**: *'Each foreman is responsible for quality, plan fulfilment, if he needs to encourage particular employees, somebody to carry out uncharacteristic work, above-plan work, there is an emergency, repair work, something with the chemicals, he sends me a list: for carrying out such work we will reward such and such an employee, a proposed sum. I gather everything together in a heap, I look to see whether or not I can cover it, then I give it to the foreman, the foreman gives the incentive'* (shop chief). At **SM4**, which makes reinforced concrete fabrications, the position and authority of brigadiers has been increased due to the introduction of 'brigadiers' payments'.

However, these cases are the exceptions. Although there has been a substantial relative increase in bonus payments and corresponding reduction in the guaranteed part of the wage, and there is a proliferation of regulations that prescribe bonuses and incentive payments for anything and everything that the enterprise wants to encourage, the attempt to centralise control of expenditure and impose uniform payment systems has meant that line managers often have no influence over the size of the bonus. In about half the case-study enterprises the shop chief has the right to determine bonuses, and in a few cases bonuses are determined by the foreman, but in 40 per cent the bonus is determined by the director or central administration. Moreover, even where line managers have the power to determine the bonus, it is not a very effective form of incentive payment because it is nearly always regarded as a part of the regular wage, many workers not even knowing how much of their wage is accounted for by the bonus. This means that any attempt to reduce the bonus would be likely to provoke severe conflict.

The shop management has some control over the distribution of wages if the shop has its own wage fund. However, in many enterprises the material incentive funds and shop wage funds have been liquidated as a part of the centralisation of control over resources. Shop wage funds still exist in only just over half of the traditional enterprises and in very few of the new private enterprises in our sample. Only about a third of shops had their own material incentive funds, with rather more in independent enterprises, and such funds are very rare in new private enterprises. Only one in six foremen in independent traditional enterprises, one in ten in new private and one in twenty in holding companies had foremen's funds.

> *'It would be good if the shop chief had a system of incentives in his hands. I worked in the past with such a system. When there is the possibility of giving people who deserve it an incentive, that is a big lever. The present system suffers from many inadequacies'* (chief of repair shop, *NKhZ1*).

The chief of the ice-cream shop at **KhDK1** also complains that in the past there were many more levers of influence than she has today. *'In the past there was socialist competition, in the past we took account of the quality of labour. If I saw that one of my workers worked badly I gave her a minus. We only gave them a few roubles, but it was an incentive. Now I do not have any of that, there is nothing. I cannot even punish. The only punishment is a reprimand or the sack, they are upset, but it would be much more effective with roubles. We have absolutely none of that. All the time I say . . . I drop in to the shop – there is a mistake: not that weight, not that label . . . someone goes into the toilet in her overall, she has not washed her hands, then she has violated the sanitary regime, but I cannot punish her. I shout, I scold, but that is all. Or they pack 120 grams (instead of 100), they have exceeded the weight, or the mixture began to leak, once even into the sewer, that is a loss, again I cannot punish anyone for that. . . . It is very difficult to work with people now. In the past there was a stimulus, the bonus, if you take it away it will be worse, they made an effort. Now people, of course, are completely different. . . . The system of KTU disappeared because of perestroika twelve years ago'.*

At the bakery **KhBK1** serious problems have arisen in the transport section, which is a relatively new department established to handle the delivery of bread. The problem of payment for additional responsibilities leads to constant conflict. The drivers refuse to carry out tasks of unloading, for which they are not paid, the loaders refuse to clear snow from the roads on the territory of the factory. Line managers have to find a way of solving these problems for themselves: *'There is not any kind of monetary fund to* *encourage the workers, even to carry out any kind of additional work, for example, to clear ice from the entrance to the place where we load bread. The director said that I should ask somebody to do it. I asked the loaders. Once they cleared it, but they would not do it again, nobody wants to do it without payment. It turned out that we had to use the trade union money for this, that is given to our department once every three months for visiting the sick (300 roubles). I paid 150 roubles to the lads twice'* (head of the sales department).

When line managers do not have control of bonus funds, the most effective ways in which they can influence workers' earnings are the traditional mechanisms of the distribution of tasks and internal transfers, by which line managers can assign the most loyal and reliable workers to the best-paid tasks to enable them to earn the best wages, but this can also create problems because it deprives others of the chance to earn.

> In the same transport section of **KhBK1** a group of drivers who have worked there for a long time has become established. These people comprise the core of the labour collective of the section on whom the chief can rely. Newly arrived drivers get the less profitable routes and they are given the older equipment, so their incomes are relatively low. These conditions do not encourage them to stay in their jobs and many new employees leave the enterprise, so this is the one area of the enterprise which faces problems of high labour turnover.

The very limited ability of line managers to provide positive incentives for their workers means that the main levers of management at their disposal are negative, disciplinary measures. '*In the hands of middle management there is only the stick in the form of fines. The carrots, in the form of bonuses, are in the hands of the owners*' (*SO1*). As an illustration of the asymmetry in the power of line managers to punish and reward their workers, in just over half the cases shop chiefs and foremen could influence the bonuses to be paid to workers, while in over 80 per cent of cases it was they who imposed fines and punishments.

The limited powers of the line manager are not a major problem in prosperous enterprises which pay good wages, where people value their jobs. At the new telecommunications company **TK1**, a verbal reprimand is enough: '*Well, a rebuke is appropriate, but it is all basically verbal. It works. But they never punish with money; an informal warning – that is already a very strict form. There is nothing more*' (head of the design-licensing section). But in most enterprises, as noted by the chief of the ice-cream shop above, punishments are much less effective. Reprimands are ineffective, and dismissal is too draconian a punishment, particularly where the line manager needs to hold on to all the experienced workers to cope with fluctuating (and often increasing) production demands. The most widespread form of punishment available, that is most commonly imposed for wastage and for failure to meet quality standards, is deprivation of some or all of the bonus. But, as noted above, such a punishment can provoke a disproportionate response. Moreover, many line managers are reluctant to impose any monetary punishments because their workers have such low wages that it is impossible to live on any less.

The management policy at the construction company *ST2* is that monetary punishments in present conditions are an unduly harsh measure because even without any loss of their bonus the workers receive low wages. Instead they emphasise the responsibility of workers and make them stay on late to rectify faults. In the view of the management such a 'humanistic' approach has proved itself.

MZ7 suffers from a high level of breakage, but the director does not impose monetary penalties. *'I have not yet held back the pay of a single worker for breaking a machine or a mould; if I begin to do this, they will not be able to earn'.*

The most commonly used forms of punishment are informal warnings and deprivation of bonus, each used in more than 80 per cent of enterprises. Shop chiefs are more likely than are foremen to use dismissal as a disciplinary sanction, but even then, particularly in independent traditional and new private enterprises, they prefer to encourage workers to quit voluntarily rather than to dismiss them 'under article'. Line managers are also reluctant to impose a strong reprimand with an entry in the worker's labour book, which would make it difficult for the worker to get another job.

In addition to having diminished resources at their disposal, line management is often cut off from information flows, particularly if there is a formalisation of management structures and processes. The traditional source of information for lower-level managers and workers in a soviet enterprise, apart from rumours and the factory newspaper and radio, was the regular meetings and informal discussions at which information would be passed down the line. The shop chiefs would typically have a weekly meeting with the general director and a meeting at least once a day with the production director, which would address current production issues and provide information about broader developments. The shop chief would meet with the foremen at the beginning of the day, and the foremen would similarly meet with their workers and report on current issues while assigning the day's production tasks. These meetings still typically occur, but the downward flow of information has been significantly reduced. As middle managers are increasingly excluded from managerial decision-making, they are cut off from access to information, which correspondingly chokes off the flow of information to the workers. Where computerised management information systems are introduced, line managers either do not have access to the system, or their access is restricted to the information directly relating to their managerial tasks.

Among our respondents, the majority of shop chiefs got information at planning meetings and directly from the top management of the enterprise, foremen got information from their shop chiefs, and workers from their line managers. Rumours were a significant source of information only for workers. The more highly centralised is decision-making, the more restricted is the downward flow of information.

At the knitting factory *TF2*, only the director has access to the full range of information and other managers only have the information that they require to carry out the responsibilities of their posts. The subdivisions have to provide complete operational information upwards, but information comes back down only in small doses. Information about the ownership of the enterprise, the composition and activities of the Board of Directors, and about the external relations of the enterprise in general, were all very well hidden.

Very much the same situation was found at the bakery *KhBK1*, although here information flows primarily through informal channels: *'Everyone has worked here a long time, everyone knows everyone else, so why create bureaucratic barriers between one another?'*

At *SM1*, where decision-making is very centralised, there are problems with the flow of information in both directions. From the bottom up, the problem is that there are discrepancies in filling internal forms reporting the state of affairs in the shops. From the top down, there is insufficient information, as the management team demands unconditional execution, while those below often do not understand what this or that decision requires, and how it is related to the activity of the enterprise or their particular subdivision.

The autonomy of line management

Line managers are under severe pressure from above to persuade the workers in their shops and sections to achieve plans and targets from the formulation of which they have largely been excluded, while they have very limited resources with which to achieve their aims. The fact that their wages are also much closer to those of the workers with whom they interact every day leads them in the majority of cases to identify with their workers rather than with senior management.

At *MZ1* there is no significant hierarchical distance between the positions of shop chiefs and foremen. Both are excluded from strategic decision-making, have limited access to information, their authority is confined to the production divisions and is restricted by the rigid centralisation of planning and financing. Though the pay of the shop chiefs is higher, they do not consider themselves representatives of senior management and are not perceived as such by foremen. Moreover, shop chiefs do not have separate offices; they work in the same room as the foremen.

At *TF1* foremen, brigadiers and even chiefs of shops position themselves as working class. Notwithstanding the fact that all shop chiefs are shareholders of the enterprise, they do not identify themselves with the group of managers, even less do they identify themselves as owners.

When we asked line managers what qualities they needed to do the job, the most important, in order of significance, were ability to organise the work, ability to fulfil the plan on time and knowledge of the specific features of production. The ability to adapt to constant changes was rated only marginally more highly than the ability to earn the confidence of their workers. Twice as many foremen and four times as many shop chiefs nominated being able to earn the confidence of the workers as nominated being able to earn the confidence of higher management (not one of the thirty-nine shop chiefs in enterprises owned by holding companies cited the latter quality). In traditional enterprises the shop chiefs and foremen still have the high status in the eyes of workers that they enjoyed in soviet times (especially when, as is usually the case, they have made their career at the same enterprise).

At *SM4* the older generation of workers, who are the majority in the enterprise, relate respectfully to their chiefs as '*the same as us*': '*He* [the shop chief] *is closer to workers. We have good relations. He worked as a welder earlier, as a mechanic. I have known him for a long time, since '83'*.

Shop chiefs are particularly close to the workers where they relate to them directly.

At *TF2*, a textile combine, there has been a considerable reduction of the management apparatus. As a result of restructuring, the main shops were combined and the post of head of production was abolished (the director of the enterprise took over responsibility for the management of the main shops, the chief engineer is responsible for the auxiliary shops). The sharp reduction in the staff of the organisation also led to the elimination of brigadiers and foremen and the widening of the functional responsibilities of the remaining line managers. For example, in one of the auxiliary shops (the water purification shop) only one line manager, the shop chief, remains. The shop chiefs here consider themselves to be closer to workers than to management.

In some cases the day-to-day management of work is entirely in the hands of foremen and brigadiers, whose increased managerial authority might be expected to increase their distance from the workers, particularly as foremen have a higher level of education and generally less work experience than do the workers under their command. Nevertheless, foremen and brigadiers generally identify themselves as workers and not as managers.

At *LPZ1*, a new private sawmill, in the drying shop, notwithstanding the fact that formally the foreman is responsible for ensuring the productivity of the shift, his functions are practically the same as those of the workers. In his interview he identified himself as one of the skilled workers (despite earning double their wages) because he has been deprived of any real levers to encourage or punish the workers and because he is not integrated into the structure of management.

In total, more than 70 per cent of seventy-eight foremen considered themselves to be workers or closer to workers, while only three considered themselves to be managers. In holding companies almost a third of foremen defined themselves unequivocally as workers, while not one foreman in a new private enterprise defined him or herself as a manager.

In soviet enterprises workers tended to look to the management rather than the trade union as the main defender of their interests and this continues to be the case in the enterprises that we studied.

The last increase in job rates at *SM4* was in spring 2004. According to the brigadier of the moulding shop, the initiative for the pay increase came from the workers: *'We gathered the whole shop, the director came. We raised the question of increasing pay, pay was small, the job rates were weak. He promised to increase the job rates, and he did that, job rates were raised. We felt that pay had improved'*. How did that happen? *'First we went to the foreman, then the foreman went to the shop chief with the brigadiers, and she invited the director along'*.

The majority of workers interviewed saw the management of the enterprise as their most reliable defence in relation to questions of pay, working conditions, work regime, health and safety, and even benefits and social welfare questions. Only in relation to the latter two issues, which are the specific sphere of responsibility of the trade union, did a significant number of workers cite the trade union as defender of their interests and even there more workers responded that nobody or they alone could best defend their interests. In all but these last two issues it is striking that more workers cited the enterprise management than their line management as the best defenders of their interests and that there was no significant difference between independent enterprises and enterprises which are part of a holding company (and even new private enterprises, which generally do not have a trade union organisation) in this respect. This is not so much an indicator of greater confidence in enterprise management than line management as confirmation of the extent to which the discretion of line management has been reduced so that they only really have control in dealing with social and welfare questions (distribution of privileges, benefits and so on), where they still have a great deal of autonomy.

Line managers are not the vanguard of working-class resistance to the advance of capitalism. Their commitment is to retaining their independence as production managers and to their workers as diligent producers. Line managers may make representations on behalf of their workers, but they do not usually lead their workers into outright resistance to senior management (although they have an interest in pressing for their workers to be adequately paid and they can play a decisive role if there is a struggle for power in the enterprise).[1] They are more likely to ignore, avoid, subvert or transform inconvenient instructions that are handed down from above, very often on the basis of informal relations within the shop and informal connections with managers of other divisions. This is frequently the case if senior management demands a tightening of labour discipline, often with a policy of zero tolerance for drinking at work, but line managers do not want to lose skilled, reliable and loyal workers just because they have a drink now and then.

> *'If somebody* [he is referring to the loaders] *comes to work drunk, if he has worked well for a long time, then usually we won't betray him to the bosses., In the worst of cases I would give him a reduced* [coefficient]*, we will lie him down in the store room. It is a pity to punish, I grew up with them all'* (head of the sales department, **KhBK1**). *'If someone is an absentee or a drinker, I call them for an interview rather than immediately sack them. If they are completely insolent, then we hold a meeting, we criticise them and if it continues we give them a reprimand'* (**KhBK1**).

Similarly, in the event of breakages or failure to meet quality standards, the foremen and shop chiefs do not want to deprive low-paid workers of their bonuses, as is normally prescribed by the regulations. So they turn a blind-eye, or cover up the violations of disciplinary or technical regulations, which in turn puts the worker under an obligation to the line manager, providing the latter with what is often their most powerful lever of management.

If people arrive at work drunk at **MK1** this is resolved pragmatically by the foreman: *'Well, suppose somebody arrives drunk. It happens, from the evening. A hangover. For this we may impose a fine. . . . we look at how he is. Obviously, we cannot allow him on the machine, no, but* [he may be able to stay at work] *if he is responsible'* (foreman). If such a situation is repeated, then the worker will be dismissed. However, not one of our informants could remember a single case of dismissal for this reason.

At the open-cast coal mine **U1** some disciplinary violations are hidden from the top management by the heads of subdivisions and problems are dealt with

---

[1]   Simon Clarke and Veronika Kabalina, 'Privatisation and the struggle for control of the enterprise in Russia', in David Lane (ed.) *Russia in Transition*, London: Longman, 1995.

at an informal level, but this is only possible for minor violations or accidents which can be covered up. In more serious cases there are rigorous procedures for reporting and investigation that have to be followed.

At the metallurgical factory *MetZ2*, the shop chief specifically has the right to intercede with the administration on behalf of a worker who has violated the order against drunkenness and so is subject to dismissal, but the shop chief must *'take upon himself'* some of the guilt of the worker, accepting a reduction in his own bonus: *'All our heavy drinkers – the foreman, senior foreman come here to me, and the shop chief, three people who petition to leave them alone. The shop chief has already prepared an order – 100 per cent loss of bonus for the section chief or shift chief . . . the shop chiefs lose from 10 to 25 per cent of bonus'* (deputy general director for social questions).

When problems arise, line managers do not normally refer them up the hierarchical management structure, but resolve them on their own initiative through informal relations, which regularly strengthens horizontal interaction between line managers.

At *MZ1* there is a constant interaction between chiefs of the preparatory and assembly shops: *'We work with the chief, he is a young guy, good. If something is impossible for me, I go to him, and he always tries to re-plan the activity to supply our shop. Our mutual understanding is good. We solve problems in working order. At the operational meetings we only bring up those questions which we cannot solve ourselves'* (shop chief). According to the specialists at the fertiliser factory *KhZ2*, managers there also try to resolve production problems at their own level, without involving higher management. Horizontal interaction at the level of production management also prevails at the furniture factory *MK2*. Practically all production problems are resolved there and then, without reference to higher management.

At *MZ5*, which makes cranes, there is an interesting situation in which a higher degree of formalisation of the powers and responsibilities of line managers coincides with the continued use of informal methods of management. Here the formalisation of the management system is consistent with the continuation of traditional practices. Unlike most enterprises, the shop chief has been given the power and independence to achieve the tasks assigned to him. He has control of the wage fund for the shop, so that he is able to use the funds provided by productivity increases to pay substantial bonuses to the workers of the shop. Good wages have also made it possible to tighten discipline, so that here, unlike most enterprises, the penalty for drinking at work really is dismissal. However, as in the soviet system, it is up to the shop chief to play the system successfully and here there is a sharp contrast between the situation in different shops, depending on whether they find themselves in the virtuous circle of success or the vicious circle of failure.

In the casting shop the newly appointed shop chief has managed to assemble a hard-working collective which has increased productivity and earnings substantially. The foreman is responsible to the shop chief for the fulfilment of the plan, and the new shop chief insists on the subordination of the foreman to him: *'The foreman is closer to me. There must not be any familiarity there. We must take the same line'*. The horizontal interaction of line managers, which arises informally elsewhere, has been officially recognised, as line managers have been granted wide powers which enable them to work effectively. *'Shop chiefs have been given a great deal of independence. I have not seen that anywhere. I try to resolve questions myself at my own level, so as not to burden their heads* [senior management], *they've got plenty of problems. I understood long ago that the more questions you put, you inconvenience the management, the worse all this turns back against you. And when you resolve questions at your level, in parallel with colleagues from other shops and departments, the better it turns out. Without scandals, resentment. Because if you take the question upstairs, then it looks to your opponent like a complaint. So it is better to resolve things at your level, and the management appreciates this and things go better'* (shop chief).

The shop chief is fully in support of the top management's tough line on discipline, insisting that *'there are no irreplaceable people'*, but his management methods are based on the traditional methods of manipulation of individuals rather than on any more systematic organisation of production: *'I always say to my colleagues that you have to work with cadres. You have to know each person psychologically, what he breathes. A dull person needs to be praised to excess, he will do his utmost. It is better to tease a hard-working person, to scold them to excess. It is best to encourage a conscientious person materially. You need to know the weak and the strong side of a person. You have to play on this'*. The shop chief has also resurrected traditional informal methods of encouraging collectivism, organising collective trips to the tourist base and joint celebration of holidays.

In the preparatory shop of the same enterprise the situation is very different. The shop has regularly failed to meet its production plan, which has meant that workers do not earn bonuses despite having to work long hours of unpaid overtime in the attempt to meet the target. The shop chief attributes the failure to high labour turnover, which is almost absent in the casting shop, but the high turnover is itself the result of low wages and the tough disciplinary regime. The shop also has problems with meeting quality demands because of its worn-out equipment. The shop chief has to trade on the loyalty of his experienced workers, but their patience is wearing thin. The workers complain about the working conditions and the disciplinary regime, but the key question is pay: *'If they pay well, then one can tolerate it. But here the pay is miserly and the demands are harsh'.* There are constant conflicts around the calculation of wages: *'Sometimes we do not give them the pay which people expected, sometimes they do not pay because the foreman has not signed for it. That happens'* (shop chief). *'Well, again they gave us the sheet of calculations. You have to go and look into it. You work, you work but pay does not increase. You do more but pay does not increase'* (workers). Most conflicts are resolved at the level of the shop: *'you have to have iron nerves here to extinguish all these conflicts'* (shop chief), but workers can and sometimes do appeal directly to the production director if they are not satisfied with the decision of the shop chief, and this further undermines his authority. The outcome is that relations between the workers and the shop chief are very tense. The workers consider that the shop chief wants to provide the plan at any price with the aim of receiving a good appraisal from his boss. In his pursuit of the plan he not only does not defend the interests of the workers of the shop in the face of the management, but also cannot organise people in the shop: *'he is afraid for his skin, he has a plan, he is afraid that they will swear at him. Why do we have the worst shop for turnover? He cannot work with people, he does not hold onto people... the shop chief does not know any other words, apart from "get on with it". It's like in a labour camp'.*

Quality control

One factor which has made the task of line managers more difficult is the much greater attention that is paid to the quality of the product. For most successful Russian enterprises product quality is a more important consideration than cost.

MZ3 is a new private precision-engineering company. In recent times control of quality has constantly strengthened: *'This is all they talk about, they demand more, they check, control has strengthened, this is unambiguous, we are precision engineers, and a displacement of one or two millimetres is a fault. And we ourselves look, we regulate, and the foremen control, the head of production'* (workers).

To sell on world markets Russian producers have to be able to meet international quality standards, and on domestic markets where they cannot hope to compete with low-cost grey and foreign producers, they see their competitive advantage as lying in the quality of the product, the quality demands of the domestic market being significantly lower than those of export markets. One-third of our case-study enterprises believed that their technology was above the average Russian standard and two-thirds believed that the quality of their product was above average Russian standards, with independent traditional enterprises being more and new private enterprises less modest in their quality claims. More than a third of new private enterprises claimed that their product met world quality standards. Three-quarters of the enterprises had quality management systems installed, of which just over a third were ISO certified.

The Soviet Union had quite rigorous systems of quality control, yet was notorious for the unreliability and low quality of its products. The fundamental reason for this was the inflexibility of the soviet 'planning' system, which gave enterprises an incentive to accept defective parts and materials and release defective products in order to achieve their production targets. Only in the military-industrial complex were the systems of quality control effectively implemented through a rigorous inspection regime, as demonstrated by the success of the soviet space programme, and these systems were taken as a model when systems of quality certification were developed in the capitalist west.

The traditional soviet system of quality control was based on individual responsibility and rigorous inspection. The achievement of a high quality of production was considered to be the personal responsibility of the individual workers. A record was kept of the individual responsible for each stage of the production process so that, in the event of a failure, the guilty party could be identified and, if appropriate, punished.[1] The foremen were responsible for the workers under their command and would make a visual check before signing off the production. The quality of production was monitored by the technical control department, whose staff tested samples of components and final products at all the key stages of the production process. In principle, this made it possible to ensure a high and consistent level of quality, but piece-rate payment systems and plan fulfilment bonuses gave workers and line managers an incentive to pass on defective products, and there was strong pressure on the quality control service to collude in such practices rather than compromising plan fulfilment by rejecting output. For this reason considerable emphasis was put on securing the independence of the quality control service from shop management, and in the military-industrial complex internal control was reinforced by control from outside.

A system of quality inspection can only monitor the quality of the components and the product, it does not ensure that high standards of quality are maintained in the production process. In general, achieving a high quality of production depends on having a labour force with the appropriate skills and experience using high-quality machinery and equipmen which is regularly serviced and maintained, and processing high-quality materials, within a well-managed and co-ordinated system of production. Enterprises which are serious about achieving quality pay attention to all these aspects of the quality process, investing heavily to buy modern plant and equipment; ensuring that they are supplied with high-quality materials; paying relatively good wages to recruit skilled and experienced workers and managers; and developing comprehensive

---

[1] This is very much in keeping with Sergei Alasheev's analysis of the 'untechnological' character of soviet production. Sergei Alasheev, 'On a particular kind of love and the specificity of soviet production'.

systems of training and retraining. This is all very expensive, and relatively few companies in Russia are willing or able to invest sufficient resources to ensure such high levels of quality. The majority rely on the skills and commitment of their inherited labour force to overcome the difficulties of achieving high quality standards with inferior materials and worn-out equipment and use punitive methods in an attempt to maintain quality standards and minimise losses.

All of our case-study enterprises continue to use the traditional system of quality control based on the personal responsibility of workers for the quality of their work. *'Responsibility must be personal. If there is a person who can be made responsible then he will carry out quality work'* (director for quality, **MZ5**). Generally the foreman will concentrate on monitoring the work of the younger and less experienced workers.

> *'In some cases I simply go myself to check the work afterwards, how the work was done, some I check, some I do not check. This just depends on the person. But basically the workers control it themselves'* (foreman, **NKhZ1**).

> *'When you work for several years with the same people you are able to rely on these people, that is, there is some kind of trust relationship, if it is new people the relationship with them is somewhat different – you stand somewhere where it is easier to monitor them'* (pasta shop foreman, **KhBK2**).

> At **ST2** the brigadier is supposed to monitor quality, but the foreman does not trust him to do so: *'This is the immediate function of the brigadier, but . . . . Although he should also monitor the quality, on the whole I answer for the brigadier. Basically, to be honest, he's a dead loss. So in reality I watch over what each person does. But the brigadier, all the same he lives in the brigade, he will swear for his people and might tell lies'* (site foreman).

In quite a few enterprises experienced workers or brigades have a personal stamp which gives them the right to sign off their own work, and for which they usually receive a bonus.

> Two brigades in the reinforcing shop at **ZSM4** have their own quality stamps and their work is not checked by the technical control department (OTK). A brigade can be awarded a quality stamp on the basis of a written application from the shop chief to the chief technologist. The stamp is awarded for a particular period by a commission comprising the chief engineer, chief technologist and head of the OTK. A brigade which has a quality stamp is guaranteed a monthly bonus for quality of 20 per cent of earnings. However, *'we have definite levers over them. If somewhere there is some kind of complaint, then we have the right to deprive the brigade of 50 per cent of this additional bonus for one complaint in the course of a month and by 100 per cent for two or more. If there is a repeat violation, then the question of the*

loss of the stamp is considered. But that has not happened here' (head of OTK).

As in this case, the personal responsibility of the workers is reinforced by a system of fines. In some cases this is kept within the confines of the shop and penalties are at the discretion of the line manager.

At **KhBK2** the initial punishment for poor-quality work is simply a verbal reprimand. However, every foreman has a 'black book' in which serious mistakes are recorded. Each has his own system for deciding to take more serious measures. In some cases the foreman will punish a first failure, in other cases only a third offence. In each case this is an informal system and is based on the personal intuition of the foreman. The failure has to be formally registered only if it leads to a significant wastage of production. At **ST2** too they try to avoid washing their dirty linen in public and keep matters within the shop.

Line managers may also be penalised for failing to supervise the workers adequately or for other managerial failures.

MetZ2 is a giant metallurgical enterprise which produces equipment for the oil and gas industry, which demands high quality. The enterprise employs more than 12,000 people, with 800 people working in its technical control department. The head of the technical control department in each section has the right to write out yellow, blue and red cards depending on the quality of the product. A yellow card is a warning, a blue card leads to loss of bonus and a red card indicates dismissal. Such cards are presented to the employee regardless of the post they occupy. *'Let us say the shop chief takes a decision . . . which contradicts all common sense . . . or some foreman has inflicted a loss on the whole factory. . . . As a rule we do not go as far as a red card, for us that is already a completely malevolent violator. Basically they are blue cards, when the technology, the technological instructions, are violated . . . wittingly or unwittingly'* (chief engineer).

The usual penalty for exceeding the allowable limits of wastage is a loss of bonus, but some new private enterprises (illegally) require the workers to cover some (or all) of the cost of the loss.

'A few months ago I decided that not only profits should be shared but also faults. Now at the end of the month the number of faults in production and in sales is identified. In production this is done by the head of production, in sales by the head of the sales and marketing service. A manager has not made enough effort, a designer has not drawn a design well enough, a worker has not sawn properly. We receive the total cost of faults. The guilty will pay half, I will pay half. So far there have not been any problems with this. But if somebody tries to stand up for his rights, he will do it on the

street' (director, **MK2**). At **MK1** the workers are liable for the whole of the loss.

The idea of a no-blame culture is completely alien to the soviet approach to management, but at the foreign-owned **MetZ1** there is a 'right to make mistakes' and faults that arise from ignorance or a mistake are not penalised. Systematic or malicious violation leads to dismissal, but there have not been any such cases. At the private telecommunications company **TK1**, the emphasis is also on correcting and learning from mistakes rather than seeking out the guilty.

The poor quality of supplies was a major stumbling block in the soviet system, and the problem has got more acute as high-quality materials are exported, leaving only lower quality materials for the domestic market. Maintaining the quality of supplies depends on checking deliveries, but this on its own is often insufficient.

> **MZ5** gets its hydraulic equipment from a local factory, but they were very dissatisfied with the quality and wanted to break off collaboration. They managed to preserve the relationship by placing staff of their own quality department directly in their supplier's factory. This makes it possible to ensure the quality of supplies and over the last year there has not been a single fault with the hydraulic equipment.

Our respondents claimed that the documentation accompanying the products always made it possible to trace the person responsible for any failure. *'Some things go to assembly with a thick packet of documents because the item is made of several parts, each of which has its passport. If any kind of defect occurs we can find the worker and the controller – this is tracked 100 per cent'* (deputy director for production, **MZ2**). At the vodka factory **LVZ1** the researchers decided to test a similar claim, but in discussing it with the foremen and looking through the log-books which they should have been maintaining they could not find any such records.

Some enterprises use the system of quality control to differentiate production for different markets, with products meeting the highest quality standards being sold for export and the remainder being sold on the domestic market, as branded or unbranded products depending on their quality: *'Here they consume everything, but you will not sell defective products abroad'* (shop chief, **KhZ2**).

Many enterprises producing for the consumer market claim to take feed-back and complaints from their customers into account in controlling quality. The vodka factory **LVZ1** again provides a salutary example of the limited respect for consumer rights by Russian producers.

> The production manager insisted to the researchers that the company adheres to the rule that the consumer is always right, but they also insist that they

have never received a single valid complaint from a consumer about the quality of the product or its content. The same production manager explained why it is practically impossible for the consumer to prove the validity of a complaint: '*For example, a buyer has bought our vodka, he has tried it, he did not like it, it is bad, etc. If we consider this complaint according to the law we have the right not to accept it at all. The bottle is open, we did not see in what condition it was bought, the packing has been broken, we do not know at all if he has drunk it and has poured something in and that is how black PR is started*'. In fact a former worker reported that there had been cases in the past. '*Certainly, there is spoilage. There were cases when there were flakes floating in the bottle, but I do not know whether the complaint was presented to the enterprise. I know another case, true, it was a long time ago. My friends bought some boxes of vodka for a funeral. They opened one, they were not 40 degrees, another, a third. And then they took all the boxes to the factory, they tested the other bottles, and they were only twenty, instead of forty. They replaced the box and basically the conflict was settled*'.

The system of quality control inevitably creates tension between the quality controllers and the production managers. The director for quality at *MZ5* noted that the position of the shop chiefs in relation to quality

'*is complex. The plan hangs over their heads like the sword of Damocles and the technical control department is right alongside them. The non-fulfilment of the plan risks a reduction in the size of their bonus, but for quality they can both punish and encourage. In some situations workers are more responsible than the shop chiefs. . . . In the course of the day I do not know how many times the question for us is constantly on the boundary "quantity–quality" . . . there have been serious situations when quality is not achieved but the plan has to be made*'.

Systems of Quality Assurance have increasingly been adopted around the world to provide an underpinning for quality control, the dominant standard being ISO9000. The basic principle of ISO9000 is to have documented quality management processes which meet the requirements of the standard. Certification is increasingly required to get access to export markets and some large Russian companies are requiring certification of their suppliers. Thirteen of our case-study enterprises have achieved ISO9000 quality certification and a further seven were going through the process of certification at the time of the case studies, with another four planning to seek certification in the near future, the majority being enterprises which are part of holding companies.

The process of certification is a very familiar one for Russian enterprises because it is very similar to the traditional soviet certification procedures, with the emphasis on documentation of management practices. Russian managers are therefore well practised in taking an entirely formalistic approach to ISO certification, raising the question of whether certification is rather an alternative to achieving high quality standards than a guarantee of quality.

The pay, status and careers of line managers

One indicator of the status of a particular position might be thought to be the ownership of shares in the enterprise and from this point of view it might be surprising that shop chiefs in holding companies are more likely to be shareholders than the finance and marketing directors and even than the general director. But share options are not a means of rewarding managers in Russia, not least because there is a limited secondary market for shares and most companies with minority shareholders never pay a dividend. Share ownership is rather a legacy of the original privatisation of the enterprise to the labour collective, so those with longer tenure are more likely to be shareholders, though usually with a purely symbolic holding. Thus it is those who have the longest service who are the most likely to own shares in their own enterprise.

The pay of senior managers is a closely guarded secret in most Russian enterprises today, but it is universally assumed that senior managers, particularly in market specialisms, are relatively very well paid, and that it is necessary to pay substantial salaries to attract professional managers from outside. Shop chiefs were asked to compare their pay with the heads of the marketing and financial departments and they overwhelmingly replied that they earned less or significantly less, whereas in the past they would have expected to earn more than the head of the department of sales and supply or the chief accountant (typically low-status female occupations).

> At *SM2*, which makes cement, the shop managers openly expressed their discontent with their pay in comparison with that of the staff of the sales department: *'An engineer in the sales department receives much more initially than an engineer in the shop, but they immediately conclude a contract with him for a higher sum. . . . They think that for us, here in the shop, everything is simple, and there, in the sales department, everything is difficult'* (deputy shop chief).

One feature of the soviet system of production was that foremen would very often earn less than the workers they were managing. This was partly because the foreman's position was the bottom rung on the managerial career ladder. A very significant indicator of the status of line managers is the fact that 16 per cent of foremen thought that they earned less than brigadiers and 28 per cent that they earned less than a skilled worker, even though fully half the foremen were graduates and their career prospects are much more limited than they would have been in soviet times. At *MZ1* the chief of the main production shop earned 5,000 roubles a month ($165), which was lower than the pay of many piece-workers. At *TF1* the wages of seamstresses are frequently higher than those of the foremen. Thus, line managers seem to have lost out in pay to other functional managers, without gaining at the expense of workers.

The production orientation of the traditional soviet enterprise was reflected not only in its management hierarchy, but also in career patterns. The typical career path to top management and beyond would start on the shop floor as a skilled worker, working up through the positions of foreman, senior foreman and shop chief to the posts of chief engineer or chief mechanic and then first deputy director and general director. Usually one of the main production shops would have a reputation as the 'forge of cadres', the place in which all the senior managers had begun their careers. Those working in the departments servicing production could rarely hope to rise any higher than head of their department. In soviet enterprises it was the usual practice to establish a 'personnel reserve' of people designated for promotion to vacancies once they arose, who would be given appropriate training and work experience. This practice largely collapsed in the instability of the 1990s, although it has been resurrected in some of our case-study enterprises and, even where it is not institutionalised, it persists as a traditional expectation.

It is still normal practice in almost all of our case-study enterprises to appoint middle managers from the ranks of workers in the shop.

At *ET2* there is the practice of 'nurturing cadres' in production – the majority of shop and section chiefs came to their present positions from foremen or shift foremen, although there is no special programme of work with the personnel reserve at the enterprise. Candidates for the post of foreman, shift foreman and shop specialist go through an interview with the chief engineer, after which the director issues an order confirming their appointment.

Internal promotion to senior management positions is still typical of former soviet enterprises which remain independent, with senior managers being recruited from the ranks of production management:

In 1999 the knitting factory *TF2* was in deep crisis and the chief power engineer of the enterprise was elected as the new director. He immediately created a new management team of the chief specialists of the factory and tried to find a way out of the crisis with the help of outside forces, appealing to the city administration and the regional committee of the trade union for support before agreeing to work on commission for a textile holding company, which bought a controlling interest two years later. The new senior managers have all worked at the enterprise for a long time and all have production careers. The head of the planning-economic department is typical: she was a technologist, deputy head of the technical department, technologist of the sewing shop and then head of the production-economic department. This does not mean that the senior managers have not obtained skills relevant to the new market economy. Several of them have participated in the government's Presidential Management Training Programme (in finance and credit and in marketing) and the director went on a placement to textile enterprises in northern Italy.

MZ9 makes equipment for the building materials industry. Like TF2, its senior management team was assembled in the late 1990s, before its acquisition by a holding company, and reflects the dominant role of production in this enterprise, the team consisting entirely of long-serving production specialists. The assistant to the general director for personnel and communal amenities has worked at the enterprise for seventeen years and is the former chief of a production section and head of the technical safety bureau. The head of the commercial-marketing centre was formerly head of one of the main production shops. The head of the department of labour and wages is a former mechanical engineer.

At *SM4*, which makes reinforced concrete, the senior managers have all worked at the enterprise for twenty years and more and have followed a long path of career development within the factory. The present composition of the senior management team has been stable for the past ten years, although all of the shop chiefs have been replaced through retirement over the past ten years. But even here nobody has been appointed from outside, all shop chiefs were previously workers or foremen. Half of the managers at all levels are women. For example, the head of the planning-technical department (PTO) is a 54-year-old woman, who came to work at the enterprise thirty-five years ago as a foreman, then worked as an engineer in the PTO, of which she has been the head for the past twelve years. The chief engineer began as an ordinary mechanic, the chief economist as a bookkeeper. The general director has unquestioned authority and has worked his whole life at the enterprise, beginning as an ordinary moulder. He has been regularly re-elected to the position of general director for the past twenty-two years.

However, as we have seen, in enterprises that have been integrated into holding companies senior managers are increasingly appointed from outside, on the basis of their work experience in the managing company, educational level, and qualifications, or from financial and commercial departments, so opportunities for career development of line managers have been severely restricted.

The regional mobile phone company *TK2* is perhaps an exception that proves the rule. When the holding company decided to establish an inter-regional management structure, the senior managers of TK2 were promoted to head that inter-regional structure, and line managers were in turn promoted to fill the senior management posts. However, two years later the holding company conducted an extensive review of its operations and removed the senior management of both TK2 and the inter-regional organisation, to replace local people with more loyal staff.

Integration of line managers into the management hierarchy

We have seen that line managers are in the front line in the attempt to impose new priorities on the management of production in traditional Russian enterprises. The tendency has been to increase the demands made on line managers, while restricting the resources at their disposal to meet those demands. Combined with their relatively low pay and limited career prospects, these tendencies are likely to lead line managers to identify more strongly with the workers whom they are required to manage than with the senior management which is imposing what they believe to be impossible demands on them. However, there are other tendencies operating in the opposite direction, some of which can be seen as deliberate attempts of senior management to secure the loyalty of their line managers.

In some enterprises there is a deliberate attempt to professionalise line managers, and to supplement their technical qualifications and experience with managerial skills and priorities.

At the knitting factory *TF1* the director and senior managers are all veterans of the factory, of which they are now the owners, who have embraced the opportunities presented by the market economy and have very consciously set themselves the task of strengthening and raising the status of line managers by turning them from producers into managers. As the director put it: *'Raising the importance of the middle and lower levels of management is very much a sore point at the enterprise. If earlier brigadiers were the best workers, working class, today this is absolutely not sufficient, the brigadier should be a manager and an economist, a psychologist, higher education is necessary, even two higher educations – a technologist and an economist-manager, a manager. This is today's requirement, it is vitally necessary to change it at the enterprise'.* In the long term they intend to recruit line managers with an appropriate education from outside. Already higher education and wide experience of work is required for appointment to the post of foreman, and they do not promote ordinary workers to brigadier's positions at all. It is possible for the director to consider such a radical move in this case precisely because she is a former shop chief, surrounded by a cohesive management team, who has worked at the enterprise for twenty years and knows production inside out.

Although the soviet system of training largely collapsed in the 1990s, many enterprises have developed their own training programmes. While workers are trained predominantly on the job, some companies have comprehensive training programmes for their managers, which sometimes have as much of an ideological as a substantive orientation.

ET1 is a very successful producer of electrical equipment which is independent of any holding structures. The senior management of the enterprise is committed to the development of an 'economic mentality' among the managers at all levels, although they recognise that this is only in the initial stage. *'To say that this is the aim confronting senior management and running through the whole structure of the enterprise and driving each shop and everybody is oriented to it – it would be premature to speak of this. That is why I say that everything is approximately as it was, that is it is not yet like this... in the stage of experiment some things are beginning to happen, that is, subdivisions are beginning . . . to use some of the financial indicators'* (deputy director for economics). A special management training programme has been developed to propagate the new management ideology and to bring senior and middle management closer together, which includes courses on 'economics and management' for middle managers and a series of joint seminars and round-table discussions involving both senior and middle management. The basic purpose of this training is to create a team of like-minded managers conducting their work on the basis of common principles.

In new private enterprises, which are generally small enterprises with a simplified management structure, the integration of the management body is often achieved through informal social interaction outside the workplace. At the furniture combine *MK2* the position of the foreman was finally determined both by workers and by the foremen themselves as being closer to managers by the criterion of their participation in corporate parties: *'they drink together with the managers, it means they are closer to the managers'*.

Another direction of the attempt to integrate line management into the management hierarchy is the strengthening of the role of the foreman at the enterprise. This was a perennial issue in the soviet system, but in present conditions it has a different significance.

MZ2 is a giant engineering enterprise which formerly produced for the military-industrial complex and now services the gas and oil sector. It has a minority foreign owner which has played the leading role in restructuring management, one aspect of which has been to strengthen the role of line management, building on the foreman's traditional role. The foreman has been identified as the key manager in establishing the link between production workers and the management hierarchy, with the duty of moulding a skilled production team and transmitting the voice of the worker upwards, making it possible to create a cohesive team and an integrated management system. The enterprise regularly holds competitions for the rank of 'honoured foreman' and there is a foreman's fund, whose aim is to expand the possibility of encouraging workers. The enterprise has reinstated the factory newspaper, which is deliberately used as a means of promoting the general ideology of the enterprise, including that of the role of the foreman: *'The foreman has an authority which is earned by years of hard work. The foreman can tell at a glance whether someone is a good worker or not. . . . There is no more majestic post at the enterprise than the senior foreman. . . . It is difficult to overestimate the role of the foreman in the training of the* worker. *The foreman must be not only a personal example, but also the first assistant.* . . . *The foreman is the kind of person who both pleases senior management and does not offend the worker. In work it happens that somebody should be praised and somebody should be scolded, to search for approaches and draw conclusions'* (excerpts from the factory newspaper). At the same time, there has been a marked increase in the degree of control of senior management over middle and line management with the aim of intensifying labour and cutting costs.

Although the tendency has been to exclude line managers from strategic decision-making, confining them to the role of executors, some enterprises have tried to involve line managers in wider managerial decision-making in order better to integrate line management into the management hierarchy. For example, line managers have been included in the development of plan targets at some enterprises as a conscious policy of management to increase their managerial effectiveness by including them in the decision-making process. This is most commonly found in high-tech industries, where a detailed knowledge of the technology is essential to the planning process.

Line managers are involved in the planning process at *MZ4*, which produces sophisticated (and frequently customised) industrial measuring instruments, because only they have the necessary knowledge of the production possibilities.

SM3 is a very successful enterprise which uses advanced pipe-laying technology to service the oil and gas industry. This means that its production units are spread all over the country. The managers of these units have been given an increasing degree of autonomy as more and more management functions have been transferred to them, which has tended to increase their distance from the workers. Nevertheless, although this is a fairly new enterprise with significant foreign ownership, the gap between line management and workers is bridged by the dominance of a very traditional production-oriented ideology cultivated by the general director, which stresses the division between production sites and the office. The paternalistic director also promotes the image of the enterprise as a family, but this is not a view that extends beyond senior management. Line managers and workers have a more pragmatic attitude to the enterprise. Questions about attachment to the enterprise provoke smiles, and the workers immediately transfer the conversation to the theme *'this is simply our work, for which we receive money'*.

A number of enterprises have revived the soviet practices of collective decision-making and involvement of employees in the management of the production process through the organisation of technical councils, where managers and specialists of all levels discuss technical issues related to the current organisation of production and the acquisition of new technology. Such a practice existed until recently at *ET1* and it is now proposed to reintroduce it within the framework of the company's programme of strengthening the 'market mentality' of managers referred to above. It is hoped that the closer involvement of line managers in discussing technical proposals will serve as a mechanism for their closer integration into the management structure.

Where the senior management has made a serious effort to preserve or even strengthen the status and authority of the shop chiefs in order to ensure the manageability of production, the shop chiefs are more likely to identify with senior management and to distance themselves from workers. The shop chiefs are particularly likely to be distanced from the workers in this way in large enterprises, each of whose production shops may be a factory in itself. This distancing of middle management from the workers can be found in both traditional and new enterprises.

MetZ2 is a very traditional enterprise, which has been incorporated into a large holding company as a production platform with sales and supply handled by a separate trading company. The shop chiefs, particularly of the main production shops, are unquestionably part of the factory elite and are the reserve for the top management positions of the factory. Their status is even higher than that of some heads of departments of the factory administration. The annual production plan is the key document of the enterprise and although it has to be approved by the Board of Directors, it is drawn up within the enterprise and shop chiefs play a central role in this process. The shop chief is in principle subject to multiple subordination, corresponding to different aspects of their task: *'I am administratively subordinate to the general director, functionally to the chief engineer, I resolve all those questions with the chief engineer, functionally I am also related to the head of the technical department, with the head of the production department, but all the same they are at a higher level on the ladder than me, higher than the head of a subdivision'* (chief of main shop), but this gives the chief a pivotal role in co-ordinating and integrating different aspects of the production process.

The shop chiefs are responsible for planning the production process, communicating with senior management and the heads of other shops to ensure that the resources needed to achieve the production plan are available. They leave the management of the workers to their foremen: *'I do not go to any shop to manage it, . . . that is not right. Otherwise, what is the shop chief for? . . . The same in the shops. The shop chief never interferes to give a task, say, to a worker . . . every worker has a foreman, i.e. everybody must carry out the work . . . at his level'* (chief engineer). The foremen do not have any real influence on processes occurring beyond the shop and rely almost entirely on the shop chiefs for information about outside events, which they communicate in turn to the workers. In this factory there is a strict hierarchy of status positions in the shop. The head of each shop has his own separate office, which is in a building separate from production, and his own secretary, so he has limited formal interaction with the workers of the shop, although the chief and workers will probably have known each other and worked together for a long time. The shop chiefs are paid significantly more than the foremen and even their external appearance differs – the foremen dress in work clothes, while the shop chiefs wear suits.

The new mobile phone company *TK1* is one of the few enterprises that we studied in which the real management structure corresponds to its formal representation. There is a strict decentralisation of responsibility and authority and correspondingly of decision-making. The senior and middle managers identify themselves very clearly as a separate stratum of professional managers, distinguished by their level of pay, the form of their contracts, their wide authority and high level of personal responsibility for a particular area of work.

At the open-cast coal mine *U1* there has been a recent tendency to the isolation of managers of all levels from workers. Even a shift foreman of the motor pool, answering a question as to whether he feels himself more a worker or a manager, answered that he was a manager. This situation has been encouraged by the management and, apparently, by the holding company. For example, the salary of a skilled foreman is not lower than that of workers, and it is markedly higher than that of mechanics and section heads. Moreover, the pay and compensation of managers down to section heads is stipulated by special contracts whose conditions are unknown to ordinary workers.

However, strengthening the role of middle management does not necessarily lead to their distancing from the workers, if their authority continues to be regarded as legitimate, exercised in the best interests of the workers themselves.

The reinforced concrete factory *SM4* is a very traditional enterprise in which the shop chiefs are directly subordinate to the general director, and so are effectively part of senior management. The distance between the shop chiefs and workers has been somewhat increased due to the strengthening of the role of the foremen and brigadiers. The majority of foremen have special education and their status is much higher than that of brigadiers and workers. Although the brigadiers are still elected, their authority has been strengthened and they receive additional payment. Nevertheless, foremen and brigadiers still identify themselves as workers rather than as managers, although the concept of 'management' is not much used at this enterprise, the traditional distinction between production and the factory administration still being fundamental. The main lever of line management is the coefficient of labour participation (KTU), which is applied to the basic wage to raise or lower the wage of workers according to their contribution to production, disciplinary record and so on. Although formally the KTU is set by the foreman, subject to approval by the shop chief, in practice it is determined in the traditional way by the workers themselves. *'The KTU is decided by the whole brigade, we sit and discuss it in the council. The foreman says that I propose such and such. And then I introduce my changes'* (brigadier of the moulding shop). The fact that everybody has made their career in this factory means that there are close informal relationships between all levels. *'We drop by* [the shop chief] *without ceremony almost every day, we discuss not only work, but also everyday issues'* (workers in the concrete mixing shop). There is a strong sense of belonging to the enterprise among staff of all levels: *'It would be terrible to go. This is my second home'* (worker in the concrete mixing shop).

Despite the efforts undertaken by the top management of some enterprises to integrate line management into the management team, at many contemporary Russian enterprises line managers feel themselves to be organisationally closer to the working class. This is particularly the case with foremen and shop chiefs close to pension age with considerable work experience, who are inclined to stand up for 'their' people (the workers of the shop) and to oppose the interests of production workers to those of the administration. But this is not just a matter of the persistence of traditional values and loyalties. It is also a matter of the pressures to which the line managers are subjected. When they are required to persuade the workers under their command to do things which are not technically or humanly possible because of the limitations of equipment, supplies and human capacities, or for which they are not adequately compensated, the foreman or shop chief has little choice but to take up their cause, not least because this is the only way in which the line manager can hope to avoid being blamed for failure to achieve the production plan or quality targets.

At *ST2* there are frequent disagreements around the calculation of wages. The foremen try to evade responsibility and prevent such disagreements from turning into overt conflicts by referring them upwards, confident that senior management will support them. *'In the end, when I close the books, I look at it with them, I always try to look, because if they start asking questions I can explain it to them. . . . If they are still not satisfied and say so, I start to swear, I send them off to the executive director, to the general director. There they begin to understand, of course, that I have got a case. But here, as a rule, it is also resolved in favour of the management. . . . I feel support for myself, that they support me at the top. That way there will be discipline, otherwise . . . '* (site foreman). But, according to the foremen, they will often struggle with senior management to get more money for the workers. *'If there are nuances which it is difficult to take into account, a lot of little jobs which are difficult to take into account; if I think that that is really the case, I go to the executive director and I explain that these people have really worked, the work is small, not obvious, and we have to pay for that. Depending on the situation, it might be that he will pay some more, whether or not he agrees. Sometimes we struggle with the director over pay'.*

Conclusion

Reform of management at the top has not been accompanied by significant changes in the methods of production management. Top management demands that the shops produce more at higher quality and at lower cost, the line managers have to deliver this with outdated equipment, often inadequate supplies and reluctant workers using the traditional soviet management methods based on traditional soviet labour values. However, centralisation of control of the allocation of resources has reduced the levers of management available to the shop chiefs, so that they have to rely more on negative than positive sanctions, which are not conducive to encouraging workers to identify with the objectives of the enterprise or the division. As the case of MZ5 (p. 206 above) shows, depending on their material situation and perhaps the skills of the shop chief, as in the soviet period, this can lead to a vicious or a virtuous circle. In the former situation it can lead to internal conflict in the shop, as in MZ5, with the shop chief losing the confidence of workers and senior management, or, more often, it can lead to overt or covert conflict between shop chiefs and senior management, which senior management attributes to the inadequacy of the shop chiefs, in the soviet tradition of reducing all systemic problems to personnel problems. In a minority of cases, the response of senior management is to seek to integrate line managers into the management hierarchy. This is easier to achieve in independent enterprises, where top management has more freedom of manoeuvre and line managers have greater weight in the management hierarchy. In enterprises controlled by outsiders or holding companies the more common response is to seek to replace the line managers with others who will prove more loyal to the owners and their representatives, but unless these new managers are given sufficient levers of management by being able to provide their workers with good wages, this is only likely to move the line of conflict further down the hierarchy, leading to direct confrontations between workers and line managers.

In more traditional enterprises, in which the commitment to production remains primary and shop chiefs are at the heart of management, the conflicting demands of production and the market can be resolved relatively smoothly, since even the most traditionalist of production managers understands that in a market economy the enterprise has to be able to sell what it produces. However, the traditional autonomy of line management presents the senior management of a straightforwardly capitalist enterprise with a serious problem, because here it is not a matter of reconciling technological and economic imperatives, but of subordinating the former unequivocally to the latter. In such cases we find top management complaining of the lack of professionalism of the line managers and of the need to instil in them a 'market mentality'.

The production director of the petrochemicals company *NKhZ2* complained vociferously about the quality of his middle managers, who were not always up to the tasks they were set: *'The head of one shop, it turned out, does not monitor how his tasks are carried out, the head of another checks everything, and often loses the thread, he cannot see the strategic situation'*. The general director was equally unhappy: *'ITR at the shop level do not even get onto the first rung of what I would like to see. We try to train them, but they resist. On the technical level they are professional enough, but at the same time they are completely indifferent to results'*. Above all, the director is frustrated with their deep-rooted 'soviet' stereotype of satisfactory work: *'They are used to receiving bonuses and everything. They have no criteria of good or bad work in their brains. Nobody has died, the factory has not stopped, it has not exploded, that means they have worked well, pay is big'*.

Senior management identifies the same problem of outdated values held by the middle managers at the electrical equipment factory **ET1**. *'I can say that by the highest standards we have not transformed to capitalism. When people, middle managers – chiefs of shops and departments – [expect] . . . that there will be free buses and so on, this mentality is still far from being capitalist, this is all just the same socialism and communism. When you begin to explain to people that the source of all this can only be their wages and that there are no other sources. Well, for God's sake we can reduce the wage fund and repair these roads. But who wants that? We can give everybody insurance, holidays in the Canaries, but again only from one source. They do not understand that you cannot have anything free . . . free education, free buses – people pay for everything, just in other ways. Some people say that ET1 is quite a successful enterprise, that it stands quite firmly on its feet, only thanks to the fact that it has made a transition from a socialist to a capitalist system of management, but that is not the point. We've taken one step, but it is not clear in what direction'* (deputy director for economics).

Line managers are aware of their shortcomings, but do not necessarily see them in the same light as do senior managers. We asked shop chiefs and foremen whether they thought that they had sufficient knowledge to do their jobs and only a third of shop chiefs and 40 per cent of foremen thought they did. Shop chiefs in holding companies were more confident of their ability, likewise foremen in independent traditional and new private enterprises. However, economic knowledge only came low in their list of perceived deficiencies. The leading area in which foremen and shop chiefs in all types of enterprise felt that they lacked adequate knowledge was the law, an indication of the extent to which they now have to take responsibility for a range of regulatory issues and have to manage their workers within the limits of the labour law. In holding companies and new private enterprises one in six shop chiefs felt that they required more knowledge of production management, which indicates the extent to which these enterprises have replaced experienced shop chiefs with loyal servants of the company. In independent traditional enterprises, by contrast, line managers were completely confident of their ability as production managers, but almost a third of shop chiefs felt that they needed more knowledge of economics, indicating the extent to which in these companies the shop chiefs are part of the senior management team. Elsewhere fewer than one in ten line managers felt that they lacked knowledge of economics. Foremen, in keeping with the character of their work, attached much more importance to additional knowledge of psychology than of economics.

In reality, senior managers' dissatisfaction with middle management is more often motivated by a desire to get rid of objectionable people and to remove the centre of resistance to new management principles than simply by frustration at their incompetence. At a number of our case-study enterprises we have seen how a conflict within management has reinforced the authoritarianism of the general director, who has then removed those opposing him and employed new young people as managers of production divisions, either from outside or by promoting ambitious young people from within. The outcome is more loyal, though by no means necessarily more competent, line managers.

At *MZ2* one shop has had three chiefs within two years. According to the deputy general director for production, *'there was one shop chief who was unable to organise people and he was unable to look ahead. We changed this shop chief for another. . . . But he again did not fit in with the collective, with their mobilisation and he could not see a solution for his problems. . . . And we found one shop chief who resolved these issues virtually on his own . . . he began to take up progressive measures, beginning with discipline . . . he correctly established a system for resolving issues, a system of planning in the sections. And, most important, he managed constantly to control the fulfilment of the tasks given to him'*. It may be that the previous shop chiefs had been incompetent, but the most important thing about the successful shop chief was that he did what he was told.

A similar situation of 'elimination' of objectionable line managers has arisen at *MZ1*, where a shop chief was removed from his post for failing to meet a production target, although the real reason for the failure was the absence of materials. MZ1 had been acquired in 1998 by a holding company, which had appointed the young head of sales and marketing as general director. Even five years later the employees saw the new director only as a protégé of the owners, emphasising his distance from the collective: *'We go our way, the director goes his'*. The shop chiefs are not impressed by his departure from the traditional norms *'The new director only pays lip service to the importance of the collective, that there must be a skeleton, that all this is ours. But in reality he does not even approach the workers, he walks to the middle of the shop, sees me and comes back as quickly as possible. But he never comes to speak with the workers. When Gennadii Fedorovich was the director, he mixed with the workers. The new director does not think that that is necessary'* (shop chief).

The lines of division within the enterprise are not necessarily between different levels of management. When senior management replaces shop chiefs with its own protégés, particularly in enterprises which have been integrated into holding companies, divisions between the existing line managers and the representatives of the new management team are opened up, and are expressed in different degrees of participation in decision-making and very likely in differences in salaries too.

At the cement factory **SM1** the chiefs of the main production shops are regarded as pure executors, whose sole task is to carry out the instructions of the directorate. They are almost completely excluded from decision-making, and even from consideration of the plan targets, which they are expected to fulfil without question, partly on the grounds of their low educational level but primarily because the new senior management team does not trust them. Some chiefs of auxiliary shops, on the other hand, said that they were involved in various meetings at which they could express their opinion, but these were new appointees who seemed to be protégés of the new management. The exclusion of the shop chiefs from the planning process had serious consequences for plan fulfilment, since they were not able to alert senior management to obstacles to achieving the production plan. Instead they had to use informal channels, through one of their colleagues who was trusted by senior management. For example, shop chiefs could convey their opinions to the director through the chief engineer, chief mechanic or the quality laboratory, with which they worked every day in immediate contact.

At **MZ9** there is a precise division among shop chiefs into those who have worked at the enterprise since soviet times and representatives of the new market mentality. The former are characterised by the aspiration to provide production at any cost. However, they, as a rule, do not have a strategic vision of the development of the enterprise or even of their own division. The latter have their own ideas about the development of production, and are distinguished by their flexible thinking. The first category of chiefs are closer to the foremen and the workers. The second category of shop chiefs is a future reserve for top management.

9 The distinctiveness of Russian capitalism

We have seen over the last few chapters that our case-study enterprises, even those which have been incorporated into foreign-owned multinational corporations, retain many of the managerial structures and practices and much of the organisational culture of traditional soviet enterprises. The question that we would like to address in conclusion is that of whether this is evidence for the consolidation of a specifically Russian 'variety of capitalism' which is able to harness soviet traditions to the profitable employment of labour, or whether this is an expression of the unstable coexistence of incompatible principles in which the soviet legacies will be progressively liquidated as capital consolidates its hold over production in Russia.

The question does not have a simple answer, because we have seen that there are radical differences in the form of corporate management between independent enterprises, enterprises incorporated into holding companies and new private enterprises. These differences are not necessarily the results of the different property forms, because each of these types of enterprise inhabits its own sphere of the economy. Successful independent enterprises are predominantly employing a skilled and experienced labour force, with deteriorating plant and equipment, to produce for the domestic market. Successful new private enterprises are predominantly exploiting their flexibility to fill specialised niches in the domestic (and usually local) market, based on unique technology and/or customised production. Those enterprises incorporated into holding companies are predominantly operating in the most dynamic sectors of the economy surrounding the processing and export of raw materials (metallurgy, oil and gas and chemicals) or in the mass production of branded goods for the domestic market (food processing, household products, pharmaceuticals) and making substantial investments to modernise production and achieve world quality standards.

The struggle for existence

Even successful independent enterprises are operating on the margins of profitability, not least because almost all of those with more favourable prospects have been incorporated into holding companies. These enterprises have very limited access to external finance, and even if finance was available would be reluctant to take it for fear of losing independence. All investment is therefore financed out of retained profits and even in the best of cases is barely enough to cover the costs of routine maintenance and repair of premises and equipment. When new equipment is purchased it is most commonly packaging equipment, to provide a more attractive product for consumers, or investment to increase self-sufficiency, such as establishing a transport section or constructing a boiler-house. The result is that most independent enterprises are struggling to produce with an ageing labour force and worn-out equipment in deteriorating premises, while trying to meet increased quality standards in order to command a price sufficient to maintain solvency. In order to achieve this feat, enterprises have to rely on the skills and initiative of their experienced labour force. It is indicative that among those case-study enterprises for which we have detailed data on the composition of the labour force (half of them), 27 per cent of the employees of independent enterprises, as against 13 per cent of the employees of holding companies, have worked in the company for twenty years or more and 28 per cent, as against 16 per cent in holding companies and 6 per cent in new private enterprises, are over 50 years of age, and so will have worked under soviet conditions for more than half their working lives. Most of these enterprises matched the average wage in the local labour market, but only one in eight paid above the local average, as against half the new private and holding companies.

Paying relatively low wages and making heavy demands on the labour force, these enterprises tend to rely on the reproduction of the traditional soviet social relations and culture of production to keep down costs and achieve satisfactory quality standards. They are able to survive in the market because of their commitment to traditional values of technological achievement and because of their network of connections with traditional customers and suppliers, sometimes supplemented by the novelty of a sales and marketing effort which seeks out customers and feeds back new demands on production. The management deliberately cultivates the collectivist spirit of production and the traditions of commitment and loyalty to the enterprise in the struggle to survive, now in the face of market pressures rather than of ministerial demands. There is not necessarily anything cynical in this, since the senior managers themselves are of the same generation and were brought up with the same values. The workers understand that they have to produce a marketable product, just as they used to understand that they had to fulfil the plan, and they are willing to make the effort and sacrifice necessary to survive in this hostile environment, at least so long as they are confident that their managers share their commitment and are not merely seeking to secure profits for themselves. Of course, these values were by no means ubiquitous even in the Soviet Union, but those who do not share them and had other opportunities left these enterprises long ago, while those who are not committed to these values, but have remained because they feared that they would be unable to find other work, have no alternative but to comply.

These are the enterprises which might at first sight seem to have harnessed soviet management structures and practices and the soviet culture of production to prospering in a new capitalist environment. However, this achievement is strictly limited because its material and human base is literally wearing out. The plant and equipment are old and deteriorating, with no available funds to replace and modernise them. The labour force is similarly ageing and workers are not being replaced as they retire or, all too often, die at their posts. It takes decades to acquire the experience necessary to master such production conditions, while it is almost impossible to attract young people to work long hours for low pay in derelict industrial enterprises. While 28 per cent of the labour force in independent enterprises is over 50, only 2 per cent is under 20, half the proportion of young people in holding companies and a quarter of the proportion in new private enterprises. Many of these enterprises may be a model of stability, but most of them are dying on their feet. Their only chance of surviving in the longer term is through acquisition by a holding company which will invest in premises, plant and equipment and in recruiting and training a new young labour force. But to justify such large investments it will also be necessary radically to change the management structures and practices to secure the systematic subordination of production to the expanded reproduction of capital.

The new private sector does not provide a sustainable model of an alternative variety of capitalism either. The management practices and cultures of the new private enterprises that we have studied are much more diverse than are those of traditional enterprises, reflecting the diversity of their origins, their products and their market niches. Some new private enterprises, particularly in established industrial sectors (*MetZ5, NKhZ2, MK3, MZ3, MZ7, LPZ1*), are owned by people who had been frustrated by their experience of working in soviet enterprises, who have subsequently acquired premises and second-hand equipment and have recruited their labour force from derelict industrial enterprises. In terms of their technology and the culture of the workers these enterprises are very similar to independent traditional enterprises, but they are distinctive in that they have recruited workers who have left traditional enterprises in order to earn better money and they do not have the same legacy of the past on which to draw. This makes it more difficult for them to secure the integration of the workers into a common enterprise culture and to elicit their commitment to achieving positive economic results. Although the workers are reluctant actively to resist the demands of management, for fear of losing their jobs, there tends to be a higher degree of tension between workers and managers in these enterprises than in independent traditional enterprises and a higher level of low-intesity conflict over discipline, wages and working hours.

These enterprises, like the independent traditional enterprises, are vulnerable to the problems of deteriorating equipment, an ageing labour force and a lack of funds and, because of their less cohesive culture, are likely to collapse more rapidly under competitive pressure. These enterprises have often found a market niche created by the inflexibility of traditional enterprises which made them unable to respond to the recovery of the economy from the end of the 1990s. As traditional enterprises have stabilised their position and independent producers have been consolidated into holding companies these larger companies have begun to move into the gaps in the market which had been exposed by new private enterprises, subjecting the latter to more intense competition.

Some new private enterprises, particularly those working with new or relatively advanced technology, have harnessed a rather different traditional soviet work culture. One of the researchers in the new regional telecommunications company *TK1*, now part of a holding company, noted that the atmosphere in the workplace was reminiscent of that of Komsomol construction brigades, where enthusiastic young people were drafted to remote districts to build housing, roads and railroads, and a similar atmosphere is found in other new private enterprises with a young labour force of enthusiastic professionals (*T1*), not unlike western software companies which harness the enthusiasm of young specialists prepared to work long hours for relatively low pay because of the technical challenge and dreams of the future. Of course, the enthusiasm of the Komsomol constructors rarely survived their first encounter with their new place of work, and the quality of their construction left a great deal to be desired, so the Komsomol spirit has to be lubricated by good wages and working conditions and Komsomol enthusiasm harnessed by effective management practices to ensure the co-ordination of the work.

Finally, a relatively small number of our case-study new private enterprises are probably more typical of such enterprises in Russia, indeed of SMEs in most of the rest of the world, in working on the margins of legality, cutting costs by avoiding taxes and failing to meet safety standards, paying young workers cash in hand without paying pension and insurance contributions, maintaining strict labour discipline with (often illegal) fines and dismissals, to drive costs down to a minimum in order to survive in very competitive markets (*MK1, MK2, P1, RZ1*).

Some of these traditional and new private enterprises which are still based on traditional management practices and production values and which command a market niche on the basis of their mastery of advanced technology and professional skills (*MZ7, SM3*) or which are under the patronage of their main customers (*ET2, KhZ3*) will probably retain their niche, survive and even prosper. But the majority will find their markets squeezed between imports and grey producers and threatened by competition from larger companies which can command more resources. In order to survive they will have to develop more effective systems of personnel and production management in order to get the control of costs and quality that is necessary if they are to secure investment. In general, this is only likely to be achieved through their integration into corporate structures.

No change without conflict

The case-study enterprises which have been integrated into corporate structures are not dramatically different from those traditional enterprises which have retained their independence. This is not surprising, because at the time of the research many of these enterprises had only been acquired by a holding company relatively recently. Some of the differences relate to the differences between the industries in which they operate, those enterprises which are part of holding structures being predominantly in the more prosperous export-related sectors. Some of these enterprises had undertaken substantial investment programmes even before their acquisition by a holding company and others were just gearing up for such programmes. Nevertheless, the degree of depreciation of the capital stock of the case-study enterprises which are part of holding companies was the same as that of independent traditional enterprises, at just over 50 per cent (exactly the same as that reported by Rosstat for Russian industry as a whole), with new private enterprises reporting depreciation at half this level. The distinctive feature of the enterprises which are part of corporate structures is not that they have adopted a radically different level of technology or radically different management structures and practices than have the independent enterprises, but that they are in the course of doing so. Although many of these enterprises retain substantial parts of the traditional soviet structures, practices and cultures and, as we have seen, have made very little inroad into the traditional payment systems or forms of personnel and production management, there is no sense in which it can be said that they have established a stable synthesis of the old and the new. The process of innovation may still be at a relatively early stage, but there is no doubt that it is under way and little doubt about the direction in which it is moving, towards a decentralisation of managerial responsibility alongside a strict centralisation of financial control which has fundamental implications for all aspects of enterprise management.

We have seen that the process of change in management structures and practices proceeds from the outside inwards and from the top down. The initiators of change are the sales and marketing departments, which put pressure on production departments to deliver commodities of a quality and at a price which can be sold, and the outside owners and the Board of Directors, which demand, as a minimum, that the enterprise should achieve the financial targets set or approved by the Board. The process of change is by no means a smooth process of functional adaptation of soviet structures and practices to the new demands of a capitalist economy, it is necessarily a conflictual process, because it seeks to overturn established hierarchies of status and power, to invert traditional values and constantly to demand more while offering less.

If we look across the case-study enterprises, it is clear that the process of change has proceeded further and more deeply in some than in others. In particular, the frontier of conflict between the old and the new moves from the top of the enterprise down and from the once peripheral services of finance, sales and marketing to the former heart of the enterprise, production management.

The cement factory *SM2* has been through two phases of restructuring as it was acquired by one holding company and then sold to another. The first owner was an investment company which was just looking for a financial return, so the sales and marketing and finance departments lorded it over production. The finance director at that time explicitly belittled the role of 'mere' production: *'we not only produce, we do this properly and intelligently. In sum, from all of our activities, both managerial and productive, we must get quality* [results]*'*. The production managers complained about the pay of sales managers (see above, p. 214). When the enterprise was sold to a major cement company, the production managers rejoiced when the enterprise was reduced to a production platform and the posts of finance, sales and marketing directors were abolished, their functions transferred to the head office of the company.

At the bread and pasta factory *KhBK2*, which is a production platform in the case of its pasta production, there are two axes of tension. The first is between the directorate and the head of personnel management around the issue of the extent and conduct of organisational reforms. The head of personnel management, an energetic woman with considerable experience of personnel work, thinks that the director has been carried away with economic reform, forgetting about work with the collective, to which minimal resources are allocated: *'They do not understand that all the reforms must be done by people who will be proud of the enterprise not because it conquers the market but because professional people work here . . . staff are not involved in the problems of the enterprise'*. The second latent conflict is between the shop chiefs and chief engineer and the rest of the senior management team, because the producers are excluded from participation in drawing up the production plans or the budget.

LPZ1 is a sawmill with several subsidiary logging enterprises which was established in 2000 as a private venture on the premises of a former reinforced concrete factory by the general director of a neighbouring giant wood-processing enterprise, who brought in other outside investors. Three of the five senior managers came from the wood-processing enterprise. The initial ambition of the owners was to expand production as much and as cheaply as possible. The enterprise employs 400 people and is generally regarded as prosperous, although it has never reported a profit. The enterprise exports about 80 per cent of its product; the remaining 20 per cent, of lower quality, is sold on the domestic market for about half the export price. The enterprise grew rapidly and by 2004 had reached the limit of its technical capacity. The question of the future direction of development of the enterprise was a matter of major conflict between the production management and the marketing specialists. The producers were in favour of expanding production to reap the economies of scale, although this would imply a reduction of quality because of raw material limitations and the reluctance of the owners to invest in buying better equipment. The marketing department insisted that if they could not maintain the quality of the product, they could only sell the increased product by reducing the price. The producers claimed that they could meet any quality demands, '*we can do everything*', but when the specifications were drawn up it turned out that they could not, and a compromise had to be reached between the quality demands of the export market and the capacity of the production facilities. Another area in which the producers show their strength is that they supply customers with boards which are longer than they had ordered, so as to avoid having regularly to reset the equipment, and leave the sales people to sort out the consequences. In general it is production management that prevails, even the chief bookkeeper supporting the interests of production rather than those of marketing, so the conflict is not so much between different professional specialisms as between more fundamental ideological differences.

In each of these cases, then, tensions between different management specialisms involved demands to subordinate production or personnel priorities to financial and market calculations. In the first two cases such subordination was extended through the consolidation of holding structures, even as other management functions moved further away from production. In the third case, production managers prevailed over marketing, but the result of their continued dominance was a steady weakening of the market position of the enterprise as it had to sell an increasing proportion of the product for low prices on the domestic market, while antagonising customers by failing to meet their specifications, a situation which is not likely to be sustainable (in fact the neighbouring giant wood-processing enterprise, now under foreign ownership, is expected to construct its own sawmill and displace *LPZ1* in the near future).

Thus, the outcome of the contest between the different functional specialisms is determined by the top management of the enterprise, the Board of Directors and/or the general director and the senior management team, but it is conditioned in part by the character of the technology and the principal customers and is ultimately determined by the objective requirement to produce profits. The balance of power over decision-making between the production departments and the economic departments, for example, does not necessarily reflect the outcome of a struggle between the old and the new, between the traditional soviet production orientation and a new capitalist orientation to the market. For example, in capital-intensive production with high overheads, and especially in continuous process production, the costs of below-capacity operation of a plant are substantial and the pressure is on the sales and marketing departments to dispose of the full-capacity output. In labour-intensive or materials-intensive production, by contrast, the pace and rhythm of production is more likely to be dictated by sales, and in the case of reduced capacity working the production departments are likely to come under pressure to reduce costs, to allow a reduction in the selling price, or to improve the product quality or specification in accordance with proposals from the marketing department.

A much more significant indicator of the extent of the real subordination of labour to capital is the extent to which the top management of the enterprise has managed to construct a cohesive management team, integrating all the managers from the general director to the foreman into a common structure oriented to a single aim. Very few enterprises have got anywhere near to this situation and in most there are still more or less obvious fundamental divisions within the management team. We have seen in the previous chapter that line managers identify themselves more often as workers than as managers and that attempts to integrate line managers into the management hierarchy have met with limited success.

But in many enterprises the divisions are still to be found within senior management, or even between the senior management of the enterprise and the owners. We have already discussed the case of *LPZ2* (above p. 110), whose new foreign owners brought in expatriate senior managers who found themselves completely out of their depth trying to manage a giant soviet production complex. Two other enterprises in which the senior management was most vociferous in criticism of the owner were both nominally state-owned.

The frozen food factory *KhDK1* remained in majority state ownership because of its role in the strategic reserve, but the State Property Ministry, as manager of the state shareholding, not only deprived the enterprise of investment funds, but insisted on extracting dividends which drove the enterprise to the verge of bankruptcy. As the general director complained, *'The State Property Ministry will never invest money, it has other functions. They plunder. Our business is to earn profits and theirs is to divide them up and take them away. . . . Few people listen to my opinion. . . . When I say that what we need is not to have to pay dividends but to deal with all the issues in the enterprise, such as that production is dangerous, the capital stock is already forty years old, the market situation demands capital re-equipment of the factory, new equipment, nobody listens to me. Every year I speak about this, but I remain in a minority of one'.*

The vodka factory *LVZ1* is owned by the regional government and sales tax and excise duty is an important source of government revenue. The position of the state owners of the company is ambiguous. The state body which is formally the owner has an interest in the profitability of the company because they get 30 per cent of the net profit, but the regional authorities are interested in maximising production regardless of sales, because the excise duty, which is about 30 per cent of the cost of a bottle, is payable on production, not on sale, though sales bring an additional 20 per cent in VAT. It has taken the company some time to explain to the authorities that the company cannot pay tax on products which it cannot sell, but it has still not managed to persuade them to provide funds for investment. *'In my opinion, the proprietor is completely inefficient. . . . I need not this proprietor, but a normal investor, who would invest and calculate the returns from various investments. But for officials the problem first of all is to hand over a report, to receive some reports, that is what the solidity of their position depends on. The better the report, the better they look. But the results of the report do not always coincide with my interests. And if one is honest – they do not coincide at all, they are the opposite'* (general director).

The conflict between production and marketing is inherent in capitalism, an expression of the constitutive contradiction between the production of things and the production of profits, but, as noted in the case of LPZ1 above, this conflict often takes the form of a conflict between the old and the new, between soviet and capitalist managerial approaches and mentalities. We find such a division running through the senior management team in many enterprises, typically between new young senior managers appointed by a holding company and the other senior managers, veterans of the enterprise, who are kept on because of their knowledge of production and of the specific features of the enterprise. Usually this tension is not articulated explicitly, because the old managers know only too well where power lies and do not want to compromise their careers, so they pay lip service to the new values and priorities, but in some cases it defines a clear fracture within senior management, as in the case of MetZ3 (above p. 96).

MZ1 (above p. 93) was a very traditional soviet enterprise, whose general director sold out in 1998 to a regional holding company, to which he was then appointed vice-president. The holding company makes all the strategic decisions and is responsible for planning, finance and marketing. The senior management team comprises the general director, a recent appointee, who is only 31 and looks after the economic management of the enterprise (including sales), a young chief engineer who is also a recent arrival, and the deputy director for production who has worked at the enterprise for twenty years. However, the former director visits the enterprise every day and does not hesitate to interfere, so that there is effectively a situation of dual power. The deputy for production shows a commitment to traditional paternalistic values and is used to working with a hyper-controlling authoritarian director. The new director could not be more different, with a purely economic orientation to high profits and wages rather than social protection and support for the community, preferring a democratic style of management, working with a team on which he can rely and delegating authority. He radically distances himself from the management style of the former director: *'When the general director sits and writes down how many screws need to be brought in to the factory today, on the whole this is simply stupid. The director must concern himself with strategic development, monitor the block of problems and they in turn must be monitored by his deputy. On the whole, the director should not often discuss things with the shop chiefs as well. He must discuss things with his deputy, distribute the tasks and concern himself with strategic planning, prospects and contacts with the outside world'.* The presence of the former director means that the traditional orientation has the upper hand, and this is the basis of the culture which keeps people working long hours for low wages. However, the new director clearly finds the traditional attitudes a burden which it is difficult to change: *'The trouble with old enterprises, when a young team comes there, is that people are impregnated with this atmosphere at the factory, and even intelligent people quite often turn into unconcealed boors. I do not like this way of interacting. . . . I do not want to operate in the ways to which people here have been traditionally accustomed – to stamp feet and to humiliate each other. I said to them – I have the levers of sticks and carrots. I shall not shout, I shall simply leave you without your bonus. Whether I shout it at you or tell you in a normal voice, it won't make any difference'.* The employees see the new director only as a protégé of the owner, emphasising his distance from the collective: *'We go our way, the director goes his'.* Thus the division within senior management is reproduced in conflicts between senior and line management (see above, p. 194).

New owners often find that the only way to achieve a cohesive management team is to replace all of the senior managers, although often this will be by promoting ambitious young people who have some roots in the enterprise, rather than drafting people in from outside. But after a cohesive team of senior managers who are committed to subordinating production to the dictates of capital has been established, the problem still remains, as we saw in some detail in the last chapter, of harnessing line management to the objectives of the senior management team. The problem is that it is line management which confronts the real technical and human barriers to the realisation of the ambitions of senior management and the capitalist owners. Thus tension, if not overt conflict, between line managers and senior management is ubiquitous.

At the road-building enterprise *ST1* there is constant conflict between middle and senior management over the traditional soviet issue of supply, as a result of the tardy delivery of parts and equipment, which is expressed in terms of the conflict between production and finance. *'Everybody wants to do things more quickly. We make out an order, we send it to supply* [a centralised department in the holding company], *supply immediately transforms it into financial questions. These questions are not resolved, there is a delay'* (head of repair-mechanical workshop). The finance department considers that a store of parts is 'dead money'. Moreover, spending on spare parts, which includes tractors, motor vehicles and every kind of machinery, is limited to 8 per cent of the money earned in the year, which is never enough.

At the petrochemicals enterprise *NKhZ2* the senior managers have been brought in from the holding company and there is a lot of tension between the senior managers and line management, which is sometimes expressed in overt conflict (see above p. 178). The director is frustrated by the adherence of local managers to outdated practices, their lack of initiative and their weak receptivity to managerial innovation. The local managers resent the high pay and privileged position of the senior managers, feel a definite frustration at their exclusion from strategic decision-making and are anxious about their own prospects.

SM5 is a large enterprise which originally made wall panels but has expanded in to housing construction. It was privatised in 1992 and the director, an authoritarian paternalist with a legendary production career, owns a majority of the shares, with other managers as minority shareholders. The senior management team is made up of 'tested people', long-standing owner directors, but they have begun to promote promising young people who head newly created subdivisions (a commercial service, sales department, financial service, personnel management) to the senior management team. The young managers are ambitious and consider the development of sales to have priority over production tasks. *'Until the creation of the department the basis of management was the production cycle, everything was directed at production, that is at the growth of productivity, the growth of labour productivity, the growth of production capacity. Today the task is to target financial management somewhat. That is profits, it is the final result. . . . When I was taken on for this post, my first task was to write a strategic plan for the development of the sales department, correspondingly, and also the enterprise as a whole . . . the enterprise completely depends on the sale of products. We understand this clearly, that the development of the whole enterprise completely depends on the development of our department'* (head of sales department). This is leading to growing contradictions between senior management and middle management as middle managers have been excluded from planning, but they accuse the young managers of not being able to organise stable work of the enterprise with their obsession with sales. Periods at which a large part of the equipment is at a standstill alternate with rush jobs. *'[I would participate in planning] with pleasure but, actually, we are a bit separated from it, that is people consider, that they will earn money for us, well, for the factory, but nobody takes any account of our interests. So much is wasted, sometimes there is nothing . . . well it is feast today, fast tomorrow . . . there is no stability of production'* (shop chief).

Although there is often a high degree of tension on the shop floor, overt conflict between workers and their capitalist employers is still relatively rare. One major reason for this is that workers' resistance is usually expressed by their line managers, who make representations to senior management when the workers' resistance presents an obstacle to the achievement of their production tasks. As we saw in the last chapter, workers generally look to their line managers to represent their interests, and in many cases of overt conflict the line managers explicitly support their workers, as at SM1 (above, p. 184).

Apart from the dispute over social welfare provision (p. 159 above), a collective labour dispute broke out at the open-cast mine *U1* during the research. The management of the holding company had decided to transfer the employees of all its mines from a twelve-hour working day to an eight-hour day, to reduce payment for overtime and increase the intensity and quality of work. Such attempts are made by mine management about once every five years, especially at open-cast mines, and always provoke fierce opposition from the workers because the change would increase the number of shifts they have to work and, consequently, the amount of unpaid time they have to spend travelling to and from work, by the equivalent of one month's working time a year. The trade union committee took up the issue and as a result of an extended and embittered discussion with the management were able to defend everybody, except for the dump truck drivers. The management of the holding company found a document from soviet times which prescribed that drivers should not work more than nine hours a day. But now the drivers are offended and indignant that they alone have been moved onto an eight-hour working day, which they see as an attempt to infringe their rights and to defend the privileges of the excavator section.

Conflict is endemic at the crane factory *MZ5* (see above p. 207), where the general director does not have the highest opinion of his employees. *'I was already sure that we could not break these people with punishments, nor with incentives, nor with persuasion, nor by breaking them up, not with anything. You can use them as an executive mechanism. You cannot demand independent movement from them. Their thinking, performance, and desires are inert. You cannot imagine what a sea of contradictions and conflicts there are in our factory as a result of what those at the top want and those at the bottom do not want'* (general director). He tries to discipline the workers using quasi-military methods: *'I have tried to ensure that people form up in the shops in the morning. The next step they will do gymnastics for me. That will be great. We are struggling with smoking. I do not smoke any more, that means my subordinates should also not smoke'* (general director). Workers are only allowed to smoke in special separate places at precisely determined times and the joke is that they need to apply in writing to go to the toilet. The workers have a mass of grievances, they criticise management's failure to pay enough attention to working conditions and technical safety, they consider that the administration does not create the necessary conditions to increase the productivity and quality of labour and, particularly, adequate incentives to work well. There are many complaints about the work schedule and the demand that they clean their special clothing every day. In the view of the workers, the management has gone too far in questions of discipline, particularly in the struggle with drunkenness: *'The engineer for technical safety, I call him "the chief narcologist of the factory". In the past there were raids after wages had been paid. They came to the shop, breathe into the tube. Many were sacked under article. Whether or not it was appropriate. There was a comrade, he had worked at the factory for more than thirty years. It was boiling hot, more than 30°, the man was tired, he went into the street to smoke. The director came: "why are you smoking in working time?" He was sacked under article. The shop chief tried to interfere in this matter. He kept him on with a month's probation . . . okay, if someone is noticed drinking spirits on the job, one can agree without discussion. But if there was a birthday the evening before, do you not drink because you have to work tomorrow? Well someone arrives with a smell, so what?'* (worker).

The development of capitalism in Russia is still at a relatively early stage. The soviet system was destroyed as the expansion of market relations undermined the control of supplies through which the authorities had secured, however inadequately, the conditions for the reproduction of the productive apparatus. The 1990s were witness to the 'formal' subsumption of labour under capital as capitalist intermediaries diverted state revenues and appropriated the enormous profits to be obtained from selling Russian natural resources on world markets. The 1998 default redirected Russian capital from financial towards productive investment, oriented primarily to renewing the production facilities for the extraction and processing of natural resources, but also extending to production for the dometic market, which initiated the 'real' subsumption of labour under capital as management structures were established to ensure that money invested in production would be returned with profit. However, this process is still only in its early stages and, as we have seen, has barely penetrated beyond the senior management levels so that it has barely even begun to transform personnel and production management.

There are certainly substantial residues of soviet institutions, soviet culture and soviet practices to be found in even the most capitalist of contemporary Russian enterprises, not least indicated by the gulf of (mis)understanding that often arises between Russian and expatriate managers in foreign-owned companies operating in Russia. There are even plenty of examples of the resurrection of traditional soviet institutions and practices, usually renamed but otherwise completely familiar, by unambiguously capitalist managers. But it is much too early to say to what extent these values, institutions and practices will survive, and to what extent they will survive as one of the cultural variants of adaptation to global capitalism or will be integrated into a distinctively Russian model of capitalism which articulates the distinctive legacy of Russia's soviet (and pre-soviet) past.

One distinctive feature of Russian capitalism since the collapse of the soviet system has been the relative absence of class conflict, despite the catastrophic decline in living and working conditions and deterioration of public services. The traditional trade unions have lost half their members, and the new (and more militant) alternative trade unions have made very little headway. After the wave of strikes and protests of public sector workers over the non-payment of wages in the middle of the 1990s, the reported level of strikes has declined year by year. Some put the relative quiescence of Russian workers down to a fatalism that supposedly lies at the heart of Russian culture, but the analysis presented above suggests that this apparent quiescence is a reflection of the limited extent of the subsumption of labour under capital in Russia.

The incomplete subsumption of labour under capital means that class conflicts are still diffused through the structure of management, appearing primarily in divisions within the management apparatus rather than in a direct confrontation between capital and labour. The completion of the subsumption of labour under capital is only really possible where there is substantial new investment, which makes it possible on the one hand to reduce reliance on the commitment of skilled and experienced workers by introducing more reliable modern production technologies and, on the other hand, to pay relatively good wages to provide workers with positive work incentives and line managers with effective levers of management.

Such a modernisation of production facilities does not result in the elimination of class conflict, but facilitates the assimilation of line managers to the management structure so that patterns of class conflict take on a more familiar form, as conflicts between labour and management rooted in the conflict over the terms and conditions of employment. We can see an example of such a development in the Ford plant at Vsevolozhsk, near Saint Petersburg, (not one of our case-study enterprises) where the traditions of the Ford Motor Company have been reproduced. Substantial investment in a greenfield production facility paying relatively good wages was associated with a management structure in which line managers are unequivocally part of the management apparatus. But over the past year the traditional trade union has been replaced by a more militant union which has been aggressively pursuing demands for higher wages with a series of strikes and work-to-rules, attracting the attention of workers in neighbouring greenfield plants established by multinational companies. It would be foolish to exaggerate the significance of this development, let alone to imagine that history is repeating itself, but it is indicative of the fact that capitalism in Russia is not so different from capitalism everywhere else.

The case-study enterprises

Pseudo-nym	Number employed	Controlling interest	Industry	Page references
ET1	5,205	Outsider	Electrical equipment for oil and gas industry	84, 86, 140, 149, 153, 156, 198, 217, 220, 224
ET2	582	Insider	Maintaining power stations	69, 81, 140, 172, 215
FNP1	950	Insider	Synthetic fabrics for the auto industry	69, 72, 78
KF1	700	Holding	Confectionery	83, 86, 167
KhBK1	500	Insider	Bakery	35, 69, 71, 78, 80, 130, 143, 148–9, 151, 158, 172, 192, 199–200, 202, 205
KhBK2	750	Holding	Bread and pasta	97, 104, 108, 130, 149, 153, 191, 210–11
KhDK1	395	Outsider	Frozen foods	81, 85–6, 142, 148, 151, 167, 172, 175, 199
KhZ1	807	Foreign	Detergents	105, 109, 114–15, 131, 138, 145, 150, 153, 156, 180, 182
KhZ2	1,448	Holding	Fertiliser	92, 94, 177, 198, 206, 212
KhZ3	300	Insider	Design of production facilities for chemical industry	69–70, 136, 183
KhZ4	140	Insider	Rubber footwear and auto components	69, 74, 81, 174
LPZ1	300	New private	Sawmill	194, 204
LPZ2	5,526	Foreign	Timber processing	99, 102, 110, 113, 153, 161, 192
LVZ1	404	Outsider	Vodka	81, 85–6, 212
MetZ1	246	Foreign	Metal tools	103, 108, 114, 131, 152, 153, 167, 194, 212

Continued …

Pseudo-nym	Number employed	Controlling interest	Industry	Page references
MetZ2	12,551	Holding	Equipment for the oil and gas industry	145, 178, 195, 206, 211, 220
MetZ3	7,469	Now foreign	Metal fabrications	27, 96, 113–14, 137, 152, 157, 196
MetZ4	7,065	Holding	Refining non-ferrous metal	87, 104
MetZ5	260	New private	Recycling non-ferrous metal	124, 229
MK1	65	New private	Furniture	121, 205, 211
MK2	65	New private	Furniture	118–20, 147, 172, 181, 186–7, 206, 212, 218
MK3	550	New private	Furniture	121
MZ1	422	Holding	Electrical equipment	91, 93, 95, 104, 148, 183, 194, 197, 202, 206, 214, 225
MZ2	7,000	Holding	Advanced engineering, now supplying oil and gas industry	91–2, 111, 133, 137, 140, 145, 153, 157, 160, 174, 182, 212, 218, 225
MZ3	135	New private	Precision engineering of machine parts	116, 172, 208, 229
MZ4	1,007	Insider	Industrial measuring instruments	69, 72, 75, 136, 147, 181, 187, 219
MZ5	450	Insider	Cranes	81, 86, 102, 105, 136, 160, 170, 206, 210, 212, 213, 223
MZ6	200	Holding	Industrial gas installations	88, 107, 177, 180
MZ7	52	New private	Precision engineering	120, 147, 201
MZ8	11,000	Insider	Advanced engineering, now supplying oil and gas industry	69, 79, 130, 155, 157, 165
MZ9	1,156	Holding	Machinery for building materials industry	215, 226
NKhZ1	2,127	Holding	Petrochemicals	94, 98, 105–6, 197, 199, 210

Pseudo-nym	Number employed	Controlling interest	Industry	Page references
NKhZ2	626	Holding	Petrochemicals	91, 130, 150, 166, 168, 178, 223
NKhZ3	4,614	Holding	Petrochemicals	105, 112
RZ1	200	New private	Fish processing	142, 164, 186
ShF1	135	Insider	Clothing	69, 75, 171
SM1	573	Outsider	Cement	82, 86, 130, 134, 141, 148, 151, 184, 198, 202, 226
SM2	1,086	Holding	Cement	95, 108, 178, 214
SM3	400	New private	Laying oil and gas pipelines	168, 219
SM4	406	Insider	Reinforced concrete	69–70, 73, 76, 151, 156–7, 170, 191, 198, 203–4, 216, 221
SM5	1,010	Insider	Prefabricated construction units	69, 77
SO1	240	New private	Disinfection services	120, 200
ST1	372	Holding	Road building	91, 97, 192
ST2	130	Insider	High-quality construction	69, 74, 76, 79, 143, 175, 184, 193, 201, 210–11, 222
ST3	900	Insider	Construction	69
T1	36	New private	Printing and publishing	124, 146, 186
TF1	1,320	Insider	Knitted goods	69, 74, 137, 140, 145, 194, 203, 214, 217
TF2	350	Holding	Knitted goods	87, 168, 202–3, 215
TK1	621	Holding	Telecommunications	106, 131–2, 136, 139, 154, 173, 200, 212
TK2	6873	Holding	Telecommunications	107, 216
TP1	584	New private	Household fittings	121
U1	700	Holding	Open-cast coal mine	159–60, 193, 205, 221

Index